JOYCE, CHAOS, AND COMPLEXITY

JOYCE, CHAOS, AND COMPLEXITY

Thomas Jackson Rice

UNIVERSITY OF ILLINOIS PRESS *Urbana and Chicago*

Manufactured in the United States of America
1 2 3 4 5 C P 6 5 4 3 2
This book is printed on acid-free paper.
Library of Congress Cataloging-in-Publication Data
Rice, Thomas Jackson.
Joyce, chaos, and complexity / Thomas Jackson Rice.
p. cm.
Includes bibliographical references and index.
ISBN 978-0-252-02279-1 (alk. paper). — ISBN 978-0-252-06583-5
(pbk. : alk. paper)
1. Joyce, James, 1882–1941—Knowledge—Science.
2. Literature and science—Ireland—History—20th century.
3. Mathematics and literature—Ireland—History—20th century.
4. Chaotic behavior in systems in literature.
5. Complexity (Philosophy) in literature. 6. Postmodernism
(Literature)—Ireland. 7. Science in literature. I. Title.
PR6019.09Z78455 1997
823'.812—dc20 96-9969 CIP

FOR DIANE

CONTENTS

PREFACE: POSTMODERNISM AND SUPERSTITION

Two books published within a few months of each other as this study neared its completion, John Brockman's *Third Culture: Beyond the Scientific Revolution* (1995) and Paul Gross and Norman Levitt's *Higher Superstition: The Academic Left and Its Quarrels with Science* (1994), present similarly dismal pictures of the present relationship between the humanities and the sciences. Brockman's thesis is as simple as it is straightforward: the contemporary literary intelligentsia has abandoned its traditional function of "rendering visible the deeper meanings of our lives, redefining who and what we are" (17). "Quite often proudly (and perversely) ignorant of many of the truly significant intellectual accomplishments of our time," literary scholars have virtually ignored the major achievements of modern science and have thus ceded their role as "people who shape the thoughts of their generation" to "the new public intellectuals," an "emerging third culture" of scientists such as Murray Gell-Mann, Stephen Jay Gould, Stuart Kauffman, and Roger Penrose, who can and do write for a large popular audience (17, 19). Brockman has concluded, with a logic that escapes me, that these "scientists are communicating directly with the general public" *because* "literary intellectuals are not communicating with scientists" (18).

Nevertheless, Brockman has a point. Literary intellectuals have not been doing a good job of communicating either with the general public or with scientists. He is completely wrong, however, when he claims that science has been "invisible" in the humanistic disciplines (18), as the reader can judge by a quick check of the articles and books I cite at the end of this study.

Lately, as a matter of fact, there has been so much discussion of twentieth-century science in the humanities and social sciences that Gross and Levitt devote their *Higher Superstition* exclusively to a review of this literature. Beyond this blind spot, there is a more basic problem with Brockman's book. By dividing modern intellectual life into two or three distinct "cultures," he contradicts what he himself recognizes as one of the greatest insights offered by those new scientific intellectuals who are "shap[ing] the thoughts of their generation," the contemporary scientists of complexity: "there's an enormous variety of things and phenomena in the world . . . , [and] in such a complex self-organized world, all properties of things are relational" (31). As I argue in the introduction, this insight reminds us that literature, science, and the communities working within and affected by both disciplines inhabit an even larger relational "field" of activity; literature and science are fundamental constituents of *one* culture, the only one we have.

Because literary intellectuals have not been doing a good job of communicating either with the general public or with scientists, this study of the manifold relations among mathematics, science, Joyce's fiction, and its reception suggests two remedies for this situation, one stylistic and one conceptual. True, I have not sought the most direct remedy; I have not written this book primarily for common readers or professional scientists. Rather, I address a more specialized readership here, one comprising those who are familiar with the works of James Joyce and interested in the broad cultural context of his fiction, few of whom are likely to be professional scientists or extensively trained in the sciences. I have written to this audience, however, not as a specialist to specialists but in a style that should be accessible to a general readership, for I am convinced that the increasingly opaque language of recent literary and cultural studies, rather than any inherently revolutionary viewpoint that these studies may offer, has isolated literary intellectuals from both the general audience and the scientific community. (As a logical subset of structuralism, poststructuralism represents no essential paradigm shift in late twentieth-century thought.) In this book I have written as clearly and concisely as possible about complex subjects, for three increasingly compelling reasons: (1) I would like my study to be as accessible to the nonspecialist as the best work by Brockman's "new public intellectuals," books the nonprofessional can enjoy reading. (2) Since I argue in this book against the theoretical premises that underlie and determine the "indeterminate" language and style of much recent literary criticism, I generally avoid the (rarefied) vocabulary and (passive) voice that tend to dominate poststructuralist criticism. Although I have benefited greatly from this body of work, my study disputes the basis of much postmodernist thought—on which its intransitive vocabulary ("emplaced," "imbricated," "reified," etc.) and indeterminate voice depend—from the vantage offered by contemporary sciences that reaffirm *grounds, origins,* and *design* in the phenomena they study. And (3), because the metaphysical consequences of this revolutionary reaffirmation of origin in the emergent sciences of chaos and complexity are so important for contemporary culture, they demand, as I have sought here, the most lucid and precise formulation possible.

This leads me to the second, "conceptual" barrier—actually a yawning chasm—that has isolated the literary intelligentsia most especially from the contemporary scientific community, provoking increasingly hostile responses to humanistic studies from the scientifically informed. As I make clear at several points in this book, the prevailing ideology of uncertainty in postmodernist thought—the exaltation of relativism and the denial of referential meaning that contemporary science refutes—has implicitly and often explicitly sought its justification through the misrepresentation of scientific concepts or in science *misunderstood* (i.e., via fundamental misconstructions of both Albert Einstein's theories of relativity and Werner Heisenberg's uncertainty principle in quantum physics). The works of James Joyce, as I demonstrate, reject indeterminism and finally resist the appropriation of the poststructuralist. Joyce remained a realist throughout his career, progressing from a literary mode to a scientific conception of realism and arriving ultimately at a view of "underlying objective, independent reality" analogous to that of Einstein's relativity theories—properly understood—and of scientific realists today (Peat, *Einstein's Moon* 68); Joyce rested as secure in the existence of "*objective truth about the world,*" of certainty, as did Heisenberg, properly understood (Gross and Levitt 52).

Paul Gross and Norman Levitt's *Higher Superstition* focuses on precisely this contemporary ideology of uncertainty to present an even more disturbing view than Brockman's of the interactions between science and (specifically) poststructuralist literary intellectuals and social scientists such as Jean Baudrillard, Jacques Derrida, Michel Foucault, and Jean-François Lyotard, among others. Gross and Levitt describe the characteristic poststructuralist response to mathematical and scientific thought as a logically incoherent assault on "Western modes of knowledge and their claims to objectivity" (38), an openly hostile rejection of "the totalizing propensities" of the empirical sciences, which itself promotes the "emphatically *totalizing*" point of view of postmodernism (89). But Gross and Levitt attack even those nonscientists who have written positively about the cultural significance of science, claiming that they so often mislead their readers by their "distended misreading[s] of science, in equal measure grotesque and condescending," that their "approbation . . . is hardly distinguishable from hostility" (100). They reserve their strongest condemnation, however, for the cultural "constructivist" or relativist who contends that science is merely "a highly elaborated set of conventions brought forth by one particular culture (our own) in the circumstances of one particular historical period." The full logical consequences of this constructivist rejection of science's "privileged position in respect to its ability to 'know' reality" are that science and superstition come to have equally valid claims to *truth*, that the scientific concept of objectivity becomes "meaningless outside the community that endows [it] with meaning," and that the picture of reality provided by science amounts to no more than one of our culture's many synthetic constructions (45). As two early contributors to the cultural constructivist reading of science, Paul Feyerabend and Thomas Kuhn, both admit, this approach breaks down into nonsense when "rigorously applied" to the activities of science and to the assumptions underlying those activities: science works; superstition does not (45). "How can an enterprise depend on culture in so many ways, and yet produce such solid results?" Feyerabend wonders. "Movements that view quantum mechanics as a turning-point in thought—and that includes fly-by-night mystics, prophets of a New Age, and relativists of all sorts—get aroused by the cultural component and forget predictions and technology" (qtd. in Gross and Levitt 49–50).

Gross and Levitt's indictment of cultural constructivism may seem to be eminently reasonable and even persuasive, but their argument is seriously flawed by their failure to distinguish between the rigorous relativist who views science and reality as purely social constructions, with no privileged claims on knowledge and truth, and the cultural critic—such as myself—who finds significance in the way that scientific thought conditions the modes of seeing and the *constructions* of reality that function in a particular society in a given historical epoch. (This is why the theoretical perspective of postmodernism—as a particular cultural construction of reality—still has much to tell us about the complexity of critical response, although it has less to tell us about the complexity of literature that does not share its metaphysical assumptions.) There is a fundamental difference, then, between criticism of science and criticism of a scientific culture, a distinction Cheryl Herr emphasizes in her felicitous phrase "people create their culture and in turn are created by it" (147). Ironically, Gross and Levitt themselves prove to be exemplary cultural critics, because they particularly attend to the ways in which contemporary misconstructions of science affect their audience. Their only motivation for writing their devastating exposure of the nonprofessional blunders and the misconceived, inaccurate, incoherent, fraudulent, or hostile responses to science and mathematics in the writings of humanists and social scientists is their conviction of the pernicious influence of such views as they enter our culture ("Does It Matter?" 234–57). So, although deeply suspicious of cultural criticism, Gross and Levitt tacitly accept its central premise: the "synergy" of creation and self-creation (Herr 147).

Were *Higher Superstition* to achieve the result that Gross and Levitt envision, Brockman's illusion that science has disappeared as a concern in the humanities would become a reality, for they demand that anyone who attempts to assess the cultural impact of science be a trained scientist: a "scholar" who undertakes a "serious investigation of the interplay of cultural and social factors with the workings of scientific research in a given field . . . must be, *inter alia*, a scientist of professional competence, or nearly so" (235). Moreover, although the relations between the arts and sciences may indeed be turning hostile, Gross and Levitt's rejection of the qualifications of the historian or philosopher of science or of the literary or cultural critic to assess science's impact on society more than reciprocates the hostility toward empirical science they find in postmodernist thought.

My qualifications for writing about the interplay of mathematics and science in the formation of James Joyce, literary artist, and the similar influence of recent developments in these fields on our reading of Joyce today are not those of a professional scientist; rather, they are those of a professional literary scholar and cultural critic who has a background in mathematics and science (the "road not taken"), an abiding interest in these subjects, a decidedly nonhostile appreciation for their contributions to twentieth-century thought, and a fascination for the ways in which people—Joyce and his readers—are created by this culture. This book, as I argue in the introduction, is both a complement and a supplement to several recent works that have sought to place James Joyce as a product of his contemporary culture, such as Herr's analysis of the impact of the media, the theater, and the church on his writings in *Joyce's Anatomy of Culture* (1986), R. B. Kershner's discussion of Joyce's assimilation of "bourgeois popular culture" (9) in his early fiction in *Joyce, Bakhtin, and Popular Literature* (1989), Margot Norris's decanonization of Joyce as an ahistorical and apolitical modernist (6) in *Joyce's Web* (1992), and

Maria Tymoczko's identification of the traces of Celtic myth, language, and folklore in *Ulysses* in *The Irish Ulysses* (1994), all of which are studies that reground Joyce in his historical context. Moreover, my approach complements the emphases of recent postcolonial critics of Joyce who find a "political trajectory" for *Ulysses* within the "historiographic matrix of decolonization" (21), as Enda Duffy does in *The Subaltern "Ulysses"* (1994), or who recognize a "symptomatic representation of the various ideological positions on [colonial] issues in turn-of-the-century Ireland—in very specific, cultural and historical detail and accuracy"—throughout the fiction (9), as Vincent Cheng does in *Joyce, Race, and Empire* (1995). The recent surge of interest in a postcolonial Joyce, as much as the ongoing attention to Joyce's interactions with popular and "high" culture, has moved us a great deal closer toward the rehistoricization of James Joyce as an early twentieth-century author. What these studies lack and what this book offers is an argument for a broader understanding of how, at the turn of the century, during the years of Joyce's intellectual and artistic formation, new developments in mathematics and science penetrated "high" and "popular" culture and contributed significantly to the reactions against the hegemony of received political, racial, and intellectual paradigms, as I argue in my first and second chapters. Moreover, my study of the cultural contexts of both Joyce and his readers today leads to a critique, not unlike Gross and Levitt's, of what I see as the essential limitations of the ahistorical, postmodernist criticism of Joyce's fiction that flourished in the 1970s and 1980s and remains potent today. (For representative examples, see the essays by Jacques Aubert, Hélène Cixous, Jacques Derrida, Stephen Heath, and Jean-Michel Rabaté collected by Derek Attridge and Daniel Ferrer in *Post-Structuralist Joyce* [1984]). This argument emerges from my consideration of the reader's response to *Dubliners* and *A Portrait of the Artist as a Young Man* in my first and second chapters and gains strength as I turn to the discussion of *Ulysses* and *Finnegans Wake* in my last two chapters.

Several people have contributed to my completion of this work. I would like to thank especially A. Walton Litz, my teacher and friend, who responded enthusiastically to the first manuscript version; Robert Spoo and Craig Werner, whose careful readings of subsequent versions of the manuscript provided me numerous suggestions for its improvement; and David Hayman, who kindly read and commented on my discussion of the *Wake* in the fourth chapter. I wish I could also thank the late Bernard Benstock, a mentor to so many Joyceans, who initially urged me to pursue this study. I owe a special debt to

John Palms, the president of my university and a physicist intrigued by science's impact on literature, who took a personal interest in my work and gave me the opportunity to meet some of the members of the Santa Fe Institute for the Study of Complexity by asking me to speak about literature and chaos theory at the Southern Universities Conference (Santa Fe, 1994); I particularly thank Stuart Kauffman of the institute for his words of encouragement. I am also grateful for the research support I have received from the University of South Carolina and the German Academic Exchange Service (DAAD), which accelerated my completion of this study. I would also like to thank Ann Lowry, Terry Sears, and Bruce Bethell, all of the University of Illinois Press.

Earlier versions of portions of this book first appeared in the following publications:

"*Ulysses*, Chaos, and Complexity," *James Joyce Quarterly* 31, no. 2 (Winter 1994): 41–54.

"The Complexity of *Finnegans Wake*," *Joyce Studies Annual* 1995, ed. Thomas F. Staley (Austin: University of Texas Press, 1995), 79–98. Used by permission of the University of Texas Press.

"The Geometry of Meaning in *Dubliners*: A Euclidean Approach," *Style* 25 (1991): 393–404.

"Paradigm Lost: 'Grace' and the Arrangement of *Dubliners*," *Studies in Short Fiction* 32 (1995): 405–21. Copyright 1995 by Newberry College.

And for their constant conviction that I must be doing something important to spend so much time in the office, I thank my children and my wife, Diane, to whom I dedicate this book.

ABBREVIATIONS

Titles of Joyce's works and the standard biography of Joyce—entered parenthetically in the text or in the notes—are abbreviated as follows:

CW	*The Critical Writings of James Joyce*. Ed. Ellsworth Mason and Richard Ellmann. New York: Viking, 1959.
D	*Dubliners: Text, Criticism, and Notes*. Ed. Robert Scholes and A. Walton Litz. New York: Viking, 1969.
FW	*Finnegans Wake*. New York: Viking, 1959.
JJI	Ellmann, Richard. *James Joyce*. New York: Oxford University Press, 1959.
JJII	———. *James Joyce*. Rev. ed. New York: Oxford University Press, 1982.
Letters I	*The Letters of James Joyce*. Ed. Stuart Gilbert. New York: Viking, 1957.
Letters II–III	*The Letters of James Joyce*. Ed. Richard Ellmann. 2 vols. New York: Viking, 1966.
P	*A Portrait of the Artist as a Young Man: Text, Criticism, and Notes*. Ed. Chester G. Anderson. New York: Viking, 1968.
SH	*Stephen Hero*. Ed. Theodore Spencer. New York: New Directions, 1959.
U	*Ulysses*. Ed. Hans Walter Gabler. New York: Random House, 1986.

Ulysses citations will provide chapter and line number(s) in the Gabler edition; *Finnegans Wake* citations will provide page and line number(s) from the Viking edition. All other citations will provide page numbers only.

INTRODUCTION: JAMES JOYCE, FROM "SCIENTIFIC" REALIST TO SCIENTIFIC "REALIST"

To Joyce reality was a paradigm, an illustration of a possibly unstatable rule.
—*Samuel Beckett* (JJII 551)

The striking fact is that every fruitful scientific revolution has forced a profound revision of the categories of the real. What is more, realism never precipitates such crises on its own. The revolutionary impulse comes from elsewhere, from the realm of the abstract.—*Gaston Bachelard* (THE NEW SCIENTIFIC SPIRIT 45)

Examining the record of past research from the vantage of contemporary historiography, the historian of science may be tempted to exclaim that when paradigms change, the world itself changes with them.—*Thomas Kuhn* (THE STRUCTURE OF SCIENTIFIC REVOLUTIONS 111)

Some of the themes of the new sciences of complexity . . . portend a new synthesis of science that will overturn our traditional way of organizing reality.—*Heinz Pagels* (THE DREAMS OF REASON 12–13)

Once upon a time in Zürich, presumably during one of their peripatetic conversations, James Joyce and Frank Budgen discussed the work of (remarkably) an author other than Joyce himself. "You find him difficult to understand because his thought is deep and strange," Joyce remarked, adding, "If there is any difficulty in reading what I write it is because of the material I use. In my case the thought is always simple" (Budgen, *James Joyce* 291). In this study of Joyce I pursue precisely this interplay of simplicity and complexity in his fiction both locally and globally. The emergence of complex narrative behaviors, arising from simple initial premises, both determines the complexity of Joyce's mature works and defines the pattern of his overall artistic development, as the straightforward naturalism of *Dubliners* progresses toward the intricate symbolic and linguistic labyrinths of *Finnegans Wake*.

In the last few decades natural scientists have turned their attention to physical systems that similarly tend to generate enormously complex behaviors out of simplicity, detecting emergent patterns of order in nonlinear dynamic systems that demonstrate such "sensitive dependence" on simple initial conditions. Although originating in the physical sciences, this discovery of order in chaos, this new recognition of embedded design or spontaneously occurring patterns of organization in systems previously considered to be random, lawless, and incomprehensibly complicated, has consequences that have extended outward to influence the study of complex social and cultural phenomena. The maturation of chaos theory in the natural sciences thus has legitimated and intensified the broader study of complexity in both natural and social sciences.[1] In this book I explore the consequences that this new way of "organizing reality" in the sciences has for the humanistic discipline of literary criticism by examining the fiction of James Joyce, a writer who was affected by some of the same initial conditions that determined the development of chaos and complexity theories, who anticipated the emergent worldviews of these late twentieth-century movements in the sciences, and who contributed to the "sensitively dependent" cultural context that promoted their emergence. (One result of the new organization of reality in chaos theory is that one can argue, as I do here, that small perturbations in a dynamic system can generate massive consequences in the later history of the system.)[2] Although the "profound revision[s] of the categories of the real" in the early twentieth century may have been stimulated "from elsewhere, from the realm of the abstract," as Gaston Bachelard observes, assessing the crucial significance of non-Euclidean geometry for the new physics, it is equally true that the current "revolutionary impulse" in the sciences owes at least a partial debt to another such abstract realm, namely, to those reconceptions of reality found among the nonscientific intelligentsia who had adjusted to the "changed," post-Cartesian world of the new sciences. James Joyce's fiction well represents this symbiotic relationship of the "two cultures," the literary and the scientific, which have never been as isolated from one another as C. P. Snow seems to think (9–26 and passim). Joyce's early works, as I demonstrate, show his considerable familiarity with both traditional and revolutionary mathematical ideas, the "realm of the abstract" that Bachelard considers to be "the wellspring of contemporary experimental thought" (*New Scientific Spirit* 134). His later fiction illustrates informed, yet intuitive, responses to the new conceptions of reality offered by modern science that, in a reciprocal interaction, anticipate recent perspectives in the sciences of chaos and complexity.

Snow's contention that the arts and the sciences had evolved into two distinct cultures by the mid-twentieth century (rather like the Eloi and Morlocks of H. G. Wells's *Time Machine* [1895]) reflects a contemporary sense that modern art and technology had both surpassed the comprehension of the common person, caught between these two cultures; the artist and the scientist, moreover, seen accelerating in opposite directions of specialization within their distinct cultures, could no longer be expected to communicate with each other, let alone understand what each other was doing. Snow's conception of two cultures, however, is both one of the most entrenched myths to emerge from the modern era and, ironically, a myth that he himself, a man equally at home in literature and science, disproves. His influential attack on the parochialism of working scientists and the nonscientific intelligentsia in *The Two Cultures and the Scientific Revolution* (1959)—the consequence, Snow believes, of educational specialization—is at best a half-truth. A cursory inspection of the writings by scientists and about the sciences from the turn of the century to the present will uncover numerous examples of literary sophistication, from Niels Bohr, Werner Heisenberg, Henri Poincaré, Bertrand Russell, and A. N. Whitehead to John Barrow, James Gleick, Stephen Hawking, Douglas Hofstadter, Heinz Pagels, and Ian Stewart (most of whom are cited in this study). It is true, however, that the major modernist writers, although often pursuing recognitions that parallel the notions of the new physics, such as the "descriptive inadequacy" of language (Papin 1255), often seem to be less overtly aware of contemporary issues in the sciences. Both Marjorie Perloff and Garry Leonard describe modernist writers' apparent isolation from the nonliterary concerns of contemporary culture, which for Perloff is the direct result of the modern author's characteristic assumption of the *autonomy* of art (158, 171) and for Leonard is the immediate consequence of T. S. Eliot's example and influence: "Eliot's theorizing about modernism made the literary text a privileged space, immune to, and therefore removed from, economic, social, and ideological influence" ("Joyce and Advertising" 580). In addition, the literary criticism of modernism, the "new" critical methodology created by and applied to the modernist writers and the preeminent critical mode when Snow published his essay on "the two cultures," only reinforced this conviction that writers were isolated from extraliterary concerns (Perloff 156 and passim). As my study demonstrates, James Joyce's fiction discredits this modernist paradigm.

The governing assumption here is that "the models of physics and mathematics, the theories of the philosophy of science and [literature], and the structure and strategies of literary texts" of an era constitute, in Katherine Hayles's term, a broad cultural "field" (*Cosmic Web* 9).[3] This field in turn both determines and ultimately embraces the responses of the readers of the literary text. The revolutions of twentieth-century mathematics and science in particular have generated one of the most broadly influential fields of cultural action at a distance; indeed, as Hayles argues, it is modern science itself that we owe for the field model:

> Perhaps most essential to the field concept is the notion that things are *interconnected*. The most rigorous formulations of this idea are found in modern physics. In marked contrast to the atomistic Newtonian idea of reality, in which physical objects are discrete and events are capable of occurring independently of one another and the observer, a field view of reality pictures objects, events, and observer as belonging inextricably to the same field; the disposition of each, in this view, is influenced—sometimes dramatically, sometimes subtly, but in every instance—by the disposition of the others. (*Cosmic Web* 9–10)

The most important developments in contemporary science have challenged a major component of the "Copenhagen interpretation" of quantum theory on which Hayles bases her field model by reinstating, with a difference, the Newtonian assumption that reality exists "independently of . . . the observer" (see Gross and Levitt 261–62). Nevertheless, since they confirm the balance of the quantum paradigm—the assertion that events are incapable of occurring independently of one another—chaos theory and the sciences of complexity still employ the field concept, and thus the field model remains central to my book's literary discussion of the interactive relations among Joyce's fiction, his cultural context, his readers, and their context. Katherine Hayles excellently describes the new perspective offered by such a conception of the cultural field as a complex interactive network:

> One of the many ideas that the field view revises is the notion of a one-way chain of reaction between the event labeled as the "cause" and that labeled the "effect." Although I spoke earlier of the "influence" of the field view on modern literature, I do not mean to imply by this that the literature . . . is "caused" by scientific field models. Rather, the literature is an imaginative response to complexities and ambiguities that are implicit in the models but that are often not explicitly recognized. Thus a comprehensive picture of the field concept is more likely to emerge

> from the literature and from science viewed together than from either one alone. In this sense the literature is as much an influence on the scientific models as the models are on the literature, for both affect our understanding of what the field concept means in its totality. (*Cosmic Web* 10)

Ideally this field model for reading demands more than a study of the interactions among literature, mathematics, science, and the audience to situate Joyce's fiction fully in context, or in current terms, to "rehistoricize" Joyce, that is, to counter an ahistoricism that, as Margot Norris observes, is both "a defining feature of Joyce's place within modernism" and, ironically, the target for his own subversion of the modernist aesthetic (*Joyce's Web* 6). In this study I attempt no more than a delineation and clarification, for further cultivation, of one section of the Joycean "field" that has often been dismissed as infertile. Nonetheless, as the field model itself maintains, any events in this sector should generate reaction (a "sympathetic response," I hope) in other components of the field.

There are dangers of misconstruction and misrepresentation whenever a nonspecialist in one discipline appropriates its concepts and language for specialized discussion of another, dangers that cannot altogether be avoided by placing terms in quotation marks, as I have just done in transmuting scientific terminology into metaphors in the concluding sentences of the previous paragraph. In this study I explore Joyce's similar assimilation of contemporary mathematical and scientific ideas into the forms and language of his early work and the possibilities of rereading his later work in the light of current developments in mathematics and the sciences; nevertheless, although the focus in both dimensions of this book is on the sources and value of such appropriation of the ideas of two related disciplines by a distant third (be it Joyce's literary creation or my literary criticism), this is no excuse for not getting the facts right. One of the most pleasant discoveries of my research is that Joyce seems to have grasped a great deal of the specifics and significance of contemporary mathematical and scientific developments, and I have attempted to be as accurate as Joyce in my representations of the details of, as well as the larger cultural implications of the recent surge of interest in, the study of chaos and complexity. The horror stories recounted by Paul Gross and Norman Levitt in their *Higher Superstition* (1994), an excellent survey of current misrepresentations of scientific thought in the humanities and social sciences (and particularly rife in "culture studies"), show that cultural critics have rarely succeeded in such acts of appropriation. To the trained mathematician and scientist, all too common factual errors and misreadings of significance make the "results" of the work of sociologists and anthropologists of science such as Stanley Aronowitz (*Science as Power* [1988]) and Bruno Latour (*Science in Action* [1985]), for example, or literary and cultural critics such as Andrew Ross (*Strange Weather* [1991]) and Steven Best ("Chaos and Entropy" [1991]) merely "grotesque" (Gross and Levitt 95).[4]

I believe that the present study will avoid such censure because it accurately represents some of the fundamental facts of Euclidean and non-Euclidean geometry—and Joyce's understanding and use of these facts—and the ideas and principles at work in chaos theory and complexity science. I even believe that Gross and Levitt would approve this work, because I join with them in arguing that the ideology of uncertainty in postmodernism rests on both a major misconstruction of quantum theory (one of their major themes) and a fundamental confusion of relativity and quantum theories (which, short of a grand unification theory, are not only distinct but irreconcilable, much to the chagrin of physicists). Simply put—and I return to this issue in chapter 3—those individuals who promote the un-Einsteinian and "unblushingly relativistic" concept of undecidability in postmodern literary and cultural criticism implicitly and often explicitly claim the sanction of Werner Heisenberg's uncertainty principle in quantum physics (Gross and Levitt 51), despite the fact that "when viewed as a law of physics, the uncertainty principle is a very certain item indeed. *It is an objective truth about the world*" (52).[5] "Now, the uncertainty principle," Gross and Levitt observe,

> is undoubtedly one of the cornerstones of quantum mechanics and one of the most philosophically provocative developments in the history of science. [To the postmodernist], however, it seems rather to refer to a kind of epistemological and spiritual malaise, plaguing the minds and souls of contemporary physicists. The argument, roughly but accurately paraphrased . . . , is that since physics has discovered the uncertainty principle, it can no longer provide reliable information about the physical world, has lost its claim to objectivity, and is now embedded in the unstable hermeneutics of subject-object relations. This, alas, demonstrates depressingly well the connotative power of words when they are allowed to drift apart from their contextual meaning. . . . [The uncertainty principle] is not some brooding metaphysical dictum about the Knower versus the Known, but rather a straightforward statement, mathematically quite simple . . . [that] has been triumphantly con-

> firmed. It has been verified as fully and irrefutably as is possible for an empirical proposition. (51–52)

One of the chief contentions of my study is that postmodernist criticism has enlisted the James Joyce of *Ulysses* and *Finnegans Wake*, as much as the Heisenbergian uncertainty principle, to argue for an intensely subjectivist reading of our culture. It is true that the Stephen Dedalus of *Ulysses* sees himself as "a conscious rational reagent," "ineluctably construct[ing meaning] upon the incertitude of the void" (*U* 17.1013–15), but it does not follow, as I show in chapter 3, that Joyce shares or endorses Stephen's "quantum" view of reality. (As I do when I return to the consideration of Stephen's subjectivity, I use quotation marks here to distinguish the postmodernist concept of incertitude, the "pseudo-uncertainty principle," from "the genuine uncertainty principle" [Hofstadter, "Heisenberg's Uncertainty Principle" 455]). In *Ulysses* and *Finnegans Wake*, and in fact throughout his career, Joyce more nearly resembles his character Leopold Bloom as "a conscious reactor against the void of incertitude" (*U* 17.2210–11). Moreover, in their mutual reaction against indeterminism, both Joyce and Bloom markedly resemble the physicist Albert Einstein.

The initial condition that determines Joyce's first fiction, the stories later collected in *Dubliners*, and dictates the aftercourse of his career is his sense of the artist's obligation to reality, his conviction that the artist dare not "alter in the presentment . . . whatever he has seen and heard" (*Letters II* 134). In other words—and this thesis should startle no one—Joyce began his career as a realist, emulating his admired Ibsen and, as much from his aborted medical training as from his reading, accepting the "scientific" conception of naturalist fiction, "the experimental novel" tradition of Zola, wherein writing becomes a mix of empirical observation and diagnosis of symptoms.[6] A more startling contention here, however, is that Joyce remained a realist throughout his career, an assertion that will make more sense if one important qualification is kept in mind: Joyce clearly moves away from the conventions of literary "realism" as early as his second work of fiction, his autobiographical novel *A Portrait of the Artist as a Young Man*. In doing so, however, he adopts the position of a scientific "realist," sometimes pejoratively called a "naive realist" (a label he can share with Einstein), by continuing to accept the existence of a concrete, aboriginal real that exists independently of the subjective individual's act of observation. For Joyce, as I argue in this study, reality exists "without you" (*U* 3.27) in both senses of that phrase, as a paradigm of a possibly unstatable rule. Einstein likewise "firmly held that beyond the world of appearances there exists an independent, objective reality. Whatever scientists measure and observe may be a function of the object's velocity and location in the universe, yet these appearances are nevertheless founded on an underlying objective, independent reality. It may never be possible to obtain a direct perception of that reality—for appearances are relative to the observer—yet it is possible to grasp some essence of that reality through science" (Peat, *Einstein's Moon* 68). Joyce's *nonlinear* development, then, is from "scientific" realist to scientific "realist."[7] Joyce's progress toward the inordinately complex, orderly chaotic "chaosmos" (*FW* 118.21) of *Ulysses* and *Finnegans Wake*, although unpredictable in prospect, follows a route, discernible in retrospect, that is determined by the initial conditions of his art.

A second way of recovering Joyce for the realist tradition in fiction—a semantic recuperation, perhaps—is to argue that the nature of reality, but not the real itself, changes during the course of Joyce's career. Joyce wrote his *Dubliners* stories confident that the artist, relying on the traditional strategies of literary re-presentation, could achieve both an objective and, therefore, a "true" presentment of reality in fiction. In *A Portrait of the Artist as a Young Man*, however, Joyce demonstrates his recognition that the strategies of literary realism offer no more than a convenient "convention" for representation, a subjective perspective on the real that masks its subjectivity with the illusion of objectivity. *Ulysses* and *Finnegans Wake*, paradoxically, constitute objective analyses of this inescapable subjectivity of literary representation. Both works curiously affirm a real that, although unreachable or unrealizable through representation, nonetheless exists; in effect Joyce plays Mr. Tate, arguing the "[im]*possibility of ever reaching*" the real, which is different altogether from the heretical schoolboy who argues the "[im]*possibility of ever approaching nearer*" to reality (P 79).

Thomas Kuhn, clarifying his view of the epistemological consequences of paradigm shifts in the sciences in a passage quoted as one of this introduction's epigraphs, remarks that "though the world does not change with a change of paradigm," scientific and technological developments transform the way the world looks: "the scientist"—and the novelist—"afterward works in a different world" (121). As I show in chapter 1, in *Dubliners* Joyce reflects his thorough assimilation of the Cartesian paradigm of his youth, a result of his having received a Jesuit education, which after the curriculum revision of 1832 emphasized mathematical and scientific studies. Coincident with his completion of the last story of *Dubliners*, "The Dead," and his return to the composition of *A Portrait of the Artist as a Young Man* in 1907, Joyce looked on "a different world," a world transformed by his realization that non-Euclidean geometry had destablized both this Cartesian paradigm and "the spectator theory of knowledge" based on it (John Dewey's phrase).[8] As I show in the second chapter, Joyce's recognition of the "aliments of jumeantry" (*FW* 286.4) profoundly affected both his conception of the subjective subject of his novel, Stephen Dedalus, and his manner of representing Stephen in the novel.

Critics have ignored the extent and subtlety of the influence of contemporary developments in the sciences and mathematics on Joyce's early works, perhaps because of his admittedly indifferent performance in these subjects in school. Nonetheless, Leopold Bloom's confused notions about science ("refracts is it?" "Law of falling bodies," "Parallax" [U 4.80; 5.44–45; 8.110]), muddled calculations (e.g., U 5.307–12), or futile attempts to solve geometry puzzles (e.g., "the problem of the quadrature of the circle" [U 17.1071–72]) are not new interests for the Joyce of *Ulysses*. Although Bloom's limited familiarity with science and mathematics does establish him as a counterfigure to the artistic Stephen, enhancing Bloom's status as "a cultured allroundman" in Dublin (U 10.581), at the same time it both sustains Joyce's ongoing concern with the impact of the scientific and mathematical revolutions on the modern world into his third work of fiction and accurately represents the popular awareness of this impact, circa June 1904, a few weeks prior to the publication of his first story. (The initial version of "The Sisters" appeared in *The Irish Homestead*, 13 August 1904 [Scholes, "Further Observations" 109]). And as several Joyce scholars have already observed, *Finnegans Wake* illustrates an even greater reflection of the different world picture generated by new developments in science and technology (see appendix A).

Consequently, this study opens by exploring the cultural context of Joyce's first two works of fiction, demonstrating his unquestioned assumption of the Cartesian perceptual model for knowledge of reality in *Dubliners* and his move to a post-Cartesian awareness of subjectivity in *A Portrait of the Artist as a Young Man*. There has been remarkably little comment on contacts between *Dubliners* and *A Portrait* and early twentieth-century scientific culture, despite the fact that the best recent criticism of Joyce's early fiction has enormously broadened our awareness of his historical contexts, social, economic, political, and artistic (for representative examples, see Cheng, Herr, Kershner, Norris [*Joyce's Web*], and the "Joyce and Advertising" issue of *James Joyce Quarterly* [ed. Leonard]). The current critical focus on the hierarchical relation of "high culture" and "popular culture" in his works has overlooked the dynamic lateral interaction of those other two "cultures," literature and science, in a society that was well aware of the contemporary technological revolution.[9] The first and second chapters of this study supplement current projects to rehistoricize Joyce by showing (1) that recent developments in mathematics and science had penetrated mass culture by the turn of the century; (2) that a reasonably intelligent and educated individual of the era was certainly as likely, if not more likely, to be scientifically "literate" as a similar individual today would be; and (3) that Joyce was not only aware of current developments in mathematics and science but exploited their implications for his fiction.

Other than offering a few adjustments to the picture of Joyce's relation to twentieth-century science already available in the discussion of *Ulysses* and *Finnegans Wake*, however, the last two chapters of this study shift the emphasis to the context of Joyce's readership today, reciprocating the rehistoricization of Joyce by historicizing these readers. The "different world" pictured in contemporary science, the view of natural and social phenomena that Heinz Pagels predicts "will overturn our traditional way of organizing reality," has unique affinities to the worlds created in Joyce's later fiction. It is now possible, for example, to read in *Ulysses* the dialectical synthesis of chance and determinism found in chaos theory or to see in *Finnegans Wake* a prototype of the evolutionary models of complexity science. *Ulysses* and *Finnegans Wake*, in fact, confirm Hayles's contention that as an integral component of the larger, sensitively dependent cultural field and as an "imaginative response to complexities and ambiguities" in contemporary science, "literature is as much an influence on the scientific models as the models are on the literature" (*Cosmic Web* 10). The third and fourth chapters of this study, therefore, show that the chaos and complexity theories that have emerged as the future states of this sensitively dependent cultural system return this influence by providing new vantages on the nature and significance of Joyce's achievement in his last two works. The advantage of this approach to the later fiction, reciprocating the focus on Joyce's context by considering the "profound revision in the categories of the real" in the reader's context, is that it reinforces what is already explicit in the first part of the book: if the rehistoricization of the literary work ultimately affects the present reading of that work, the historicization of the present reader, positioning this reader within the cultural field of the work, will likewise open new possibilities for reading in a "different world." Patrick McGee has called this reciprocal relation "the transferential effect—

the way in which the reader positions a text in relation to his or her own historical context. Reading from this perspective constructs a dialogue between past and present, including not only the reader and the text but the two historical contexts that define their positions" (2).

Rather than see such transferential reading as a license for critical relativism, in this study I argue, as does Thomas Kuhn (who has rejected the label of historical "relativist"), for a critical relativity:[10] the object scrutinized by the text, the "real," does not shift and change under the influence of the act of observation; the transformations take place in the community of observers, the field composed of the text, its author, and its audience. This is what the "naive realist" Einstein was saying; this, too, is what the scientific "realist" James Joyce has to say.

1

THE ELEMENTS OF GEOMETRY IN DUBLINERS

I said softly to myself the word paralysis. *It had always sounded strangely in my ears, like the word* gnomon *in the Euclid and the word* simony *in the Catechism. But now it sounded to me like the name of some maleficent and sinful being. It filled me with fear, and yet I longed to be nearer to it and to look upon its deadly work.*—(D 9)

The young James Joyce "detested mathematics," his brother Stanislaus recalls. Math "was his weakest subject," Stanislaus adds, and although "he tackled it resolutely because he wanted to win an exhibition," he retained "not a particle of personal interest" in the subject in later years (*My Brother's Keeper* 72). Joyce's examination totals for mathematics, it is true, were usually his weakest scores, yet his skillful handling of geometry in both the "Ithaca" episode of *Ulysses* and the "night lessons" chapter of *Finnegans Wake* (II.2) suggests that Joyce continued to find a use for, and a "personal interest" in, at least this branch of mathematics.[1] Moreover, Joyce's two earlier works, *Dubliners* and *A Portrait of the Artist as a Young Man*, show that his mind, regardless of interest, was as "supersaturated" by the mathematics he detested as by the religion in which he said he disbelieved (P 240). Both saturations were the product of Joyce's Jesuit education, for religion and mathematics—Euclidean geometry in particular—constituted mutually supporting "logical and coherent" systems commanding belief (P 244) in late nineteenth-century educational theory and in the Jesuit *Ratio Studiorum*. Thomas Smith, for instance, in his turn-of-the-century introduction to *Euclid, His Life and System* (1902), advocates geometrical study in the schools "as a corrective of prevalent false reasoning" (176) that "pervades much of what is most popular in the literature, the science [especially evolutionary theory], the philosophy, the politics, the economics, the ethics, and . . . what we feel most painfully of all . . . [,] the theology of our day, and the religion based on it" (162). Joyce seems to have observed much the same confidence in the value of mathematics in his Jesuit teachers, judging from his student essay "The Study of Languages" (ca. 1899).[2] Clearly writing to please, to satisfy his teacher's expectations, Joyce admits that the study of mathematics, rather than languages and literature, is "most important" for the development of "mental precision and accuracy . . . [and] a zest for careful and orderly method" (*CW* 26). Joyce makes this claim less from personal conviction—"We, the pluralized essayist, say this, who were never an ardent votary of the subject" (*CW* 26)—than from his obvious awareness that this was exactly what his instructor, who evidently demanded that he adopt the first-person plural voice, *expected* him to say. (This instructor, however, did cross through Joyce's impertinent appositive—"the pluralized essayist"—in the quoted sentence [*CW* 26, n. 1].) Joyce, still the model student, "admit[s] that the most important study for the mind is Mathematics, and our vindication of Literature will never venture to put it before Mathematics" (*CW* 27), because doubting the primacy of mathematics "for the building of an intellectual man" (*CW* 26) would surely be considered "false reasoning," as Smith puts it, provoking much the same response from Joyce's teacher as would any questioning of the logical and coherent order of the church's doctrines.

Consequently, when the exotic word "*paralysis*" in the opening paragraph of *Dubliners* triggers associations with "the word *gnomon* in the Euclid and the word *simony* in the Catechism" in the mind of a schoolboy (*D* 9), the child is not free-associating geometry and theology; he is merely reflecting the equivalent status of Euclid's *Elements* and religious doctrine in both secular and Catholic education, circa "July 1st, 1895" (*D* 12), an equivalence evident in the parallel methodologies of the *Elements* of Euclid and the *Maynooth Catechism*, which further constrains the "freedom" of the boy's association: these two texts present similarly rigorous deductive systems of explanation, both derived from first principles. Moreover, by expressing a desire "to look upon [the] deadly work" of paralysis (*D* 9), the boy reveals his assimilation of the essentially Euclidean "perceptual model of objective knowledge" inculcated both by Scholastic theology and by Cartesian empiricism: "Cartesian science is . . . grounded in an *a priori* intuition of space, the clear and distinct perception of extension which guarantees the truth of the axioms of Euclidean geometry" (Tiles 50, 30).[3] Like Euclid (and like Descartes, as I show later on), the boy in "The Sisters" assumes that by looking at things you can understand them. Euclidean geometry, likewise, "sets out with, and proceeds throughout on, the postulate that truth, objective truth, exists, that it should be sought for, [and] that in many cases it may be ascertained" (T. Smith 162). The Catholic philosophic tradition, in turn, formulated a corollary to this Euclidean postulate of truth, maintaining that spiritual truth, too, exists and in many cases may be ascertained by an extension from the perceptual analysis of its parallel and complementary forms in reality. (Such is the logic of Aquinas's version of the "ontological proof," the argument from experience [Copleston, *Medieval Philosophy* 2:56–65].) As Euclid provided the "catechism" for Western mathematics and science, the unquestioned and unquestionable perceptual (and fundamentally *visual*) basis for a rational and objective knowledge of the external world, St. Thomas Aquinas, the "spiritual Euclid" of Catholicism who conceived all forms of intellectual perception in terms of sight, provided the "realist and concrete" system upon which Catholic education rested (Kline, *Mathematics in Culture* 96; Noon 25–26, n. 9; Copleston, *Medieval Philosophy* 2:26 and passim).[4] Ultimately, as I will show, Stephen Dedalus's choice to "forsake" religion as "an absurdity," despite its logic and coherence (*P* 244), entails James Joyce's rejection of *both* Catholicism and the Euclidean worldview.

The Alexandrian geometer Euclid (ca. 330–275 B.C.) himself seems to have resembled a product of Scholastic education, for like Joyce, who credited the Jesuits for training him "to arrange things so that they can be grasped and judged" (Suter 64), Euclid, "the greatest systematizer of his age," chiefly arranged rather than formulated his geometry: "Few, if any, of the theorems established in the *Elements* are his own discoveries. His greatness lies in his organization, into a deductive system, of all of the geometry known in his day" (Blumenthal 2). Euclid's achievement was a synthesis. The fifteen books of his *Elements of Geometry* (the *Stoicheia*, ca. 300 B.C.) build on the prior achievements of Thales of Miletus (640–546 B.C.), Pythagoras (ca. 580–500 B.C.), and Eudoxus (408–355 B.C.).[5] Fortified by Plato's endorsement of geometry's value ("it tends to facilitate the apprehension of the idea of good" [*Republic* 7.526e]) and employing the syllogistic method of Aristotle's *Posterior Analytics* (W. D. Ross 47), Euclid's *Elements* became what Morris Kline has called the "most influential . . . textbook in history":

> The creation of Euclidean geometry was more than the contribution of some useful and beautiful theorems. It engendered a rational spirit. No other human creation has demonstrated how much knowledge can

> be derived by reasoning alone as have the hundreds of proofs in Euclid. The deduction of these numerous and profound results taught the Greeks and later civilizations the power of reason and gave them the confidence in what could be achieved by this faculty. Encouraged by this evidence, Western man was inspired to apply reason elsewhere. Theologians, logicians, philosophers, statesmen, and all seekers of truth have imitated the form and procedure of Euclidean geometry. (*Mathematics in Culture* 42, 53–54)

More than this, Euclid's geometry seemed to be "unquestionably true of the physical world" it described, both to the Greeks and to its students for over two thousand years; his rigorously consistent axioms were "universally acceptable" formulations, statements of "absolute truths" (Kline, *Mathematics in Culture* 43). Thus the study of geometry became the pursuit of divine truth itself, as both the Platonic and Christian traditions transformed the contemplation of geometrical forms into a ritual activity, unwittingly reciprocating geometry's remote origins in ancient Greek and Hindu religious rites.[6] To Plato (ca. 427–347 B.C.), "geometry is the knowledge of the eternally existent" and provides the basis for the perception of divine order (*Republic* 7.527b). In his account of creation in the *Timaeus*, Plato's god is a geometer, fashioning the world, for example, as a "cube" and the things of the earth—the elements—and all bodies out of "triangles" (53c-55e).[7] Legend has it, and for good reason, that the inscription over the entrance to Plato's Academy read, "Let no one ignorant of mathematics enter here" (Kline, *Mathematics in Culture* 54). The Christian Platonist St. Augustine (A.D. 354–430) similarly considered an understanding of mathematics, particularly geometry, to offer access to the mind of God. Augustine argues that the study of "ideal geometrical figures," promoting the discovery of "objects of knowledge which are above the human mind," leads to the apprehension of the "eternal truths [that] are in God. 'The ideas are certain archetypal forms or stable and immutable essences of things, which have not themselves been formed but, existing eternally and without change, are contained in the divine intelligence' " (*De Ideis* 2; qtd. in Copleston, *Medieval Philosophy* 1:74–75).

To St. Thomas Aquinas (1225–74), who played Aristotle to St. Augustine's Plato, geometry was less the "study of an ideal order [than] a science of the real world," yet the analyses of the geometer were nevertheless valuable as a preliminary exercise in a spiritual education. The "abstraction of form from matter"—a process that was to influence Stephen Dedalus's theory of art in

A Portrait of the Artist as a Young Man—trained the mind to discover the "essence, species, definition, quiddity" of the mathematical object (V. Smith 65, 24, 29). Aquinas's chief relation to Euclid, however, is his comparable role as the systematizer of Christian theology, forging a rigorously deductive vision of order by means of an Aristotelian (syllogistic) method. It was left to the great "continuator of the work of St. Thomas," Duns Scotus (ca. 1265–1308), to make explicit the pedagogical importance of Euclid in the Scholastic intellectual tradition in his *Opus Oxoniense* (ca. 1300): "Scotus's ideal of science was mathematic[s]. . . . Scotus is clearly taking geometrical science as the model of science" (Copleston, *Medieval Philosophy* 2:204, 217). (Very likely Scotus also knew the *Opus Maius* [ca. 1266–70] of Roger Bacon [ca. 1214–94], which, by emphasizing the importance of mathematics for scientific inquiry, was a major influence on the medieval mathematization of science.)[8] The greatest stimulus to the eventual "geometricization" of Western science, however, was the achievement of the French philosopher and mathematician René Descartes (1596–1650). Independent of, yet simultaneously with, another French mathematician, Pierre Fermat (1601–65), Descartes formulated an analytic geometry by which "the universe could be quantified and objectified" and thus the "real" world's mysteries could yield to mathematical analysis (Peat, *Philosopher's Stone* 24).[9] By making it possible to quantify space in terms of numerical coordinates, Descartes overcame the limiting abstraction of Euclidean geometry, which ignores quantity—a square is square regardless of its size ("scale invariance")—and by making quantity visible and concrete, he overcame the limiting abstraction of idealized mathematical calculation. Descartes's innovative synthesis of the descriptive power of geometry and the computational power of algebra provided "the basis of all modern applied mathematics" (Kline, *Mathematics in Culture* 163).

Descartes, a product of his Jesuit education at La Flèche, seems like Joyce to have developed an appreciation for coherent systems of thought, more perhaps from his training in Euclid than from his study of a theology that he pictures as intellectual sophistry, only distantly related to the logical clarity of Aquinas (Copleston, *Descartes to Leibniz* 74–75). In the autobiographical account of his intellectual formation with which he opens his *Discourse on Method* (1637), Descartes describes his early ambition to recast all learning, including scientific knowledge, as the medieval Schoolmen had formed Catholic theology, into a rigorously deductive Euclidean system employing the "long chains of reasoning, so simple and easy, which enabled the geometricians to reach the most difficult demonstrations" (15).[10] Like the naive young boy in

"The Sisters," and like the skeptical adult Joyce who stands behind this boy's naïveté, Descartes was driven in his ambition to reestablish learning on the perceptual model by his recognition that his teachers were skilled in making "complex and mysterious" those matters that he "had always regarded as the simplest acts" (*D* 13). Descartes's experience of teachers like Fr. Flynn led him, he recalls, to distrust "speculations which produce no effect, and which have no consequences to [the scholar] except perhaps that the farther they are removed from common sense, the more they titillate his vanity, since then he needs so much more wit and skill to make them seem plausible" (9). As Herbert Butterfield has remarked, Descartes's *Discourse on Method* provided the archetypal pattern—the discovery of a clarity in geometry that was conspicuously lacking in the "sophistries and obscurities" of theological discourse—that recurs in the biographies of the leading scientists in the *philosophe* movement: Bernoulli, Varignon, Boerhaave, and so on (174–75). This pattern is also imminent in the boy's nascent skepticism in "The Sisters" and complete in the matured Cartesian skepticism of the objective author, Joyce, who stands behind this boy. Descartes's contempt for such sophistry is evident in his third rule for the pursuit of knowledge, a clear extrapolation from his study of geometry: "to think in an orderly fashion when concerned with the search for truth, beginning with the things which were simplest and easiest to understand, and gradually and by degrees reaching toward more complex knowledge" (15). His Cartesian system, consequently, moves "by chains of reasoning," by the principles of both geometrical and philosophical "extension" (Butterfield 125), from the simplicity of sense perception to a physics and ultimately to a metaphysics, all of which Descartes grounds on "vision as [the] paradigm for sensation" (Caton 87), much as Euclid's geometry relies on vision as the paradigm for the understanding of space.[11]

Thus geometry, which had retained a prominent place in the Scholastic quadrivium from the twelfth century on, not only restored an earthly equivalent to the logical and coherent order of Christian doctrine but also emerged as the foundation for all applied mathematics, the essential preparation for all scientific study in the Cartesian tradition. Accordingly the study of geometry was central in the Jesuit *Ratio Studiorum* and most especially in the revised *Ratio* of 1832, which, with an intensified emphasis on mathematics and science, dictated James Joyce's curricula at Clongowes Wood and Belvedere College (Sullivan 73). In "The Jesuit System of Studies" at Clongowes, for example, "the entry into scientific studies was made through Plane and Solid Geometry into Astronomy. From 1835 at Clongowes, scientific studies [were] always based on mathematical processes" (Corcoran 85, 88). This "hegemony of Euclidean geometry" in European education, as Joan Richards has observed, was to remain unchallenged into the early years of the twentieth century (*Mathematical Visions* 198).[12]

The late Victorian schoolboy James Joyce came to know his Euclid in truncated form. Thomas Smith observes that in "the universal usage of mankind . . . [,] at least of juvenile mankind . . . [,] *Euclid* means not a man but geometry; and geometry means 'the first six books'" of the *Elements* (56). Otherwise, nineteenth-century texts differed little from the *Stoicheia* of the third century B.C. Augustine, Aquinas, and Duns Scotus had known only Latin translations from corrupt Arabic texts of the *Elements*, one version of which was among the first printed books (1482); the discovery of a surviving Greek version in 1533, "soon followed by others . . . brought from Alexandria before the destruction of the great library," made more accurate translations possible (T. Smith 81).[13] The first rendering of Euclid into English was from these Greek manuscripts, by Henry Billingsley in 1570, whose work provided the basis for countless later school texts. The most influential and popular English edition, however, was John Playfair's 1795 version, which included his treatise on the first six books, as well as his famous modification of Euclid's problematic fifth postulate (the so-called parallel postulate—non-Euclidean geometry, as I discuss in the next chapter, springs from this problematic fifth postulate). Playfair's *Euclid* went through ten editions, the last appearing in 1846 (Blumenthal 11); it is safe to assume that whatever Euclid text Joyce studied was close to the spirit and letter of Playfair, whose reconception of the parallel postulate he alludes to in *Ulysses* (17.2085–89).

Although we have no way of knowing what edition of Euclid Joyce used at Belvedere College, we do know that he believed that both an "improperly arranged" (U 17.1358) and a proper personal library would be incomplete without a copy of the *Elements*; Leopold Bloom has an early eighteenth-century edition of the *Short but yet Plain Elements of Geometry* among his volumes (U 17.1397–1407),[14] and Joyce himself had Hall and Stevens's *Text-Book of Euclid's Elements* (1900) in his Trieste library, which he evidently purchased in Zürich sometime between 1915 and 1919 and which he probably plundered for his geometrical allusions in the "Ithaca" chapter of *Ulysses*.[15]

We can be sure that James Joyce was as thoroughly grounded in Euclidean geometry through his education as he was in Catholic theology, given the emphasis on Euclid in both secular and Jesuit pedagogy. Beyond referring to Euclid in the first paragraph of *Dubliners*, Joyce demonstrates the extent of his own acceptance of a Euclidean worldview by repeatedly employing the Cartesian perceptual model of objective knowledge—that is, by assuming that an aboriginal reality can be accurately discerned and objectively described—throughout his collection. Joyce also manifests a Euclidean Scholasticism in his compulsion to order and arrange his stories to give the appearance of a rigorously systematic representation of reality, appropriating the model of the syllogism as a structure among and within individual stories, emulating the order of Euclid's *Elements* in the four-part organization of his "chapter of the moral history of [his] country" (*Letters II* 134), and embedding in the text a pattern of geometrical allusions that tie his original and final endings in "Grace" and "The Dead," respectively, to his beginning, "The Sisters." It could also be argued that Joyce's decision to write *Dubliners* "in a style of scrupulous meanness" (*Letters II* 134)—the "clear hard prose" Ezra Pound so greatly admired (399)—owes as much to the rigorously objective style of Euclid as it does to the positivist diction of literary naturalism. Ultimately, however, the correlation between geometry and theology found in Scholastic tradition and in the first paragraph of "The Sisters"—Euclid and the catechism—does more than reflect Joyce's unquestioned assumption of Euclid's worldview and method. This correlation also provides the key—*Eucleides* means "*the happy key*" (T. Smith 5)—for what Edward Brandabur calls Joyce's "Catholic sense of the reality of a spiritual world" in his stories (165). Indeed, Joyce embeds a Euclidean figure in his collection, the "rectangular parallelogram" (Euclid 30), to represent the "parallel lines" of the real world and the spiritual or symbolic world in *Dubliners*, inviting a reading of the surface and subtext of his narratives in terms of Euclid's problematic fifth axiom (Euclid 2), the "parallel postulate."

THE PERCEPTUAL MODEL

The extent to which Joyce uses the perceptual model of cognition is readily evident even to beginning readers of *Dubliners*. Story after story culminates in the moment of vision—or failure of vision—as Joyce's characters and readers attempt, in parallel, to read the meaning of their experiences in reality. In "The Sisters" the boy gratifies his desire to "look upon [the] deadly work" of paralysis when he views the corpse of Fr. Flynn: "There he lay, solemn and copious" (*D* 14). As the boy learns from this funereal viewing, as he literally and intellectually *sees*, he cannot evade the objective reality of death, even by fantasy: "The fancy came upon me that the old priest was smiling as he lay there in his coffin. But no" (*D* 14). Similarly, the boy in "An Encounter" visually discovers the perverted reality that counters his romantic fancy of adventure when he meets the "gaze of [an old josser's] pair of bottle-green eyes" (*D* 27), and the boy in "Araby" experiences an ambiguously blinding insight into himself while "gazing up into the darkness" at his story's conclusion (*D* 35). Eveline's blank stare ("Eveline"; *D* 41), Lenehan's "gaze" at the coin in Corley's palm ("Two Gallants"; *D* 60), Polly Mooney's insensible "gaze" at the pillows on her bed ("The Boarding House"; *D* 68), and such conspicuous later moments as when the blindfolded Maria fails to see what her hand feels ("Clay"; *D* 105) or when Fr. Purdon urges the businessmen in "Grace" to "look" into their spiritual "accounts" (*D* 174) mark the moments of vision, or failure of vision, throughout the collection. Each of these visual events, culminating in Gabriel's epiphanic view of Ireland in the final story, although generating an often-noted motif in *Dubliners*,[16] is most significant for a self-evident and thus infrequently emphasized reason: the effectiveness of the Joycean "epiphany" rests on a still unquestioned assumption, shared by Joyce and most of his readers, that something like an objective reality exists, that the individual perceives and understands the orders of reality by a concentrated visual attention. Whether or not we choose to call these moments of vision "epiphanies," after Stephen Deadalus's definition of the concept in emphatically *visual* terms in *Stephen Hero*—the early version of *A Portrait of the Artist as a Young Man*—as one's perception of a "thing" as "*that* thing which it is" (*SH* 213; also see *P* 213), it is clear that Joyce structures his stories to present climactic recognitions of the real, achieved or missed by his characters, throughout the collection.[17] To the Joyce of *Dubliners*, the verb *see* clearly means, as it has always meant in the Cartesian tradition, both "to look" and "to understand."[18]

A similar, unquestioned "common sense" view of concrete reality provided the original basis for the formulation and systematization of geometry, the most pragmatic and least abstract of the mathematical disciplines. Whatever its ritual origins, the Greeks and the Egyptians before them valued geometry for its practical use in delineating property lines (the Greek roots of *geometry* mean "the measure of the earth"); for generations before and since Euclid, there was no question that measurements, literally *grounded* in the real, represent an objective truth about reality. Complexity could be resolved into simple geometrical figures, and simple geometrical figures could generate a complexity (e.g., the mosaic). Employing only two concepts, the circle and the line, and their corresponding tools, the compass and the straightedge (the only implements permitted, for example, to those who sought to "square the circle" [Kline, *Mathematics in Culture* 50]), geometers could discern the order of reality.

This clear and persistent certainty of the geometrical order of the real, moreover, underlies the development of realism in Western art, as Rudolf Arnheim observes in *Art and Visual Perception* (265–84 and passim). Early in the Italian Renaissance both Brunelleschi (ca. 1377–1446) and Piero della Francesca (ca. 1420–92), the "great master of perspective and, incidentally, one of the best mathematicians of the fifteenth century," established their new "science of painting" on the principles of Euclidean geometry (Kline, *Mathematics in Culture* 132–33). Leonardo da Vinci (1452–1519), in turn, was to echo both the motto of the Platonic academy and Piero's emphasis on geometry for rendering optical perspective by opening "his *Trattato della Pittura* with the words, 'Let no one who is not a mathematician read my works'" (Kline, *Mathematics in Culture* 133; also see Leonardo's inscription and circumscription of the human figure, within the square and circle, in his famous sketch of the proportions of the human body, *Proporzioni del corpo umano*).[19] In the north Albrecht Dürer (1471–1528) both constructed "drawing machines" to facilitate the artist's rendering of perspective and wrote a highly influential treatise about the geometrical representation of reality, *Underweysung der Messung mit dem Zyrkel und Rychtscheyd* (1528) (Arnheim 279–80; Kline, *Mathematics in Culture* 133–34).

The artists' and geometers' mutual confidence that their measuring was simply a discovery of order, rather than the subjective imposition of human orders on an "other," seems not to have been seriously threatened until well into the nineteenth century. Even Immanuel Kant (1724–1804), despite his considerable influence on the growing awareness of human subjectivity, considered the axioms and theorems of geometry to be truths, at least to the extent that our minds possess the forms of space as prior conditions for our perception of an objective reality: "Geometry is a science which determines the properties of space synthetically, and yet *a priori*" (*Critique of Pure Reason* [1781], 44). (It is not easy to follow Kant's explanation of how geometry can be both synthetic and a priori, but his argument resembles Plato's doctrine of the *anamnesis* of geometrical forms in the *Meno*'s "geometry lesson" [82b–86b].)[20] In his *Prolegomena to Any Future Metaphysics* (1783) Kant repeats his assertion "that certain pure synthetic knowledge *a priori* is real and given, namely *pure mathematics*" (29), offering a fuller commentary on the truths of "pure mathematics" (36–51), of which geometry, "the pure intuition of space" (39), is his prime exemplar: "It follows that the propositions of geometry are not determinations of a mere creature of our poetic fantasy which could not be reliably referred to real objects, but that they hold necessarily of space . . . because space is nothing other than the form of all outer appearances under which alone objects of the sense can be given to us. Sensibility, the form of which is the ground of geometry, is that on which the possibility of outer appearances rests; hence these can never contain anything other than what geometry prescribes to them (43).[21]

As I already mentioned, St. Augustine and St. Thomas Aquinas had similarly accepted the Euclidean assumptions that reality, no "mere creature of our poetic fantasy," both exists and can be understood and described visually, while they appropriated Platonic and Aristotelian psychology, respectively, to account for the role of the remaining senses in the soul's progress toward an understanding of existential reality. The full perceptual model of objective knowledge in Christian philosophy, and in the Western scientific tradition as well, asserts that the individual grasps objective reality primarily by vision but may also do so by any and all of the remaining senses. As vision provides a general "paradigm for sensation" for Descartes (Caton 87), for St. Thomas vision stands for all orders of perception: "The word 'sight,' for Aquinas, referred to all knowledge obtained through the intellect" (Noon 25–26, n. 9). Correspondingly, although stressing the visual access to an aboriginal reality throughout *Dubliners*, Joyce also emphasizes the nonvisual access for character and reader alike to a "morphomelosophopancreate[d]" world (*FW* 88.9; Joyce's portmanteau word conflates most of the sensory processes by which we grasp the "audible-visible-gnosible-edible world," "cognitively" [*FW* 88.6–7] and universally ["pan"], by vision ["morpho"= form], hearing ["melo" = sound], understanding ["sopho" = wisdom], and taste ["pancreate" = suggesting both that which the cooking "pan" creates and that which the pancreatic juices digest!]). Thus in the third paragraph of "Araby" ("When the short days of winter came . . ." [*D* 30]), Joyce, anticipating the synesthesia he achieves by a single word in the *Wake*, suggests that his central character's nascent sensuality proceeds inevitably and apparently hierarchically from his full sensory response to the real: in the early winter evening, before "we had well eaten our dinners" (taste), when the sky was "the colour of ever-changing violet" (sight), the "cold air stung us" (touch), and the children's "shouts echoed in the silent street" (hearing), as the boys ran "to the back doors of the dark dripping gardens where odours arose from the ashpits, to the dark odorous stables" (smell), and so on. Joyce evokes his readers' sensory responses, too, although the medium of fiction limits what he can do with taste, touch, and smell to the audience's vicarious participation. A model paragraph from "The Dead," however, illustrates how Joyce can exploit a variety of auditory devices—alliteration, assonance, consonance, onomatopoeia, phonetic intensives ("nudge," "unsettlings," "pushed"), and even punctuation ("A pause followed," followed by a comma)—to make his visual description audible (note my emphases):

> The raisins and almonds and figs and apples and oranges and chocolates and sweets were now passed about the table and Aunt Julia invited all the guests to have either port or sherry. At first Mr Bartell D'Arcy refused to take either but one of his neighbors nudged him and whispered something to him upon which he allowed his glass to be filled. Gradually as the last glasses were being filled the conversation ceased. A pause followed, broken only by the noise of the wine and by unsettlings of chairs. The Misses Morkan, all three, looked down at the tablecloth. Someone coughed once or twice and then a few gentlemen patted the table gently as a signal for silence. The silence came and Gabriel pushed back his chair and stood up. (*D* 201)

One might say that in this marvelous paragraph, bracketed by the parallel sequences in space (the cornucopia of fruits and sweets) and in time (Gabriel's rising), the "noise of the wine" is the least audible sound present, even if the filling of D'Arcy's glass *is* "allowed." Within a "rectangular" block of text, bracketed by unbroken parallel "lines"—unpunctuated sequences in space and in time—the reader experiences the auditory dimension of a represented, visual real, "the ineluctable modality of the audible" contained within the "ineluctable modality of the visible" (*U* 3.13, .1). As I will show, the geometrical figure of the rectangular parallelogram in this paragraph also operates in "The Dead" as a whole and globally in the collection of *Dubliners*.

THE ART OF ARRANGEMENT

Joyce's schooling in Euclidean geometry, even more than his training in Scholastic argumentation, taught him to value the syllogistic method as a structure for rational thought, the logical model that Euclid appropriated from Aristotle's *Posterior Analytics* and passed on to Aquinas. Whatever its primary source for Joyce, the syllogism often governs the relations among stories in *Dubliners* and dictates the structure of several individual stories.[22] The thematic connections among the first three stories in particular generate a syllogistic argument as their central characters come to "see" what it means to be a Dubliner:

A. a boy learns that paralysis is the condition of the Dubliner ("The Sisters");
B. a boy learns to appreciate that he is a member of the community, Dublin, which he had to this point "always despised . . . a little" (*D* 28) ("An Encounter");
C. a Dublin boy is paralyzed in and by his attempt to achieve integration with this community ("Araby").

The fourth story, "Eveline," embodies a straightforward syllogism:

A. in Eveline's experience, relationships between men and women are abusive;
B. Frank offers Eveline a relationship;
C. Eveline withdraws in terror from a potentially abusive relationship with Frank (who may not be altogether "frank").

Virtually every story in *Dubliners* falls into three natural divisions, equally inviting syllogistic readings: Mrs. Mooney's, Bob Doran's, and Polly's narratives in "The Boarding House"; the parallel office-pub-home sequences in "A Little Cloud" and "Counterparts"; Maria's journey from laundry, to shops, to the Donnellys' home in "Clay"; Tom Kernan's progress from pub, to sickroom, to chapel in "Grace"; the three-act structure of "The Dead"; and so on.[23]

Joyce's Euclidean worldview is equally evident in his concern for the form of his collection, his decision to arrange the original twelve (of fifteen) *Dubliners* stories in four groups containing three stories each of "childhood," "adolescence," "maturity," and "public life" (*Letters II* 134).[24] Joyce's arrangement of *Dubliners*, as I will show, is an essentially geometric act of construction. His critics, however, have universally overlooked the Euclidean basis of his compulsion to arrange his materials, his "desperate need for principles of order and authority" in all his works (Litz, *Art* 24), from this four-part organization in *Dubliners* or his "rhythm[ic]" and "analogical" structure in *A Portrait of the Artist as a Young Man* (Litz, *James Joyce* 66; Kenner, *Dublin's Joyce* 129) to his elaborate Homeric and Viconian schema in *Ulysses* and *Finnegans Wake*. The standard assumption in Joyce criticism is that his structuring impulse was the consequence of a Jesuit education that had "developed habits of mind which placed a premium on intellectual order and thoroughness, and on the systemization and schematization of knowledge" (Sullivan 10), a view Joyce himself generally supports by crediting the Jesuits for teaching him "to arrange things so that they can be grasped and judged" (Suter 64). What is missing from this picture is the specific and central role of geometrical study for the development of "mental precision and . . . a zest for careful and orderly method" in Joyce's Jesuit education (*CW* 26). If Fr. Noon is correct in finding Joyce's "exposure" to Scholastic philosophy to have been casual and derivative ("there is no proof that Joyce ever took any formal courses in philosophy at all" [2–3]), there is even more reason to believe that it was not so much Joyce's familiarity with Aquinas as his extended exposure to Euclidean geometry, an exposure he shared with his modernist contemporaries, that was the primary source of his attraction to intellectual order and schematization. This compulsion to arrange his materials, to *construct* the work of art, is clearly one of the defining characteristics of Joyce's modernism that associates him with other major modernist writers—Yeats, Eliot, Pound, among others—none of whom shared his Jesuitical background but none of whom could escape, any more than he, the "hegemony of Euclidean geometry" in nineteenth-century education (Richards, *Mathematical Visions* 198). As David Lachterman has argued in his *Ethics of Geometry* (1989), the central "'idea' giving significant shape to the 'constellation' of themes ingredient in modernity . . . is the [traditional geometrical] 'idea' of construction or, more broadly, the 'idea' of the *mind* as essentially the power of making, fashioning, crafting, producing" (4), a view of creativity that the study of classical geometry clearly fostered. To this Joyce would add that the artist, employing this constructive power of the mind, "forg[es] anew in his workshop out of the sluggish matter of the earth a new soaring impalpable imperishable being" (*P* 169). Joyce's metaphor of forging is but one of many modernist "idioms" for construction and constructing, for the construct as a concept and construction as an activity, and for the postmodernist act of deconstruction, all of which "enjoy the . . . protective authority" of their traditional, Euclidean geometrical origins and their "essentially mathematical roots" (Lachterman 5, 6, 7).

The specifically mathematical roots of Joyce's four-part arrangement of *Dubliners*, although not immediately obvious, become clear when we consider the timing of his original conception of the collection's organization in the fall of 1905, coincident with his composition of what was to be his twelfth and concluding story, "Grace," and with his important revisions of his opening story, "The Sisters." Furthermore, Joyce retained his geometrical model for *Dubliners* as his collection expanded, for he sustains his Euclidean strategies in his ultimate concluding story, "The Dead." In a review of the origin and after-history of Joyce's four-part plan for *Dubliners*, three things become clear: (1) Joyce himself seems to have been chiefly responsible for providing his critics with his original schema; (2) the "protective authority" of Joyce's statement of his intentions has prevented his critics from considering the apparently bizarre "logic" of his arrangement; and (3) by this failure to question Joyce's design, combined with our general loss of the late nineteenth-century Euclidean worldview, we have lost sight of how thoroughly Joyce appropriated the logical order and central figures of Euclidean geometry, both for the overall structure of his collection and for the elemental geometrical patterns that join his end(s) in his beginning.

In late September 1905 James Joyce wrote from Trieste to his brother Stanislaus in Dublin, requesting (as ever) some personal favors and describing for the first time his plan for arranging in a coherent sequence the short stories that would eventually become *Dubliners*: "The order of the stories is as follows. *The Sisters, An Encounter* and another story ["Araby"] which are stories of my childhood: *The Boarding-House, After the Race* and *Eveline*, which are stories of adolescence: *The Clay, Counterparts*, and *A Painful Case* which are stories of mature life: *Ivy Day in the Committee Room, A Mother* and the last story of the book ["Grace"] which are stories of public life in Dublin" (*Letters II* 111). During October and November Joyce composed "Araby" and "Grace," the two remaining stories of this original twelve-story sequence, and reversed the order of his "stories of adolescence."[25] At the end of November 1905 he mailed this early version of *Dubliners* to the English publisher Grant Richards, little suspecting that he would endure nearly a year of frustrating and ultimately futile negotiation for their publication. On 26 October 1906 Richards, who feared that both he and his printer could be prosecuted for publishing an "indecent" book (Scholes, "Grant Richards" 149), finally returned Joyce's manuscript, which had grown to fourteen stories in the interim with the addition of "Two Gallants" and "A Little Cloud." (Richards would eventually accept the collection for publication eight years later.)[26]

This "curious history" of the publication delays for *Dubliners*, as Joyce called it (*Letters II* 324), is most interesting not for the often exaggerated story it tells of Joyce's defense of his artistic integrity, or for the lesson it offers on the power of censorship, but for the way in which Joyce's descriptions of his artistic intentions in his letters to Richards in 1905–6 have entered and come to dominate the critical discussion of his short fiction. Midway in his correspondence with Richards, for example, on 5 May 1906, Joyce identified a central theme in his work, defined his literary style, defended his refusal to compromise either his text or his artistic conscience, and once again described his conception of the four-part arrangement of the stories:

> My intention was to write a chapter of the moral history of my country and I chose Dublin for the scene because that city seemed to me the centre of paralysis. I have tried to present it to the indifferent public under four of its aspects: childhood, adolescence, maturity and public life. The stories are arranged in this order. I have written it for the most part in a style of scrupulous meanness and with the conviction that he is a very bold man who dares to alter in the presentment, still more to deform, whatever he has seen and heard. I cannot do any more than this. I cannot alter what I have written. (*Letters II* 134)

Countless critical studies of *Dubliners* have focused on the thematic and symbolic implications of paralysis in Joyce's stories, usually citing both this letter to Richards and his earlier, August 1904 letter to Constantine Curran ("I call the series *Dubliners* to betray the soul of that hemiplegia or paralysis which many consider a city" [*Letters I* 55]), together with the trio of symbolically suggestive, italicized terms, "*paralysis,*" "*gnomon,*" and "*simony,*" in his opening paragraph for "The Sisters" (*D* 9). Likewise one book—by its title—and countless articles and chapters on *Dubliners* have invoked Joyce's own phrase, "a style of scrupulous meanness," to characterize the narrative objectivity and scientific naturalism in the stories (see Brandabur). And hardly any substantial critical commentary on *Dubliners*, from Harry Levin's *James Joyce: A Critical Introduction*, published in 1941, to the present, fails to mention his collection's four-part organization.

Actually, there was remarkably little substantial critical commentary on *Dubliners* prior to Levin's work. Nicely illustrating what Elizabeth Hardwick calls the "infiltrative powers" of an author's "self-representations" (85), Joyce's descriptions of his intentions not only have come to dominate the discussion of his literary achievement in his collection but seem to have directly stimulated the belated critical attention to *Dubliners* in the early 1940s. The source of this stimulus, clearly, was Herbert Gorman's publication of Joyce's letters to Richards in his account of the young artist's painful "struggle . . . against prejudice, against compromise, against the shoddiness and hesitations of the British bourgeoisie" in his 1939 biography, *James Joyce* (147). The James Joyce who assisted Gorman throughout his preparation of the "authorized" biography, who characteristically erased his presence by withdrawing the authorization, and who knew Gorman's account of his difficulties with

Richards well enough to allude to the biography—before its publication—as "the *Martyrology of Gorman*" in *Finnegans Wake* (349.24) was the same James Joyce who, as recent studies have reaffirmed, worked covertly to direct the reception of both *Ulysses* and *Finnegans Wake* in the 1920s and 1930s and who seems to have used Gorman to orchestrate at a distance the critical reclamation of *Dubliners*.[27] Certainly Joyce realized that if his description of his intentions in his letters to Richards were made public, his admirers would see *Dubliners* as a precursor to his later fiction, an early example of his conscious, architectonic craftsmanship. They did, immediately. Whether or not Joyce was the "artist . . . within or behind or beyond or above [the] handiwork" of Gorman's account of his negotiations with Richards (*P* 215), two facts remain indisputable: (1) commentary on *Dubliners* suddenly took off in the 1940s, directly in the wake of Gorman's *James Joyce*, and (2) Joyce's correspondence with Richards, particularly his letter of 5 May 1906, instantly became and has continued to be an extraordinary influence on critical discussion of *Dubliners*.[28]

The most powerfully "infiltrative" representation in this letter has been Joyce's claim that he arranged his story collection in four parts. Levin became the first of many to quote or paraphrase the letter to Richards from Gorman's biography (without acknowledgment), citing Joyce's arrangement of "his book under four aspects—childhood, adolescence, maturity, and public life" (40). Not long after, in 1944, Richard Levin and Charles Shattuck quoted the same letter to open their discussion of the book's "architectural unity" in the first major journal article on *Dubliners* (49). From the mid-1940s to the present critics have invariably resurrected Joyce's fourfold division to describe the "architecture of the collection" (Litz, *James Joyce* 53) and have often structured their own discussions of the stories on "The Plan" of the book (Kenner, *Dublin's Joyce* 53).[29] Joyce's May 1906 letter, the locus classicus of his conception of a "structuring pattern" to be "imposed" on his fiction (Benstock, *Joyce* 26), has so long remained a force in Joyce criticism that, as Michael Patrick Gillespie remarks, the division of *Dubliners* "into stories of childhood, adolescence, adulthood, and public life" has "become the standard outline of the collection's structure" (146).

Yet would this standard outline ever have emerged in Joyce criticism from a direct reading of *Dubliners*? That is, if Gorman had not made available the author's architectural organization of the book by publishing his May 1906 letter to Grant Richards, would anyone now argue from *Dubliners* that the "James Joyce who habitually thought in terms of patterns and structures was now in full control of his material" (Benstock, *Joyce* 26)? No one prior to 1939, including Gorman in his critical study *James Joyce: His First Forty Years* (1924), seems to have had the barest notion of the book's arrangement of its contents. William York Tindall, one of the few influential early critics of Joyce who fail to invoke the four-part organization of *Dubliners* explicitly, touches indirectly on this question. Tindall contends that the careful reader of *Dubliners* will grasp the "unity" and "sequence" of the collection's "parts": "the fifteen stories proceed from the individual to the general and from youth to an approximation of maturity by degrees" (*Reader's Guide* 7–8).[30] By omitting the fourth term in Joyce's arrangement—stories of "public life"—Tindall admits that this reader, who might perceive pattern in the general organization of *Dubliners*, would be unlikely to see more than an ongoing concern with mature life in "Ivy Day in the Committee Room," "A Mother," and "Grace." Tindall tacitly acknowledges what few Joyceans have been willing to recognize: the fourth category in Joyce's four "aspects" of Dublin life *does not seem to fit the pattern*. The infiltrative power of Joyce's May 1906 letter to Richards, containing as it does his firm and eloquent statement of his intentions for *Dubliners*, has prevented most of his critics from noticing, and all of them from discussing, the apparently arbitrary logic of the fourth term in his schema for the collection. This fourth category of "public life" is a kind of *quartum quid*, a fourth part that neither matches nor grows out of the previous three, as stories, say, of old age or death ("The Dead"?) would; but does it, like a *tertium quid*, arise somehow from a dialectic among the previous three categories?

Without addressing this issue directly, a few critics have glanced at the logic of Joyce's arrangement and come close to answering the implied question of how Joyce's focus on public life in Dublin connects to his three-part sequence, ordered by the stages of private life.[31] Levin and Shattuck, for example, tracing the (dubious) connections between *Dubliners* and Homer's *Odyssey* in their "First Flight to Ithaca," suspect that Joyce's move to public life in "Ivy Day in the Committee Room," "A Mother," and "Grace" was his incomplete transition to "the materials of the second [public] half of the *Odyssey*," although Joyce "falls short of exhausting the possibilities" of his parallel (50). Both Margaret Church (150–56) and Jean-Michel Rabaté, importing the perspective of *Finnegans Wake* rather than *Ulysses*, see Joyce anticipating the organization of the *Wake* "with his four-part pre-Viconian scheme" (Rabaté, *Joyce* 35). Mary Reynolds, however, offers a more persuasive parallel between *Dubliners* and Dante's *Inferno*, arguing that Joyce's enlargement of focus for his fourth group of stories replicates Dante's movement from individual forms of depravity to the "anti-social quality of injustice in human malice and fraud" as he descends to the lowest depths of hell (162). Joyce's transition from his "basically tripartite structure: childhood, youth, and maturity" to "stories representing public life in Dublin . . . allow[s him] to suggest, as Dante does, a progression from the less culpable forms of moral failure to the most unregenerate evil" (163).

This is plausible, but it seems equally credible to argue that the Joyce of *Dubliners*, although "habitually" inclined to think "in terms of patterns and structures," was less in "control of his material" than Benstock believes (*Joyce* 26). The asymmetry of Joyce's arrangement scheme—with the peculiar fourth term, public life, joining the trinity of childhood, adolescence, and maturity—could simply mean that Joyce integrated his architectonic impulse less fully into his governing design for *Dubliners* than in his subsequent fiction. His habitual desire to arrange, his "desperate need for principles of order and authority" (Litz, *Art* 24), seems to have compelled him, like the Misses Morkan in "The Dead," to mix "apples and oranges" (*D* 201). Nonetheless, there *is* a logic operating in Joyce's arrangement of his stories, an important sense of a system underlying the collection, although the largely uncritical acceptance of Joyce's statement of his intentions for *Dubliners* has kept his readers—unconscious of Euclidean geometry's precarious hegemony in the first decade of the twentieth-century—from recognizing the original paradigm that provided him his four-part pattern. The timing of Joyce's two statements of his plan of arrangement, September 1905 for his less often quoted letter to Stanislaus and May 1906 for his letter to Richards, provides the context for the recovery of this Euclidean paradigm. Within this same eight-month time span Joyce composed "Grace," the last story in his original plan for *Dubliners*, and extensively revised his first story, "The Sisters." Without speculating on consequences, Hans Walter Gabler expresses the suspicion that it "is significant that a first reconsideration of the opening of the book apparently coincided with the composition of the concluding story, 'Grace' " (Preface xxviii). The greatest significance of the joint composition of "Grace" and the opening of "The Sisters" is that it enables us to date with accuracy the stage of the construction of *Dubliners* when Joyce realized that Euclidean geometry—which he could still consider to be logical, coherent, and *true*—could provide him with both a major motif within his stories and a model for the overall shape of the collection.

When Joyce wrote "Araby" and "Grace" in the fall of 1905 and solicited publishers for their interest in *Dubliners*, he had clearly begun to consider those patterns and structures of arrangement that could justify his story collection, in his own mind, as something more than a dozen disparate tales of Dublin life. As Joyce brought his volume to its preliminary completion, he returned to its opening to make the first of two substantial revisions in his first completed story, "The Sisters" (initially published in 1904). He sent this intermediate version of "The Sisters" to Richards in November 1905, only to revise it once again, sometime before 9 July 1906 (Gabler, Preface xxviii–xxix). In this later revision he reconceived his opening for the story, adding the now famous first paragraph in which the boy narrator free-associates, and Joyce underlines those exotic sounding terms "*paralysis*," "*gnomon*," and "*simony*" (*D* 9). Since this stage of revision coincides with Joyce's growing concern for the form his book would take—during these months he wedged two more stories, "Two Gallants" and "A Little Cloud," into his arrangement—there is every reason to assume that the reworked opening of "The Sisters" has as much to do with his conception of *Dubliners*'s four-part design as it clearly does with establishing his principal theme of paralysis, with its intertwined thematic and symbolic associations. When we also consider that Joyce looked at "Grace" as the structural complement to "The Sisters," the end that would join with this new beginning (at least until he conceived of another concluding story, "The Dead," in 1907), we might be reminded of another word that has "sounded strangely in [the] ears" of many of Joyce's readers (*D* 9), the exotic term *quincunx*, which appears in the final paragraphs of "Grace" (*D* 172). "In his use of the odd term 'quincunx,'" Charles Duffy remarks, "we can be quite sure that Joyce is asking us to take notice, in the same way that the opening paragraph of 'The Sisters' makes 'paralysis,' 'simony,' and 'gnomon' jump out at us" (487).[32]

A quincunx, Don Gifford notes, is an "arrangement of five points, one at each of the four corners of a square and one in the center, associated with the pattern of wounds which Jesus received on the cross" (*Joyce Annotated* 109).[33] Gifford concludes his annotation for *quincunx* with an essentially irrelevant quotation from the *Maynooth Catechism* ("the Son of God died for our sins"), implying some connection between Joyce's use of the quincunx in "Grace," his provisional close for *Dubliners*, and his reference to the catechism in the opening paragraph of the collection. The configuration of the quincunx, however, its *shape* rather than its possible religious symbolism, provides a far more convincing association with the first paragraph of "The Sisters." Since the quincunx inhabits a *geometrical* form (a square), its more plausible connection to the opening paragraph of *Dubliners* is to that other exotic word denoting a geometrical figure, "the *gnomon* in the Euclid," rather than to "the word *simony* in the Catechism" (*D* 9).[34]

Tom Kernan's return to church at the urging of his friends in "Grace" entails, among other things, a geometrical resolution of the gnomon figure, its completion as a square (see fig. 1). By sitting with Martin Cunningham in "one of the benches near the pulpit," with Mr. M'Coy seated "alone" in "the bench behind" them, and Mr. Power and Mr. Fogarty seated together behind M'Coy (*D* 172), Tom Kernan fills the final corner of both a quincunx and a square, the rectangular parallelogram toward which the gnomon tends (Euclid 30). As a supplement to and completion of the gnomon, as a design inhabiting a second design, the quincunx of "Grace" provided Joyce a "geometrical" conclusion for his original version of *Dubliners*, joining his end with his beginning by means of a Euclidean inscription exercise (superimposing one geometrical design on another). In the study of Euclidean geometry the student proceeds to such inscription problems only after mastering the postulates and propositions concerning basic geometrical forms, much as Joyce's readers move to the consideration of public life only after mastering the individual figures of Dublin in the successively more complex stages of childhood, adolescence, and maturity.

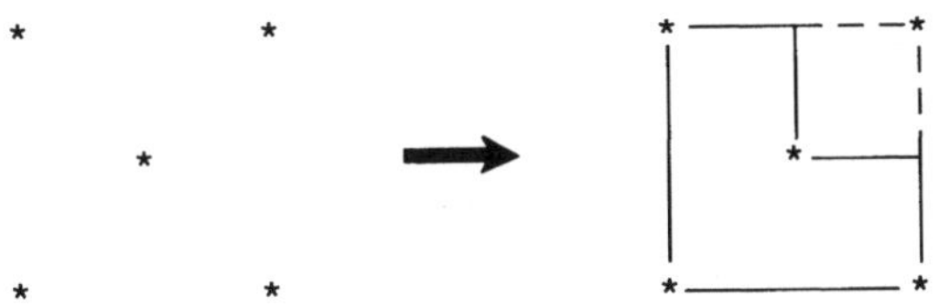

Figure 1. From quincunx to gnomon in "Grace."

To say that Joyce uses the quincunx in "Grace" geometrically, as a sign of completion both for his story and for his collection, does not mean that the ending of "Grace" is any less ironic than readers have traditionally seen it to be. In other words, although Kernan fulfills both the artist's and his friends' designs by taking his seat in church, Joyce, by emphasizing the specious morality of Fr. Purdon's "Jesuitical" sermon (Boyle 18), implies that Kernan will find no genuine fulfillment, no true grace or *place*, no integration or reintegration within the spiritual community, in this businessman's retreat. Joyce's decision to situate Kernan in the corner of the design rather than at its center, moreover, both clarifies and intensifies the irony of this ending of "Grace," contrasting Kernan's false salvation to the mystical union of the redeemed in Dante's *Paradiso* in yet another dimension of the story's geometrical allusion.

In an often cited remark in his memoir *My Brother's Keeper*, Stanislaus Joyce calls "'Grace' . . . the first instance of the use of a pattern in my brother's work," claiming that Joyce modeled the three parts of his story on the "inferno-purgatorio-paradiso" of Dante's *Divine Comedy* (228). Stanislaus need hardly add that this pattern "is ironical" (228). Although Stanislaus is not the most trustworthy source of information about Joyce's intentions, his comments seem to be entirely plausible in light of the connection between Joyce's composition of "Grace" and his reconception of his opening for "The Sisters." Joyce might well have decided to invoke the inscription above the portals of Hell from the *Inferno*—"ABANDON EVERY HOPE, YE THAT ENTER" (canto 3:9 [Dante 1:47])—in the opening line of "The Sisters" ("There was no hope for him this time [*D* 9]) to foreshadow his later allusion to the structure of the *Divine Comedy* in "Grace." He could thus join his opening to his close for *Dubliners*, in characteristic Joycean fashion. Most Dantean readings of the final version of *Dubliners* see the frigid concluding vision of "The Dead," corresponding to the ninth circle of the *Inferno*, as Joyce's similar complement to the opening line of "The Sisters" (Reynolds 161–62; Rice, "Dante" 35–36; also see Boldrini).

There is less agreement, however, about how seriously to take Joyce's supposed allusion to the *Divine Comedy* in "Grace."[35] Although Kernan's progress from the foot of the stairs, to the sickroom, and then to the "Jesuit Church in Gardiner Street" (*D* 172) clearly parallels Dante's tripartite structure, as Stanislaus Joyce says (228), there seems to be little in the story's conclusion that otherwise supports a connection to the *Paradiso*. Fr. Purdon's businesslike sermon, for example, could easily suggest that Kernan has entered the eighth circle of Hell—among the "Simonists"—rather than any paradise (Reynolds 159). If we recognize, however, that Joyce has associated the quincunx with a geometrical form, as the fulfillment of a gnomon and a sign for the completion of his collection, we can see that he concludes "Grace" with both a clear parallel and an ironic contrast to Dante's similar use of geometry for signification in the final lines of his *Paradiso* (canto 33:121–36 [3:484–85]). Only in heaven, Dante writes, where humankind joins with God, resides the solution to the most famous inscription problem in Euclidean geometry, the quadrature of the circle. The squaring of the circle, which stood for Dante as an emblem of mystical union and which Joyce visualized as a circle bounded by a square, represented a far more daunting inscription problem than the superimposition of the quincunx and the gnomon, which it only superficially resembles.[36] So, although Kernan completes the gnomon figure, fulfilling the rectangular parallelogram toward which the gnomon tends and signifying a completion of form both for the geometrical figure and for Joyce's story collection, he remains separate from the center of the design and from any Dantean suggestion of fulfillment in the ironic *Paradiso* of "Grace."

In the fall of 1905 and early months of 1906, then, as he composed "Grace," rewrote "The Sisters," and arrived at his conception of the arrangement for his stories in *Dubliners*, Joyce sought to establish his collection's ending in its beginning by embedding allusions to the *Inferno* in his opening and to the *Paradiso* in his conclusion. And although he enlarged his symbolic and thematic repertory for *Dubliners* by introducing the concepts of the gnomon and simony in his revision of "The Sisters," he may have done so principally to join his beginning to his ending, for these two terms foreshadow the Dantean "designs" embedded respectively in the quincunx and sermon of the conclusion of "Grace." Given the extent of Joyce's use of the *Divine Comedy* in the original version of *Dubliners*, it is tempting to suggest that Joyce was indebted to Dante, too, for the peculiar fourth category in his four-part arrangement of his stories, perhaps as his emulation of the medieval poet's four-stage conception of the levels of meaning inherent in myth: the literal, the allegorical (symbolic), the tropological (moral), and the anagogical (mystical) (Fletcher 313).[37] Such an argument, however, seems tenuous at best, not only because the "semantic puzzle" this "fourfold scheme of levels" has generated in literary exegesis replicates rather than resolves the problem of Joyce's arrangement—no one really seems to know what anagogy is or how it fits with the first three terms (Fletcher 313n)—but also because Joyce's schema is dynamic and linear, progressing through four stages of elaboration, whereas any one of his stories may admit analysis along a static and vertical axis, an analysis pursuing literal, symbolic, ethical, and mystical (integrative?) levels of critical interpretation (see Boyle 11–21). It is far more important to recognize that what stands behind Joyce's schema here is less Dante's example than a paradigm for the *quartum quid* shared by Joyce, the medieval poets, and ultimately Euclid, that preeminent figure who provided both Dante's symbol of the mystical union of signifier and signified in the *Paradiso* and Joyce's model for his arrangement in *Dubliners*. Angus Fletcher suspects that the fourfold scheme of levels in "medieval exegesis . . . is a translation into semantic terms of the fourfold Aristotelian scheme of *causes*" (313n), yet the most available model for this schema was not the works of Aristotle per se but the applications of Aristotelian thought found in the structure and methodology of Euclid's *Elements of Geometry*.[38]

Joyce's association of the catechism and Euclid in the opening paragraph of *Dubliners* does more than introduce two new threads of symbolism for his story collection and embed connections to the *Inferno* and *Paradiso* of Dante's *Divine Comedy* that culminate in the sermon and quincunx of "Grace"; it also reflects an unquestioned, *conventional* contemporary association between the textbook of religious doctrine and the book that had served as a "catechism" for Western mathematics and science for over two thousand years. The remarkable furor generated by any attempt to replace Euclid's *Elements of Geometry* with more modern texts in the schools in the later nineteenth century, to which I return in the next chapter, not only resembles the outcry provoked in conservative circles by perceived attacks on scriptural authority but resulted from the identical fear of any form of thought that questioned divine order. In the century that stands between today's reader and the schoolboy of Dublin on "July 1st, 1895" (D 12), not only has Euclid's *Elements* lost this canonical status "in intellectual culture" (Richards, *Mathematical Visions* 18), but the position of geometry in mathematics and mathematical education has changed so thoroughly that, for all we have gained, we have lost our sense of how completely the fundamental concepts of mathematics reside in, and were formerly taught through, Euclidean geometry.[39] (Although most math students can "square" and "cube" numbers and, less likely, solve "square" and "cube roots," few will recognize in these processes the vestiges of this geometrical approach.) Although the typical high-school student today may spend a single year in the study of geometry, the "juvenile mankind" of Joyce's generation, and the boy of "The Sisters," would have learned by rote and drill exercise, year after year, and stood repeated examinations in—as Joyce did four times in five years—the order of definitions, postulates, and propositions in the first six books of the *Elements*. A year-to-year repetition of their study thoroughly ingrained in the student's mind the arrangement of these opening books, unfolding in their inexorably logical sequence. It should come as no surprise, then, that the logic of Joyce's four-part arrangement of his stories in *Dubliners*—his progress through the three stages of childhood, adolescence, and maturity, followed by a sudden shift to the consideration of public life—owes its organization to the model of the *quartum quid* in the *Elements of Geometry*.

Simply put, Joyce's scheme for *Dubliners* parallels Euclid's arrangement of his opening books of the *Elements*. In book 1 Euclid introduces the concepts of the line and angle, proceeding to several propositions specifically concerned with the figure of the triangle. In book 2 he turns his attention to rectilinear figures (the term *gnomon* appears in definition 2 of book 2 [30]), and in book 3 he concentrates on the last principal introductory figure, the circle. With book 4 Euclid shifts to problems of inscription and circumscription (i.e., any of these shapes contained within either rectilinear or circular forms), a new consideration of the relations that exist between individual figures. We would turn to book 4, then, for axioms operating in the relation between the quincunx and the gnomon, perhaps, or in the quadrature of the circle (although neither inscription problem appears in the *Elements*).[40] Joyce's arrangement of his stories to concentrate, in turn, on individual figures of childhood, adolescence, and maturity before turning to the relations *among figures* in the "public life in Dublin" (*Letters* II 111) finds its precedent in the sequence of the opening books of Euclid's *Elements of Geometry*, the work Morris Kline calls "the progenitor of the science of logic" (*Mathematics in Culture* 55). Moreover, Joyce's *Dubliners* confirms Kline's large claim that for over two thousand years, "Theologians, logicians, philosophers, statesmen, and all seekers of truth have imitated the *form* and *procedure* of Euclidean geometry" (*Mathematics in Culture* 54; my emphases). In the major paradigm shifts in the mathematics and sciences of the twentieth century, Western culture has lost the certainties that Euclidean geometry seemed to offer for a hundred generations, much as it has lost the certitudes of religious belief found in the answers to the questions of the catechism; more than this, the collapse of this Euclidean worldview has left Joyce's readers with little sense of how thoroughly geometry had permeated the thought processes of his generation and had, much as his Catholic religion, "supersaturated" the mind of James Joyce (P 240).

THE PARALLEL POSTULATE

Although Joyce's arrangement of *Dubliners* parallels the logical order of the books of the *Elements of Geometry*, much as the tripartite structures found among and within individual stories resembles Euclid's syllogistic method, the greatest significance of Joyce's Euclideanism is that it demonstrates how thoroughly he assimilated the purportedly objective procedures for reasoning about reality common to Aristotle, Euclid, and the Scholastic tradition and still entrenched in the empirical, Cartesian worldview of the late nineteenth century. Whatever he was to "do" with aboriginal reality in his subsequent fiction, it seems clear that Joyce assumed without question the existence and knowability of the real in *Dubliners*, declaring, once again in his famous May 1906 letter to Grant Richards, that his artistic integrity rested on "the conviction that he is a very bold man who dares to alter in the presentment, still more to deform, whatever he has seen and heard" (*Letters II* 134). The skeptical reader of Joyce criticism, however, will find that the author's purported investment of spiritual or "symbolic" meaning into the reality of his accounts of Dubliners' lives is far less clear, much more open to debate. To such a reader, the symbol-hunting criticism of *Dubliners*, which finds, say, an intricate parallel to Dante in the quincunx of "Grace," may seem as much a perversion of good sense as is the insidious teaching of Fr. Flynn in "The Sisters," whose "reading" of theology shows an innocent young boy "how complex and mysterious were certain institutions of the Church which [he] had always regarded as the simplest acts" (*D* 13). Such a reader's Cartesian skepticism is reasonable, yet we will find, by remaining with Euclid a bit longer, that Joyce does in fact justify those symbolic interpretations of *Dubliners* that explore his "Catholic sense of the reality of a spiritual world" that exists, in *parallel*, with a concrete reality (Brandabur 165).

The justification for a symbolic reading of *Dubliners* has been a particularly vexing question in Joyce criticism. Although several generations of interpreters have sought and found "deeper" meanings in his fifteen ostensibly naturalistic stories, no critic has satisfactorily validated this mode of interpretation or demonstrated that the symbolic reading that Joyce authenticates in his later work should apply to his earliest narratives. For Joyce's contemporaries, this question hardly arose, and as late as 1941 Harry Levin, in his excellent overview of Joyce's achievement, echoed the well-established view that *Dubliners* is simply a technically sophisticated exercise in scientific naturalism: "The author merely watches, the characters are merely revealed, and the emphasis is on the technique of exposure" (39).[41] Thus the first readers of *Ulysses* were encouraged to recognize in this "difficult" novel a symbolic method distinctive from a one-dimensional early work like *Dubliners*. In December 1921, for example, two months before the publication of *Ulysses* in book form, the French critic Valéry Larbaud distinguished what he had earlier described as Joyce's more traditional naturalism in *Dubliners* from his symbolic method in *Ulysses*:

> Although each of these eighteen parts [of *Ulysses*] differs from all of the others in form and language, the whole forms none the less an organism, a book. . . . All sorts of coincidences, analogies, and correspondences between these different parts come to light. . . . We begin to discover and to anticipate symbols, a design, a plan, in what ap-

> peared to us at first a brilliant but confused mass . . . and we realise that we are before a much more complicated book than we had supposed, that everything which appeared arbitrary and sometimes extravagant is really deliberate and premeditated; in short, that we are before a book which has a key. (259–60)

For Larbaud, this key was not hard to find ("It is the title: *Ulysses*" [260]), and one immediate consequence of Larbaud's essay was an onslaught of symbolic readings of *Ulysses*, such as Paul Jordan Smith's optimistically titled monograph *A Key to the "Ulysses" of James Joyce* (1927), culminating in Stuart Gilbert's schematic analysis of the "thousand and one correspondences and allusions with which the book is studded" (9) in his *James Joyce's "Ulysses"* (1930). (As is now well-known, Joyce gave Larbaud his "key" for *Ulysses* [*JJII* 519] and both assisted and to some extent misled Gilbert on his exposition of the "esoteric theories which underlie the work" [Gilbert 43].)

Larbaud clearly discriminates between what he sees as Joyce's predominantly naturalistic approach to his subject matter in *Dubliners* and his symbolic method in *Ulysses*. Eventually, and apparently inevitably, all too many later critics, enthused by Larbaud's idea of a hidden symbolic agenda in *Ulysses*, extended the search for the "key" to submerged meanings back to the earlier fiction, initially turning their attention to Joyce's anticipations of his symbolic method in *A Portrait of the Artist as a Young Man* and, ultimately, arriving at this interpretive strategy for *Dubliners*. Larbaud himself invited this rearward reading of the earlier works by suggesting that a symbolic key can be found for *A Portrait of the Artist as a Young Man* in Joyce's choice of names for his central character, Stephen ("the proto-martyr") and Dedalus ("the architect of the Labyrinth") (256). The earliest important attempt to apply the reading strategies of *Ulysses* criticism to *Dubliners*, Richard Levin and Charles Shattuck's *Ulysses*-inspired exploration of the Homeric parallels in the collection entitled "First Flight to Ithaca," did not appear until 1944. Nevertheless, there now exists a considerable body of criticism on the underlying symbolic meanings of individual stories, as well as of *Dubliners* as a whole. Remarkably, despite all reasonable reservations against the practice of reading an author's early works in terms of his later techniques—implicitly denying that any development of technique has taken place—and despite a strong tradition of viewing *Dubliners* as being essentially naturalistic, as do Harry Levin and Valéry Larbaud, the quantity and quality of symbolic analyses of *Dubliners* convince their reader that Joyce may well have meant these stories to be read *both* for their indirect suggestion of "deeper" symbolic significance and for their direct treatment of slices of Dublin life. What these interpretations routinely lack, however, is anything like Larbaud's justification for seeing a symbolic pattern within surface detail ("It is the title"); they consistently fail to argue from the text itself that Joyce intended his stories to be read for their symbolism, as Larbaud has for *Ulysses*. William York Tindall, for example, takes his cue from elsewhere in Joyce, from Stephen Daedalus's definition of the "epiphany" in *Stephen Hero*, and justifies intensive symbolic readings of the stories on the assumption that Joyce's aesthetic is Stephen's, in *Dubliners* as much as in *Ulysses*: "Stephen's theory and this manuscript [*Stephen Hero*] give us a profitable way of approaching Joyce's works, all of which . . . may be thought of as epiphanies, *Dubliners* especially" (*Reader's Guide* 11).

Nonetheless, the established naturalistic approaches to *Dubliners* (e.g., Levin and Larbaud) cannot be convincingly displaced by a mere assertion, by evidence drawn from another, unpublished text. In Euclidean terms, interpretations of Joyce's symbolism in *Dubliners* rest on an undemonstrated assumption, not on any legitimating *proof*. The "decision to interpret," which to the skeptical (Cartesian) reader of Joyce criticism may sometimes seem to be prompted by a "form of paranoia" ("interpretive delirium"), must invariably be motivated by cues found *within* the text, as Tzvetan Todorov has remarked (38). A major question in *Dubliners* criticism thus remains unanswered: if the stories in *Dubliners* invite a kind of symbol-hunting reading, the search for what Todorov calls, using an intriguingly Euclidean metaphor, the "geometry of meaning" (14), do the stories themselves justify or validate this patterned symbolic interpretation?

It is tempting to seek the answer to this question, as has Larbaud, in the first "element" of the text that the reader encounters, its title. Such an argument would hold that Joyce is characteristically playing on the double entendre of *Dublin*, "doubling" his fifteen disparate, naturalistic stories with a patterned substratum of meaning; that each story has its double or doubles within the collection, as established by thematic links and symbolic clusters; and that each action or character has its counterpart or double in the symbolic or "spiritual" world of its substratum.[42] The experienced Joycean might find such a "parallel postulate" for the reading of *Dubliners* to be convincing, looking at the collection (again) from the perspective of the later work, but the uninitiated reader must suspect mostly whimsical ingenuity in the correlation, say, of the Pigeon House in "An Encounter" with the Holy Ghost, or of the "rusty bicycle-pump" (*D* 29) in the garden of "Araby" with an atrophied soul (a decayed spiritual apparatus), or of the name of Dublin with the idea of doubling.[43]

There are two serious obstacles here to seeing Joyce's title alone as a sufficient validation of his presumed symbolic method. First, *Dubliners* is a perfectly adequate and apt title for merely describing fifteen slices of Dublin life as experienced by its inhabitants. Further, *Dubliners* as a title expresses the naturalist's thesis that the stultifying environment of Dublin has determined the systematic frustration of its citizens in story after story of the collection. A second major objection to seeing its title as a key to Joyce's symbolic intentions in the collection is that *Dubliners* is as concrete and specific in its relation to reality as Euclid's geometry was taken to be in the Euclidean worldview. *Dubliners* refers to actual people in a real place, whereas the remaining titles of Joyce's major works are increasingly abstract and suggestive: *A Portrait* (a representation), *Exiles* (a condition), *Ulysses* (a mythic figure), and *Finnegans Wake* (a variety of archetypal suggestions). Nevertheless, we can make a convincing defense for seeing the parallel postulate embedded in Joyce's title for *Dubliners* as a key to, and a validation of, his correlation of discrete naturalistic accounts of Dublin life with sustained patterns of symbolism to create a "geometry of meaning," if we can show that this postulate works toward the elaboration of the full geometrical proof. Moreover, we can demonstrate this proof from within the work itself, using the limited instruments, the straightedged "lines" and defined figures of the *Elements*, to arrive at "what it was required to prove" (i.e., Euclid's *quod erat demonstrandum*, or the more familiar "Q.E.D."). Joyce corroborates the assumption that two parallel worlds of the real and the symbolic are coexistent and related in his text in a way that can be graphically illustrated by the geometrical figure of the gnomon, the incomplete rectangular parallelogram alluded to in the opening paragraph of "The Sisters."[44]

If we visualize the realistic and symbolic levels of the collection as the parallel, horizontal lines of the gnomon (A[E]C and BD, respectively, in fig. 2), then we can compare the unbroken perpendicular (AB) connecting the two horizontals—the vector projecting the reader from the level of the real to the level of the symbolic—to the emphatic invitation to seek symbolic significance in the real data of the first story's opening paragraph offered by the italicized terms *paralysis*, *gnomon*, and *simony*. As those who know the propositions and corollaries governing lines and angles are challenged to see the completed parallelogram by a small extrapolation from the gnomon, so are Joyce's readers challenged to extend and complete the figure, finding the missing angle (∠ECK) and lines (EC and KC) that connect the symbolic level

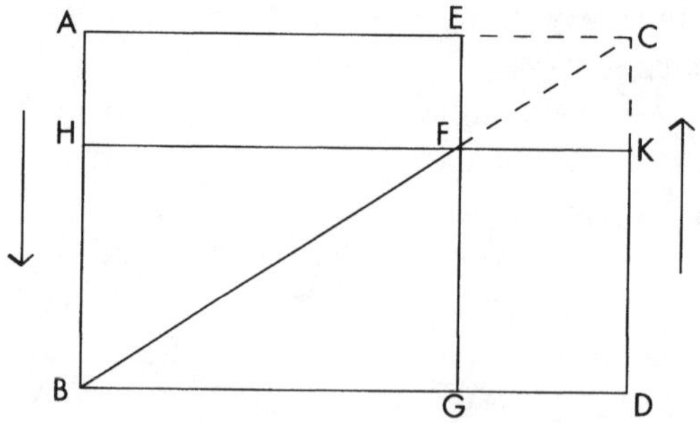

Figure 2. The gnomon, illustrating book 2, proposition 4, of Euclid's *Elements*. The lines AE and BD lie in the "planes" of the real and the symbolic, respectively. The readers' task in *Dubliners* is to complete the lines EC and (D)KC, rejoining the parallel planes in the final corner of the design. (Adapted from Robert Simson, *Euclid in Paragraphs* [1845], 43.)

back again to the real, justifying the "double" reading of *Dubliners*. And this does in fact happen, almost so easily as not to be noticed, significantly in the last "corner" of the collection, the concluding paragraph of the latest and final story, "The Dead."

If we can demonstrate, moreover, that Joyce himself in some way authenticates the symbolic interpretation of these stories, we must consider a second, similarly important issue: how far can this pursuit of symbols go before it becomes, in Todorov's terms, a kind of "interpretive delirium" (38)? Does Joyce's symbolic method give readers a license to free-associate meanings in the text, as sometimes seems to be the case in Joyce criticism? This is not a new question, although it has rarely been asked about the symbolic interpretation of *Dubliners*. Robert Adams, for example, wonders, "how far can one look for consistent meaning" in Joyce's "freely associated images" in *Ulysses*, "and how much of what one finds or creates is really relevant to the novel? Evidently there is some limit beyond which the reader is not justified in imposing *his* private associative ingenuities on the novel" (*Surface and Symbol* 26). Joyce implicitly addresses this precise issue in *Dubliners*, suggesting where this interpretive "limit" lies both for his story collection and, as I will show, for his subsequent fiction by his emphasis on the perceptual model of objective knowledge. By repeatedly bearing witness to the characters' successful and (more often) failed acts of perception in his stories, Joyce's readers develop a kind of tact, a visual/auditory acuity, an ability to distinguish between what is really being communicated and what they might wish were implied. To do this, these readers must suppress their impulse to interpret, their desire to impose meaning on their experience, until they are certain that they have attained the clear perception or apprehension of the author's statements that will ground their retrospective arrangement of the story's meaning in the text's reality. "The Dead," in particular, promotes in its readers, as in Gabriel Conroy (and, ultimately, as in James Joyce himself), a heightened awareness of the hazards of human subjectivity.

Gretta Conroy is not always thinking only of Gabriel, although he presumes she is, nor is Joyce necessarily saying what the readers would like to imagine. In *Dubliners* Joyce clearly conceives the accurate visual perception of an objective reality, the Euclidean/Cartesian model of perception, as analogous to the intellectual apprehension of objective meaning. Consequently he repeatedly interrelates vision and communication throughout his collection, especially in his final story, "The Dead." Joyce consistently ties his characters' failures of vision to their egoism—and at times to the most extreme form of egoism, solipsism—as an implied warning to readers who themselves allow fancy to occlude reality, who permit their creative imaginations to supersede the author's intentions, who fail to "hear" the words of the text. Joyce confirms this geometrical model for accurate, objective perception and affirms the parallel relation between the symbolic world and the real in his collection by resurrecting the Euclidean figure of the gnomon from the opening paragraph of "The Sisters" in the final paragraph of "The Dead" (a gesture that itself parallels Gretta Conroy's resurrection of the figure of Michael Furey).

Successful communication depends on a balance of articulateness and perception in both the communicator and the audience. Many of Joyce's Dubliners are inarticulate, for a variety of reasons. Old Cotter, in "The Sisters," speaks in broken phrases. Apprehensiveness makes the title character of "Eveline" dumb. Farrington, although he stumbles into wit on one occasion in "Counterparts," is too ignorant to speak other than with his fists. Joe Donnelly, in "Clay," can express his melancholy only by asking for a corkscrew. And Mr. Kernan, in "Grace," can hardly speak at all, for he has bitten his tongue. Those Dubliners who can speak are so blinded by egoism that they are unable to perceive their audience, and their communication rebounds on themselves: Corley, of "Two Gallants," "spoke without listening to the speech of companions. His conversation was mainly about himself" (*D* 51).

As audience, Joyce's Dubliners suffer from a variety of limitations, chiefly their inability to hear or to understand correctly what they do hear (e.g.,

Nannie and the boy in "The Sisters"). Even more prominent are the Dubliners' failures to see what lies before them as Joyce systematically correlates their limitations of vision with the limits of communication. Consider the boy and Mahony in "An Encounter." When the "queer old josser" briefly departs to do his unspecified act, presumably one of depravity, the boy narrator averts his eyes, while Mahony, who watches, is unable to describe what he is seeing: "'I say! Look what he's doing!' As I neither answered nor raised my eyes Mahony exclaimed again: 'I say . . . [Joyce's own significant ellipsis, suggesting Mahony's inability either to understand or to verbalize what he sees, other than by lapsing into the inexpressive conclusion:] He's a queer old josser!'" (*D* 26). Joyce attributes these related failures of perception and communication either to ignorance and innocence or, more disturbing, to an essential egoism that progressively moves the growing Dubliner toward solipsistic self-enclosure. In "Araby" he portrays the inarticulate and uncommunicated love of the figuratively "blind" boy for Mangan's sister. Although the boy possesses the intellectual and perceptual sophistication to "interpret [the] signs" (*D* 33) in what he hears, rightly construing the sounds of his uncle's movements on arriving home on the night of the fair as symptoms of drunkenness, he concludes his story in silence, darkness, and isolation. His culminating vision is a pseudo-enlightenment, contaminated by his unaltered egoism: "Gazing up into the darkness I saw *myself* as a creature driven and derided by vanity" (*D* 35; my emphasis). That the boy has seen something in himself is incontestable, but he is still seeing only himself. Perhaps he can be forgiven, for he is young.

Much later in the volume Joyce presents the middle-aged Mr. James Duffy, of "A Painful Case," as a less forgivable counterpart to the boy of "Araby." The egoistic Duffy initially responds to the news of Mrs. Sinico's "commonplace vulgar death" as a reflection on himself. His self-image has been tarnished by association with her: "Not merely had she degraded herself; she had degraded him" (*D* 115). On maturer consideration, however, Duffy seems to move toward an altruistic recognition of his own responsibility for her demise: "Why had he withheld life from her? Why had he sentenced her to death? He felt his moral nature falling to pieces" (*D* 117). Mr. Duffy fails to realize that his taking a perverse "credit" for a decline in Mrs. Sinico is, in fact, a sublime form of egoism. She "began to be rather intemperate in her habits" only "two years ago," the newspaper report of the inquest tells us (*D* 115), and since Mr. Duffy reads this account four years after his break with Mrs. Sinico (*D* 112), her deterioration must date from events, quite unconnected with Mr. Duffy, occurring at least two years after the end of their brief relationship. Mr. Duffy's recognition of responsibility is nothing but self-pity: "No one wanted him." He sees only himself, an "outcast from life's feast." He returns from his false moment of vision, Joyce notes, still in the darkness, "the way he had come" (D 117). Thus those Dubliners who can see, like Mr. Duffy, see only mirror images of themselves. Those who can speak and hear nonetheless listen only to the sound of their own voices: Mr. Duffy's union with Emily Sinico "exalted him, wore away the rough edges of his character, emotionalised his mental life. Sometimes he caught himself listening to the sound of his own voice. He thought that in her eyes he would ascend to an angelical stature" (D 111).

Such a self-preoccupied and sterile Dubliner as Mr. James Duffy seems to be remarkably like Gabriel Conroy in the latter's relationships to himself, his wife, and his world in Joyce's final story, "The Dead." Unlike Duffy or the boy of "Araby," however, Gabriel appears to progress toward a genuine act of communication and an uncontaminated moment of vision in the conclusion of his story, much as he ascends "from the dark" to the light (of the "heavy chandelier") in the opening two sections of the story (D 177, 186). This progress is accompanied by an escape from egoism and a new acuity of perception. Gabriel truly comes to hear his wife for the first time. Even more important, at the conclusion of the story Gabriel sees clearly for the first time (even though he has certainly taken off his glasses when going to bed). What Gabriel sees is what the perceptive reader of *Dubliners* has seen all along: the Euclidean "parallel postulate" of the collection, the simultaneous relationship of the world of reality and the world of symbolic meaning.

The examples of Mr. Duffy and the boy of "Araby," earlier in the collection, help the reader to better understand the distance Gabriel must travel during his evening. Like Duffy, Gabriel relishes the sound of his own voice, seeing himself as a gifted public speaker or the designated raconteur of the family's favorite story of Grandpa Morkan's "never-to-be-forgotten Johnny" (D 207). He too assumes that he has mounted to the stature of an angelic Gabriel in the eyes of his wife, Gretta, until shaken by the discovery of a rival angelic presence, Michael Furey. He too regards only himself throughout the story, from his early anxieties about the effectiveness of his after-dinner speech and Joyce's two significant references to his vision of himself in the mirror to the supreme egoism of his catastrophic leading question: "Gretta dear, what are you thinking about?" (D 218). Of course he presumes that she is thinking of him, not "The Lass of Aughrim" sung earlier in the evening by Bartell D'Arcy.

Joyce repeatedly correlates Gabriel's solipsistic self-preoccupation and limited vision through "The Dead" as we witness his several failures in communication. Gabriel is skilled at speaking *at* people, not communing with them. He sees his audience but does not apprehend them. Near the beginning of the story Lily's misconstruction of his apparently genuine interest in her punctures his shell. Gabriel's reassertion of their social separateness, by giving Lily a tip, quickly repairs the breech, but not before Joyce inserts a pointed reference to his limited perception: "on his hairless face there scintillated restlessly the polished lenses and the bright gilt rims of the glasses which screened his delicate and restless eyes" (*D* 178). As an audience Gabriel is equally lacking: "Gabriel could not listen while Mary Jane was playing her Academy piece." At the same time, Joyce notes that "Gabriel's eyes, irritated by the floor, which glittered with beeswax under the heavy chandelier, wandered to the wall above the piano" (*D* 186).

Gabriel's inept response to Miss Ivors's perhaps ill-timed, but nonetheless genuine attempt at communication reinforces these episodes of failed perception. The subject of her remarks, Gabriel himself, ought to guarantee his interest, yet "Gabriel tried to cover his agitation. . . . He avoided her eyes" (*D* 190). Miss Ivors, presumably an outspoken "New Woman," wants to discuss issues, not the nice music or pretty dresses that Gabriel would probably consider to be appropriate topics for a formulaic dance conversation. He cannot buy off Miss Ivors, as he has Lily. She is his social and intellectual equal. As Joyce remarks, he cannot even "risk a grandiose phrase with her" (*D* 188). He plans his payback in his after-dinner speech, when no response will be possible.

Gabriel escapes from Miss Ivors more immediately in his amusingly inconsequential conversation with Mrs. Malins. Similar to how his eyes moved from Mary Jane at the piano to the wall earlier, Gabriel first triggers the monologue of the stuttering Mrs. Malins (another limited Dubliner), who describes her "beautiful crossing" from Glasgow, her daughter's "beautiful house" and "nice friends," and her son-in-law's "beautiful big big fish"; then, "while her tongue ramble[s] on," he turns inwardly to the more important business of banishing "from his mind all memory of the unpleasant incident with Miss Ivors" (*D* 190–91). Gabriel's ideal conversation, therefore, is one he does not have to listen to, in great part because he already knows, or thinks he knows, what will be said.

The final section of "The Dead" continues this patterned juxtaposition of conversation, flawed perception, and egoism, but a significant development takes place. In a disastrous series of leading questions, provoking increasingly unexpected replies, Gabriel is forced into a communication with his wife, Gretta, a different kind of communion with her from what he had anticipated, resulting in his recognition of her otherness. The facts that she can think of someone or even something other than him, that she exists independently of him, that she has had a life before she ever met him, and that she had received the attentions, however innocent, of another male do not alone annihilate Gabriel's self-absorption, although they seriously undermine his self-possession: "A shameful consciousness of his own person assailed him. He saw himself as a ludicrous figure, acting as a pennyboy for his aunts, a nervous well-meaning sentimentalist, orating to vulgarians and idealising his own clownish lusts, the pitiable fatuous fellow he had caught a glimpse of in the mirror. Instinctively he turned his back more to the light lest she might see the shame that burned upon his forehead" (*D* 219–20). At this point Gabriel has turned his back, as well, on enlightenment. He remains turned away from the light, which enters the darkened hotel room from the lamp outside, until the concluding paragraph of the story.

Gabriel fully comes to terms with Gretta's otherness when he recognizes his failure to communicate to her the self-denying love of a Michael Furey, which she has deserved: "He had never felt like that himself towards any woman but he knew that such a feeling must be love" (*D* 223). His position is precisely analogous to that of the boy in "Araby" who has truly loved only himself, in darkness, and his recognition of this could be considered just as self-pitying as Duffy's final vision of himself "outcast from life's feast," did not Joyce preface it by noting that "generous tears filled Gabriel's eyes" and follow it with a significant moment of perception, assisted by the *generous* tears, both plentiful and altruistic, that simultaneously blur and create Gabriel's vision: "The tears gathered more thickly in his eyes and in the partial darkness he imagined he saw the form of a young man standing under a dripping tree. Other forms were near. His soul had approached that region where dwell the vast hosts of the dead. He was conscious of, but could not *apprehend*, their wayward and flickering existence" (*D* 223; my emphasis). For Gabriel's perception of these wayward and flickering existences to progress toward a full apprehension, to move from fancy to perceived reality, his ego must be suspended, as it shortly will be. Put another way, Gabriel must grasp what these flickering apparitions, these *forms*, actually are—the Euclidean act of perception—as well as what he, in his imagination, conceives them to be. Gabriel here is looking at a reflection, as Joyce will soon suggest, but at least the reflection is not now of himself.

Gabriel, an English professor, has cultivated a tendency to impose symbols on reality rather than discern the figures of reality. Earlier in the evening he stood at the foot of the stairs "gazing up at his wife. There was grace and mystery in her attitude as if she were a symbol of something." Gabriel follows this observation with the quintessential question of literary interpretation: "He asked himself what is a woman standing on the stairs in the shadow, listening to distant music, a symbol of" (*D* 210). Joyce's use of cadence, convoluted syntax (the suspended preposition), and inappropriate final punctuation in this interrogative sentence wryly suggests both the pomposity and the self-assuredness of Gabriel as the literary critic, the reader too ready to leap to symbolic meaning.[45] Gabriel does not answer his own question or offer his "reading" at this point. In the light of later events, he might interpret the visual signs in this scene, from a clearer perception of the real, as symbolic of the unknown and perhaps ultimately unknowable otherness of Gretta. At the foot of the stairs, however, Gabriel turns his attention to how, were he an artist, "he would paint her in that attitude. . . . *Distant Music* he would call the picture if he were a painter" (*D* 210), prompting the reader's association of his vision here with Little Chandler's egoistic fantasy, in "A Little Cloud," about the reviews his never-to-be-written poetry might receive. In his reverie Chandler misses his turn to Corless's; for Gabriel, it takes a moment for him to realize that the woman on the stairs is in fact his wife ("He could not see her face" [*D* 209]). Furthermore, notice Joyce's repetition of Gabriel's word of choice for Gretta's form, her "attitude," which differentiates his subjective projection of symbolic significance on Gretta from a similar act of perception earlier in the book: when the boy of "Araby" gazes up at Mangan's sister, he sees her more clearly (here he, not she, is in the "shadow"), and perhaps even more objectively (at least as a sex object), because he sees, more geometrically, "her *figure* defined by the light from the half-opened door" (*D* 30; my emphasis). Gabriel's final symbolic act of perception in his story, his vision of the "vast hosts of the dead" in the hotel room, is clearly less self-conscious than his observation of Gretta on the stairs. Gabriel is moving beyond self-fixation: "His own identity was fading out into a grey impalpable world: the solid world itself which these dead had one time reared and lived in was dissolving and dwindling" (*D* 223). Of course, what the reader realizes is that Gabriel is literally falling asleep.

But note what this realization means: Gabriel is *literally* falling asleep. At this moment in the story and in the collection, Joyce has reversed his reader's relationship to his text. Up to this point the reader so inclined has been speculatively assigning symbolic meanings to factual information presented.

At times Joyce's insistence on certain words, ideas, or motifs has encouraged this, but nowhere, at least to this point in the collection, has he validated this presumptive search for symbolic meaning. Now, however, he places the reader in the region of purely symbolic statement. Gabriel is not a "fading identity"; he is just an unsatisfied husband in a Dublin hotel, drifting off to sleep, staring at a wall, with his back to the window. While reading Gabriel's symbolic vision, the reader is aware of Gabriel, in reality, inertly lying in bed next to Gretta. The reader's ability to move from the symbolic plane to the real in this passage completes the final vector, or side, of the Euclidean gnomon (line "DC") that represents the parallel relation of the two worlds in *Dubliners* (recall fig. 2). This line leading the reader back from the symbolic to the real complements the perpendicular that leads the reader from the real to the symbolic levels of the collection in the opening paragraph of "The Sisters." Lest the reader miss this movement, Joyce has Gabriel make an identical move. At the beginning of the last paragraph of "The Dead," Gabriel hears a "few light taps" on the windowpane and turns in his bed toward the window of the hotel room. He returns to reality, emerging briefly from the twilight region of near sleep, but more is involved than simply this. Joyce provides the reader with the information to see the precise correlation between external reality and Gabriel's symbolic vision: "A few light taps upon the pane made him turn to the window. It had begun to snow again. He watched sleepily the flakes, silver and dark, falling obliquely against the lamplight" (D 223). What this tells the reader is that Gabriel's vision of the "wayward and flickering existence" of "the vast hosts of the dead" has literally been the shadows of snowflakes, projected through the window against an interior wall by an external source of light. What Gabriel has interpreted symbolically has actually been a form of cinematic projection, properly called, in the terms of projective geometry, *gnomonic* projection (see fig. 3; Kline, *Mathematics in Culture* 152).[46]

Gabriel's vision of the "hosts of the dead" is no fantasy of the dreaming ego, and this is why he is not yet asleep; although an illusion, it is also an accurate reflection of an external reality, as Gabriel *sees*. Thus Joyce brings Gabriel to the point of recognizing the interdependences of the symbolic and the real, the spiritual and the carnal, and the self and the other. As the story ends, it remains for Gabriel to complete his recognitions, to apprehend them in full consciousness, perhaps even to remodel his life on them. So also has Joyce brought his readers to the point of recognizing the interdependence of symbol and reality in the text and left them with the challenge to complete this recognition in the act of interpretation. Crucial to this task is the

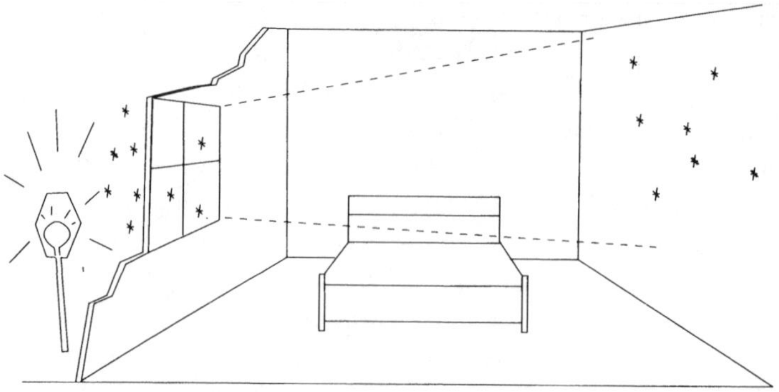

Figure 3. Gnomonic projection in "The Dead": "A ghostly light from the street lamp lay in a long shaft from one window to the door" (*D* 216).

realization that, if there exists a real correspondence to the symbolic here at the conclusion of "The Dead," by a kind of geometrical logic, by a Euclidean postulate, there also exists a symbolic correspondence to the real elsewhere, throughout *Dubliners*. Joyce has authenticated the assumption that the real and the symbolic are double, parallel planes in *Dubliners*, intersected by the opening and closing lines of the volume, which lead to and from these planes. By an act of extension, the gnomon can be fulfilled as a rectangular parallelogram by the reader's completion of this last corner of the design, much as Tom Kernan completes the embedded figure of the gnomon in "Grace," the original conclusion to *Dubliners*. Although Kernan's act of completion is ironic, denying him either fulfillment ("grace") or consciousness of his role in any larger design ("place"), Joyce's resurrection of the gnomon in the conclusion of "The Dead" shows, like so many other features of this story, an amelioration of his vision.[47] Joyce assures the reader, thematically and technically, that both the geometrical completion of the gnomon and any symbolic interpretation of *Dubliners* are not accomplished fancifully, by enthusiastic and free association; rather, they are achieved by a careful, self-effacing, objective examination of the "elements" of Euclidean reality in his text.

Neither Joyce, Gabriel, nor the reader of *Dubliners*, it seems, has been prepared to consider the possibility that this Euclidean reality itself might ultimately be just another kind of illusion, a specious form of objectivity, that all forms of perception and apprehension are necessarily and inescapably subjective. Nevertheless, it appears that precisely this realization occurred to

Joyce contemporaneous with his completion of "The Dead," in September 1907, for within a few weeks he was to begin the thorough recomposition of his objective account of his youth, *Stephen Hero*, as *A Portrait of the Artist as a Young Man*, a novel preoccupied with the nature of human subjectivity. Joyce's writing of "The Dead" could have provided the sole stimulus to his growing concern with individual subjectivity, for only in this concluding story of *Dubliners* does he abandon the detached, spectatorial narration of his first fourteen stories to fully enter the perspective of his central character (see Brown 97–103). It is equally likely, however, that his unself-conscious assumption of the Cartesian perceptual model of objective knowledge, combined with his exploitation of a Euclidean structural model for *Dubliners* as a whole, prepared him to recognize and respond in his next major work of fiction to the increasingly intense contemporary critiques of Cartesian and Euclidean subjectivity, both explicit consequences, as I show in the next chapter, of the emergence of non-Euclidean geometries.

2

THE ALIMENTS OF JUMEANTRY IN *A PORTRAIT OF THE ARTIST AS A YOUNG MAN*

"Then," said Cranly, "you do not intend to become a protestant?"

"I said that I had lost the faith," Stephen answered, "but not that I had lost selfrespect. What kind of liberation would that be to forsake an absurdity which is logical and coherent and to embrace one which is illogical and incoherent?"—(P 243–44)

Do you mean to say that you are not able to tell me what a surd is?—(P 104)

I have created a new universe from nothing.
—*Johann Bolyai (qtd. in Bonola,* NON-EUCLIDEAN GEOMETRY 98)

James Joyce's sojourn in Rome, from the end of July 1906 to early March 1907, was a watershed experience in his development as an artist. Although Grant Richards had finally rejected the intermediate, fourteen-story version of *Dubliners* in October 1906, despite having agreed to its publication seven months before, Joyce did receive a contract from Elkin Matthews in January 1907 for his first book, the volume of poetry entitled *Chamber Music*. Less immediately visible consequences of his otherwise disastrous stay in Rome, in part resulting from his disappointment with this city of the dead, were his mellowing view of Dublin and his maturing narrative art, both evident in the fifteenth and final story of *Dubliners*, "The Dead," which Joyce composed shortly after his return to Trieste in 1907. It is also clear that Joyce's original notion and title for *Ulysses* came to him while in Rome in the autumn of 1906 and, as Robert Spoo has argued, that the "inescapable presence" of the past in Rome exerted a formative influence on Joyce's conception of history, which was fully realized in *Ulysses* (482).[1] Strangely, there has been no effort to tie Joyce's "Roman holiday" to the evolution of his autobiographical novel *A Portrait of the Artist as a Young Man*. We do know that his frustrations with the composition of the early version of *A Portrait*, *Stephen Hero*, combined with his financial difficulties in Trieste in the summer of 1906, "made the city intolerable" for him, prompting his decision to seek employment in Rome (*JJII* 222). We also know that Joyce began his composition of *A Portrait*, a total reworking of the materials of *Stephen Hero*, in September 1907, six months after leaving Rome; he completed the first three of the novel's five chapters by April 1908 (*JJII* 270).[2] Richard Ellmann suspects that the birth of Joyce's daughter Lucia, in July 1907, stimulated Joyce's return to *Stephen Hero*, inspiring his reconception of his autobiographical novel as "the gestation of a soul" (*JJII* 297). Yet it is equally likely that we can associate, if not directly link, another event contemporaneous with Joyce's Roman period to his new conception of the biography of an artist's "encounter" with "reality" (*P* 159, 252–53). In 1906 Roberto Bonola, of the University of Pavia, published his now classic critical and historical survey *La Geometria Non-Euclidea*, to considerable national and international notice.[3]

There is no evidence that Joyce read Bonola, although he would very likely have been aware of him and his work in much the same way that a literate person today would recognize, say, Stephen Hawking without necessarily having read *A Brief History of Time* (1988), and he would certainly have been capable of seeing non-Euclidean geometry, as did D. H. Lawrence "as early as 1908," as a "most important scientific discovery" (Young 32). Joyce's training in Euclid, so evident in *Dubliners*, clearly positioned him to recognize that the emergence of non-Euclidean geometry, both a frequent topic in the popular press and the subject of Bonola's book, was a genuine revolution in contemporary thought, a "debacle" for the Cartesian worldview that ironically prepared the way for developments in the sciences that have obscured our sense of its revolutionary impact.[4] "The discovery that Euclidean geometry was not a unique, inevitable, and absolute truth about the world came . . . as a stunning blow" to turn-of-the-century Cartesian science, since Descartes's system depended so greatly on Euclid, yet as John Barrow further observes, the "far-reaching and irreversible" impact of this discovery extended well beyond the laboratory and classroom (*Pi in the Sky* 11). The distinguished historian Morris Kline, a man not given to hyperbole, contends that the "importance of non-Euclidean geometry in the general history of thought cannot be exaggerated. Like Copernicus' heliocentric theory, Newton's law of gravitation, and Darwin's theory of evolution, non-Euclidean geometry has radically affected science, philosophy, and religion. It is fair to say that no more cataclysmic event has ever taken place in the history of all thought" (*Mathematics in Culture* 428). It is also fair to say that non-Euclidean geometry radically affected literature in general and *A Portrait of the Artist as a Young Man* in particular. Joyce's *Portrait* is a thoroughly non-Euclidean novel in form and subject.

Joyce's notes for *Ulysses* (*"Ulysses" Notesheets* 415–89) and his allusions to geometry in its "Ithaca" episode demonstrate that he was already familiar with the history and concepts of non-Euclidean geometry by the late 1910s, and as Margaret Solomon has shown, Joyce employs four-dimensional geometry thematically and technically in *Finnegans Wake* (113–29). Joyce's internal references to geometry in *A Portrait*, however, as well as his overall reconception of both the structure and the *subjective* subject of his novel, Stephen Dedalus, suggest that we must antedate Joyce's non-Euclideanism to those formative months in Rome, from the summer of 1906 to the spring of 1907. The celebrated publication of Bonola's *Non-Euclidean Geometry* in 1906 may have been the pivotal event in Joyce's turn away from the Euclidean worldview of *Dubliners*, a turn that is imminent in "The Dead" and accomplished in *A Portrait*. True, it is equally possible that Joyce more gradually absorbed the significance of the non-Euclidean revolution from the widespread discussion of alternative geometries in popular literature and the press at the turn of the century. Non-Euclidean geometry was as "hot" a topic of popular interest from the 1880s to the second decade of this century as black holes or chaos theory is today; the non-Euclidean concept of "the fourth dimension," Linda Henderson observes, "had become almost a household word by 1910" (xix, 43).[5] Joyce seems not to have realized the full impact of the non-Euclidean revolution, however, until sometime between 1906 and early 1908, coincident with his Roman sojourn; his abandonment of both the Euclidean worldview and the related Cartesian model of the detached, spectatorial author of both *Dubliners* and *Stephen Hero* in reconceiving his autobiographical novel as a portrait of an isolated, highly subjective artist as a young man demonstrates this recognition.

In an all too common misrepresentation of early twentieth-century thought, literary historians have tended to oversimplify the transition from the cultural anxieties of the Victorian era, an "age of doubt," to the final "loss of certainty" of the modern era, locating this loss in the arrival of the "new" physics with Einstein's publication of his theory of special relativity in 1905.[6] This picture overlooks the fact that Einstein's theory was generally unknown even to the educated public until after World War I; in a far greater distortion, it entirely misses the pivotal stage in this cultural transformation, the crucial loss of faith in Cartesianism effected by the emergence of non-Euclidean geometry, one form of which, Riemannian geometry, directly led into Einstein's work.[7] Although popular literature and the press testify to the contemporary fascination with non-Euclidean geometries from the 1880s into the first two decades of this century, Einstein became a celebrity only in 1919, "at the age of forty," when astronomers experimentally confirmed some of the predictions of his theory of general relativity (1916) (Calder 1). Soon afterward Einstein became "world famous" (Calder 33), yet the public would no more have known Einstein's name or possessed even a loose conception of relativity prior to 1919 than they would have known the name or work of the Irish expatriate novelist James Joyce prior to the publication of *Ulysses*, which appeared on the day Joyce himself reached the age of forty, 2 February 1922, a few months before Einstein's Nobel Prize award in the fall of 1922.[8] Robert Graves and Alan Hodge claim that the British general public remained unaware of Einstein's achievement as late as 1921 and attribute this ignorance partly to the "popular disinterest in the more abstruse departments of science . . . and partly [to] the embarrassment of admitting that a German-speaking scientist could possibly have found anything of real interest" (94). And surely neither Joyce nor Einstein would have been aware of each other's existence, although their paths nearly crossed in Zürich, the city Einstein left a year before Joyce's arrival in 1915 (JJII 389; Calder 55). The near parallel in the dating of their early works, however, 1904–15 for *A Portrait* (P 253) and 1905–16 for Einstein's theories of special and general relativity, represents a deeper correspondence between these two men, a connection that is missing from our literary histories: both developed a new view of the individual's relationship with phenomenal reality under the shattering impact of non-Euclidean geometries, which demonstrate "that man's judgments and conclusions about space are purely of his own making" (Kline, *Mathematics in Culture* 429).

James Joyce, modest mathematical scholar though he was, would have had both sufficient knowledge and ample opportunity to follow the expositions of non-Euclidean geometry in popular literature and the press; in fact, since the topic was considered to be a species of radicalism by the guardians of orthodoxy, Joyce, the liberated young intellectual, might well have been drawn to such discussions. Thomas Smith, who in 1902, as I mention in the previous chapter, advocated the study of Euclid as "a corrective of prevalent false reasoning" that "pervades much of what is most popular in the literature . . . [and] theology of our day" (176, 162), and Lewis Carroll, who defended Euclidean geometry against all challengers in *Euclid and His Modern Rivals* (1885), were both fighting rear-guard actions against what they saw as a subversive dissemination of anti-Euclidean ideas. Smith and Carroll sound much like Gabriel Conroy, the spokesperson for conservative orthodoxy in "The Dead" who expresses alarm about the "new generation . . . growing up in our midst, a generation actuated by new ideas and new principles." To Gabriel, this "new generation" has been "educated or *hypereducated*" (D 203; my emphasis), perhaps by novel non-Euclidean ideas like *hyperspace* (i.e., four-dimensional space).

Smith and Carroll were not reacting exclusively to the emergence of non-Euclidean geometry; rather, they were resisting any attempt to displace Euclid's *Elements* as the "standard elementary textbook for all English geometry students," resistance of the sort that prompted reformist geometer J. J. Sylvester to observe that "there are some who rank Euclid as second in sacredness to the Bible alone, and as one of the advanced outposts of the British Constitution" (qtd. in Richards, *Mathematical Visions* 164). The last several chapters of Thomas Smith's *Euclid* defend Euclidean geometry against anyone who would seek to improve his system, identifying anti-Euclideanism as a symptom of a contemporary subversion of all forms of rational thought, among which Smith includes theology. Even the intellectually liberal Bertrand Russell entered this turn-of-the-century debate on the side of orthodoxy in his first book, *An Essay on the Foundations of Geometry* (1897), his attempt to reestablish Euclid's axioms in terms of projective geometry (Torretti 301–20). Generally, however, the broad-based resistance to non-Euclidean geometry at the end of the nineteenth century arose from its perceived threat to all authority, from a fear that radical thinkers exacerbated by deliberately appropriating non-Euclideanism to justify their attacks on received ideas: the new geometries "undermined absolutist views about human knowledge across a vast spectrum of human thinking," John Barrow writes, and although there "was considerable resistance to the promulgation of these new discoveries, not least amongst mathematicians" like Russell, the "term 'non-Euclidean' came to be employed in non-mathematical fields as a label for unconventional, non-traditional, or radical thinking. . . . We find articles with titles like '*Soundings in non-Euclidean economics*' and studies paralleling traditional Christian ethics with Euclideanism and its radical alternatives with the non-Euclidean paradigm" (*Pi in the Sky* 11, 12, 14).

In spite of this strong conservative resistance within and without the mathematical community, or because of it, toward the end of the nineteenth century there was already a thriving subgenre of popular fiction based on the multiple dimensions of non-Euclidean geometry. Works like Edwin A. Abbott's *Flatland* (1884), which was "the first example of popular fiction about the fourth dimension" (Henderson 17)—and which portrays a society where the penalty for non-Euclidean thoughts is imprisonment—or H. G. Wells's *Time Machine* (1895), which opens with a speculative discussion of four-dimensional geometry, are only the longest-lived survivors of a large non-technical literature that explores the "radical" ideas of non-Euclidean geometry. (Wells's "Time Traveller" is a freethinker, "one of those men who are too clever to be believed," a man whose salon allows thought to run "gracefully free of the trammels of precision" [37, 31].)[9] Several other early Wells stories—such as "The Remarkable Case of Davidson's Eyes" (1895), "The Plattner Story" (1896), and *The Invisible Man* (1897)—as well as George Macdonald's *Lilith* (1895), Joseph Conrad's and Ford Madox Hueffer's *The Inheritors* (1901), and Oscar Wilde's early spoof of the fourth dimension in "The Canterville Ghost" (1891), demonstrate the vitality of non-Euclideanism in popular and "serious" literature alike (Henderson 33–36). Perhaps the most famous fin-de-siècle work, Conrad's *Heart of Darkness* (1899), illustrates less explicit but no less relevant signs of the dissemination of non-Euclidean thought, as much by its striking moral ambiguities as by its embedded critique of "Eurocentric history" (B. Thomas 242). Conrad's equivocal response to the evil embodied in Kurtz, for example, is more a contemporary reflection of the "universal trend toward a new type of relativism, with which the downfall of Euclidean certainty struck a resonant chord," than an Einsteinian vision of moral relativity, just as his ambivalent response to imperialism reflects a realization reached by contemporary anthropologists who, in non-Euclidean fashion, "reassessed their attitude to the development of non-Western civilizations. Where once they had measured their merit by the closeness of their approach to the absolute 'ideal' displayed by the evolution of Western culture, now they recognized more forcefully the dubious nature of any such hierarchy of values" (Barrow, *Pi in the Sky* 14). From the 1880s on, then, and with increasing frequency toward the close of the nineteenth century, the demise of Euclid, a widespread subject of discussion in the press and in assorted nontechnical publications, infiltrated the popular consciousness; Duncan Sommerville's *Bibliography of Non-Euclidean Geometry* (1911), for example, lists over 3,000 titles that appeared through the first decade of the twentieth century.[10]

General interest in the new geometries was also promoted by popular "technical" books such as Jules Henri Poincaré's *Science and Hypothesis* (1902), an international bestseller and a work read, according to contemporary accounts, as avidly by the "professedly cultured" as by the "workmen and shopgirls" of Paris (Bell 530).[11] Asking his audience to imagine a "non-Euclidean world" (75), or a "world of four dimensions" (78), Poincaré popularizes his "conventionalist" philosophy for lay readers by helping them to realize that geometry is no more than a conventional conception of space, a convenient but nonetheless subjective vision of reality: "geometry is not true, it is advantageous" (91).[12] Equally popular was W. W. Rouse Ball's *Mathematical Recreations and Essays* (1892), which had reached its tenth edition by 1922 and which Joyce himself might have found interesting for its discussions of mazes, cryptographs, ciphers, and the quadrature of the circle.[13] Ball devotes several sections in early editions of his book to discussions of "hyperspace," reflecting the popular interest in the ideas of Charles Howard Hinton (1853–1907), the "first true hyperspace philosopher" (Henderson 25). Hinton, whose ideas were ultimately to influence the philosophy of the fourth dimension of P. D. Ouspensky (1878–1947) and, in turn, the development of Russian futurism, initially published his exposition of the new non-Euclidean geometry, "What Is the Fourth Dimension?" in the *Dublin University Magazine* (1880), followed by his popular explorations of hyperspace in *Scientific Romances* (1884–96), *A New Era of Thought* (1888), *The Fourth Dimension* (1904), and *An Episode of Flatland* (1907).[14] Of even more immediate influence was Hinton's most famous geometrical creation, the "tesseract," or "hypercube," a three-dimensional representation of a four-dimensional cube, which Linda Henderson argues had a substantial effect on the development of cubism in the visual arts (44–59). Joyce's allusion to the tesseract in *Finnegans Wake* (100.35) shows that he was familiar with the hypercube, which Hinton describes in detail in both *A New Era of Thought* and *The Fourth Dimension*, if not with Hinton himself.[15] Joyce could have come to an awareness of Hinton by yet another route, however: Hinton's speculations inspired several early proponents of Theosophy to incorporate non-Euclidean geometries of multiple dimensions into their conceptions of "planes of consciousness."[16] Although Joyce was derisive toward Theosophists and skeptical about their "vegetable philosophy" (*Letters* II 28), he was nonetheless familiar with Theosophist literature and retained an interest in its themes throughout his career (*JJII* 99, 121, 174).[17] Altogether the circumstantial evidence suggests that Joyce could hardly have escaped the widespread contemporary awareness of the novelties of non-Euclidean geometry, that he would have been drawn to ideas that challenged the intellectual orthodoxy of his youth, and that his training in Euclid would have prepared him to recognize the challenge non-Euclidean geometry was offering to the "powerful ontological status" of the axioms of classical geometry (Richards, "Reception" 149). Trained to view Euclid as synonymous with his Catholic catechism, as a systematic and cohesive exposition of unquestioned and unquestionable truths, Joyce was well prepared to see his geometry, like his religion, as "an absurdity which is logical and coherent" (*P* 244).

THE GEOMETRY LESSON

To paraphrase Hinton's essay title, what is non-Euclidean geometry? To answer this, we have to return to Euclid himself, who appears to have anticipated the development of alternative geometries. That seems to be the only reasonable explanation for the labored style of the famous fifth postulate, which Euclid needed to establish for the rational study of geometry. Evidently Euclid recognized an inherent flaw in his *Elements*, a problem that could undermine his entire system. Notice how he follows his first four, innocuously worded introductory postulates with the strangely formulated fifth:

> Let the following be postulated:
> 1. To draw a straight line from any point to any point.
> 2. To produce a finite straight line continuously in a straight line.
> 3. To describe a circle with any centre and distance.
> 4. That all right angles are equal to one another.
> 5. That, if a straight line falling on two straight lines make the interior angles on the same side less than two right angles, the two straight lines, if produced indefinitely, meet on that side on which are the angles less than the two right angles. (2)

Remarkably this fifth postulate, the so-called parallel postulate, contains *no* mention of parallelism. Euclid can get no further than proposition 28 of book 1 of the *Elements*, however, without employing the concept of the parallel as it was ultimately defined, in the terms familiar to elementary students of geometry, as describing "two straight lines in the same plane which do not meet even if extended infinitely far" (Wells and Hart 72; Torretti 42). (John Playfair's 1795 reformulation of the fifth postulate—mentioned in the previous chapter—provided the intermediate version that evolved into this modern wording of parallel postulate: "*Through a given point, not on a given line, only one parallel can be drawn to the given line*" [qtd. in Blumenthal 11].)

Euclid's fifth postulate is curious. It calls attention to itself in its style and manner of formulation: "It is much longer and more technical than the others and it does not possess the generality of the previous postulates" (Lanczos 58). Euclid defines parallelism implicitly by saying in effect that if two lines are *not* parallel, they will eventually meet (the test is to draw a line that crosses both other lines; if the third line creates two interior angles on one side of itself that add up to less than 180°, the first two lines will meet on that side). In other words, Euclid falls into a logical trap by attempting to establish an assumption (i.e., parallelism) on the basis of the assumption he is seeking to establish (i.e., what happens when lines are not parallel). Why does Euclid, paragon of logic, do this? Very likely he wished to avoid the full implications of parallelism; the assertion that parallel lines *never* meet would introduce the concept of infinity into the system, an abstraction that he would have found to be a repugnant defect in a mathematical science grounded in experience, in "reality." Infinity is unmeasurable, ungovernable; to describe something as infinite means no more than to say what something *is not* (i.e., not finite), not what something *is*. No respectable mathematician could allow the virus of infinity to infiltrate a calculation, and none was to attack the "problems of the infinite" successfully before Georg Cantor, at the beginning of this century (Kline, *Mathematics in Culture* 396). The rigorous rationalist Euclid, however, sought to develop a "closed and finite" mathematical system; evidently he preferred the lesser evil of a minor perversion of logic to the greater evil of an irrational concept, infinity, which would have been too much like the "irrational number," the surd, that "the Pythagorean school of mathematicians discovered to its great dismay" over two centuries before him (Kline, *Mathematics in Culture* 56, 36) (the first definition of *surd* in the *Oxford English Dictionary* is "a number or quantity that cannot be expressed in finite terms"; the OED uses the Pythagorean irrational number [e.g., $\sqrt{2}$] for illustration). Thus, in his sermon on hell in *A Portrait*, Joyce's Fr. Arnall enters where Euclid feared to tread by attempting to give spatial representation to the ungovernable concept of infinity, much as he proves to be a "geometric" theologian when he appropriates the Euclidean terminology of "extension" to characterize the torments of hell: "boundless" pain on a boundless *plane*, one might say (P 130–31). It appears that for Joyce, the "rigid lines of the doctrines of the church" (P 106) and the fixed lines of Euclidean geometry rest equally on the absurdity of infinitude.

The problem of Euclid's fifth postulate, "the scandal of geometry" (Kline, *Mathematics in Culture* 412), did not escape immediate notice; in fact, as Roberto

Bonola observes in the opening chapter of his *Non-Euclidean Geometry* (1–21), for over 2,000 years geometers sought to "improve" Euclid, either by demonstrating that his axioms and theorems could be derived independently of the parallel postulate or by rewording the postulate in some inoffensive fashion. None was successful, yet their failures were fruitful, ultimately providing the basis for the development of non-Euclidean geometry. One of the most intriguing of these "forerunners of non-Euclidean geometry" (Bonola 22) was the Italian Jesuit Gerolamo Saccheri (1667–1733), Bonola's distant predecessor as professor at the University of Pavia, whose *Euclides ab omni naevo vindicatus* (*Euclid vindicated from all defects* [1733]), took the novel approach of attempting to prove the fifth postulate by assuming it to be false, in order to

> show that such an assumption is unfeasible because it leads us to a contradiction. . . . Saccheri's method was mathematically sound; the only thing which was not sound was his attitude. When he found that assumptions about parallel lines quite different from the famous "fifth" did not lead him into the expected contradictions but into a strange and fantastic geometry which was nevertheless as consistent as Euclid's, he fell back upon his feelings instead of his brains and peppered the last pages of his work with such epithets of the logically defeated as "destroys itself," "absolutely false," "repugnant." (Reid 153–54)

What Saccheri unintentionally accomplished was to imagine a geometry "very different from that of Euclid, but just as consistent. . . . The Italian priest was unknowingly developing a new geometry" (Blumenthal 10).[18]

It took slightly less than a century for this new geometry to emerge. Not long after Kant's assertion that the truths of Euclidean geometry "hold necessarily of space" (43) in his *Prolegomena to Any Future Metaphysics* (1783), quoted in the last chapter, the famous German mathematician Karl Friedrich Gauss (1777–1855) was privately expressing his conviction "that there were no purely mathematical reasons for preferring Euclidean geometry to [a] non-Euclidean system" (Torretti 53; also see Bonola 64–75).[19] Gauss kept his reservations private, respecting "the uproar of Boeotians" that an outrageous idea such as this might provoke (qtd. in Torretti 53; also see Bonola 67). Nevertheless, "from about 1813 on" Gauss formulated his own "non-Euclidean geometry, which he first called anti-Euclidean geometry" (Kline, *Loss of Certainty* 82), and later in his career he supported and approved the foundation work of Johann Bolyai (1802–67), "a Hungarian officer in the Austrian army" and son of Gauss's former pupil, Wolfgang Bolyai (Bonola

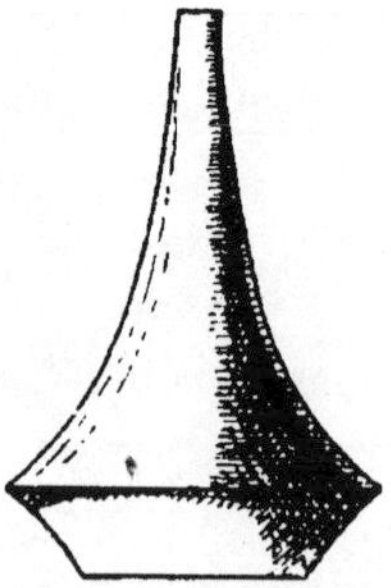

Figure 4. Bonola's depiction of the pseudosphere in his *Non-Euclidean Geometry* (132).

96). Johann Bolyai and a Russian professor of mathematics at the University of Kazan, Nicolai Ivanovich Lobatchevsky (1793–1856)—both Joyce ("*Ulysses" Notesheets* 474) and Bonola (84–96) romanize his name as "Lobatchewsky"—share the distinction of founding non-Euclidean geometry. Clearly unaware of each other's efforts, Bolyai and Lobatchevsky published remarkably similar "systematic deductive" non-Euclidean geometries by the early 1830s (Kline, *Loss of Certainty* 83).[20] Both geometers pursued alternatives to Euclid's parallel postulate, as had Saccheri, but the later men worked with figures located on a curious curved surface called a "pseudosphere" (which resembles two open-ended, curved conical surfaces joined at their wider rims; see figure 4). On a pseudosphere straight lines become curves, or "geodesics." In Bolyai's and Lobatchevsky's geometries, geodesic parallels, like Euclid's, never meet, but unlike Euclidean geometry, for any geodesic line there is "an infinite number of [parallel] lines" passing through a point not on the given geodesic "that do not meet" it (Kline, *Mathematics in Culture* 421).[21]

Orthodox mathematicians virtually ignored the new geometries of Bolyai and Lobatchevsky at the time of their publication and "completely neglected" the pursuit of their implications for several decades after. The brilliant Russian, in fact, was eventually dismissed from his post at the University of Kazan in 1847, and as Morris Kline suspects, if "Bolyai had been a professor rather than an Austrian army officer, he might have suffered the same fate" (*Mathematics in Culture* 414). Even though Lobatchevsky attempted to show how his geometry applied to real, physical space, the general opinion within the mathematical community was that his and Bolyai's non-Euclidean ideas "did not seem and [were] not intended to apply to the physical world" (Kline, *Mathematics in Culture* 417; also see *Loss of Certainty* 84–85). Georg Friedrich Bernhard Riemann (1826–66), one of Gauss's students and successor to his chair in mathematics at the University of Göttingen, surmounted this problem of perception by developing yet another non-Euclidean system, "double elliptic geometry," the geometry of outwardly curved surfaces (e.g., a sphere) (Kline, *Loss of Certainty* 86).[22] Mathematicians reluctant to accept the axioms and theorems of a pseudosphere could more readily grasp the physical relation of Riemann's geometry to the real, spherical world they themselves inhabited. With Riemannian geometry straight lines are again curves, or geodesics, yet on the surface of a sphere, unlike the curiously curved surface of the pseudosphere, *all parallel lines meet* (e.g., consider the lines of longitude on the globe); in other words, there are no parallel lines as conventionally conceived. Among Riemann's most striking non-Euclidean theorems are statements such as "*All the perpendiculars to a straight line meet in a point*" (think of the lines of longitude, which are perpendicular to the line of the equator yet meet at the poles) or "*two straight lines enclose an area*" (think of the straight seams of a football) (Kline, *Mathematics in Culture* 424; see figure 5). The non-Euclidean geometries of *A Portrait* and *Ulysses*, as I will show, are Riemannian, as is the geometry of Joyce's most "geodetic" text, *Finnegans Wake*, in which parallel lines, curving "thithaways end to end and turning, turning and end to end hithaways" (*FW* 114.15–17), diverge and reconverge to enclose an area, a "book of Doublends Jined" (*FW* 20.15–16).

Riemann first presented his ideas on 10 June 1854 in a lecture (required for

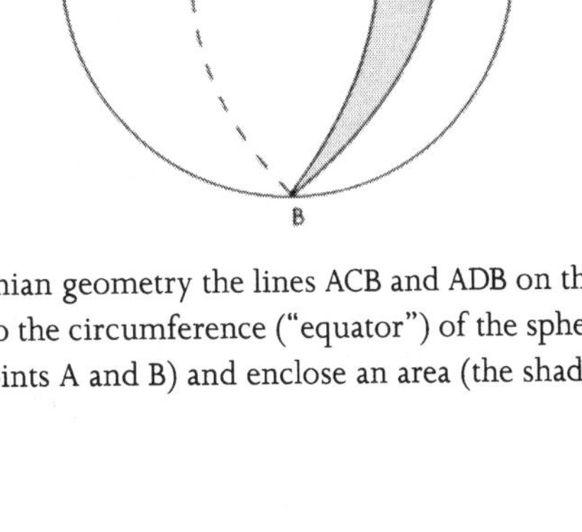

Figure 5. In Riemannian geometry the lines ACB and ADB on this sphere are parallel and perpendicular to the circumference ("equator") of the sphere at points C and D, yet both meet (at points A and B) and enclose an area (the shaded sector ACBDA).

his German Privatdozent certificate) entitled "Über die Hypothesen, welche der Geometrie zu Grunde liegen" ("On the hypotheses that lie at the foundation of geometry"). Gauss, his director of study, was in the audience (Kline, *Loss of Certainty* 85; Torretti 82; Nowak 17–46).[23] The posthumous publication of Riemann's paper in 1867, rapidly followed by translations into French (1870) and English (by William K. Clifford, in 1873) and subsequently into several other languages (Bonola 138–39, n. 2), and the amplifications of Riemannian geometry by Hermann von Helmholtz (1821–94) in the 1870s were the principal stimuli to the emergent professional and popular interest in non-Euclidean geometry.[24]

Although Riemann's geometry of spatial curvature was to provide a foundation for Einstein's theories of relativity, his translator and most enthusiastic disciple, W. K. Clifford (1845–79)—who himself formulated an early version of relativity theory—was to exert the greatest immediate influence on the dissemination of the non-Euclidean geometry in the English-speaking world by "present[ing] Riemann's ideas in more popular form as well as drawing out some of the philosophical implications of Riemann's geometrical ideas" (Farwell and Knee 98).[25] To Clifford, despite Helmholtz's resistance to this assumption, it was clear that the geometry of a curved three-dimensional space implies the existence of a fourth dimension (it does so by analogy, for the curvature of a two-dimensional plane, say of a sheet of paper, implies the existence of three dimensions). Thus, although "one might term n-dimensional geometry 'non-Euclidean,'" an intermingling of technical terms "never employed in mathematics or in knowledgeable lay treatments of the subject" (Henderson 20), the popular fascination with the fourth dimension developed in tandem and frequently in confusion with the interest in non-Euclidean geometry. Moreover, non-Euclidean and n-dimensional geometries remain conceptually linked in most discussions of Riemann's influence: "The beauty and power of Riemann's geometrical work are that it set on a firm mathematical foundation the description of arbitrarily complicated curved spaces in any number of spatial dimensions" (Pagels, *Perfect Symmetry* 141). Clifford did more than merge non-Euclidean and multidimensional geometries, however; it was he, most of all, who was to threaten the guardians of orthodoxy, such as Thomas Smith and Lewis Carroll, by making explicit the subversion of received ideas implicit in non-Euclidean and n-dimensional geometry:

> In his polemical writings, Clifford spelled out clearly the drastic implications, dimly felt by his contemporaries, inherent in accepting met-

> ric non-Euclidean [i.e., Riemannian] geometry: implications which stretched far beyond mathematics and even science, into psychology, morals, and ethics. . . . His arguments [in his speculative articles of the 1870s, such as "The Ethics of Belief," "On the Scientific Basis of Morals," and "The Influence upon Morality of a Decline of Religious Belief"] were well known and widely discussed; they were powerful and difficult to refute within their context. (Richards, "Reception" 152, 156)

What Clifford recognized, and what James Joyce too was to realize, was that the displacement of Euclid's *Elements* to the status of "a geometry," only one of many possible geometries, had transformed a system of belief, a mode of understanding that had been unquestionable and unquestioned, from a certainty into a hypothesis. Geometry, morality, and religious belief were all now to be seen as subjective, self-generated structures. "Man constructs a geometry," as Morris Kline puts it, "and decides to view space in those terms":

> Over hundreds of years . . . geometry meant the geometry of physical space and that geometry was Euclid's. With the creation of non-Euclidean geometry, however, mathematicians, scientists, and laymen were ultimately compelled to appreciate the fact that *systems of thought based on statements about physical space are different from that physical space*. . . . We should regard any theory about physical space [such as geometry or the Ptolemaic theory of the motion of the heavenly bodies], then, as a purely subjective construction and not impute to it objective reality. . . .
>
> In depriving mathematics of its status as a collection of truths, the creation of non-Euclidean geometries robbed man of his most respected truths and perhaps even of the hope of ever attaining certainty about anything. (*Mathematics in Culture* 428–30)

The Cartesian "confidence that truths would be discovered in all fields," Kline adds elsewhere, "was shattered by th[is] recognition that there is no truth in mathematics" (*Loss of Certainty* 99). As Ludwig Wittgenstein would soon observe of logic, for example, using the similarly Cartesian-Euclidean "subjective construction" of the Newtonian system for illustration in propositions 6.341–42 of his *Tractatus Logico-Philosophicus* (1921): "Newtonian mechanics . . . imposes a unified form on the description of the world, . . . [but] the possibility of describing the world by means of Newtonian mechanics tells us nothing about the world" (67–68). Likewise, when James Joyce has Stephen Dedalus in *A Portrait* reject Catholicism as an "absurdity," he is not simply dismissing the "logical and coherent" system of the church because, like Euclidean geometry or Newtonian mechanics, it is a human institution (P 244); rather, when Stephen forsakes his religion, Joyce implicates *both* Catholicism and Cartesianism in his rejection by couching Stephen's statement in specifically *mathematical* terms: remember, the *surd* at the root of his word choice, as well as the word *absurdity* itself, the intensive of *surd*, are terms used to refer to the irrational number or the irrational concept, such as infinity ("Do you mean to say that you are not able to tell me what a surd is?" [P 104]).

The difference between what Stephen thinks he is saying here and what Joyce fully implies in his statement is important because Joyce's non-Euclidean manner of presenting his autobiographical "portrait" of the artist distinguishes him from Stephen Dedalus, his former self, the artist "as a young man," who sees his world in unself-consciously Euclidean terms. Whereas Stephen might have grown capable of writing a book entitled *The Portrait of the Artist*, Joyce, more aware of the distance between "a purely subjective construction" and "objective reality," has chosen an indefinite article for his title, *A Portrait of the Artist*, to suggest this non-Euclidean sense of the possibility of several competing, logical, and equally coherent systems of representation. Thus the novel's interplay between non-Euclidean author and Euclidean character adds one more layer to the many levels of irony in the book.

THE RIEMANNIAN PARALLEL

Joyce's reconception of *Stephen Hero* in 1907 did not involve his discovery of the possibilities for irony in his material, as is sometimes mistakenly assumed. From the outset Joyce was writing an at times sardonic portrait of Stephen as antihero rather than hero. In one of his entries for 1904 in his Dublin diary, Stanislaus Joyce remarks that the title of *Stephen Hero*, as well as "the book, is satirical" (*Complete Dublin Diary* 12), a difference in tone apparent in his brother's occasionally heavy-handed sarcastic epithets for Stephen, "the fiery-hearted revolutionary" and "heaven-ascending essayist" (*SH* 80), or in his objective assessment of the "ingenuous arrogance" of "the whole-hearted young egoist" (*SH* 125) in his manuscript.[26] Joyce's maturing narrative art actually involves a lessening of his detachment from his younger self, a muting of his satire, as he moves toward a more open, equivocal presentation of Stephen as a precocious yet presumptuous undergraduate. Joyce's abandonment of his detached, third-person omniscient narrative voice in favor of a limited omniscient viewpoint or narrated consciousness centered on Stephen both lessens his distance from his subject and promotes the audience's sympathy for and identification with the young artist. Joyce's irony remains, however, and is particularly evident in the last two chapters of *A Portrait*. His irony there, however, seems intended to prevent readers from relating too closely to Stephen, from failing to see that he is, after all, a "young man," which is a very different effect from the often alienating satire of *Stephen Hero*.

Such a view of Joyce's strategic uses of tone and narration in *A Portrait*, seeing his irony as providing a counterbalance to the inherent identification promoted by his narrative techniques, might suggest that he maintains a constant aesthetic distance between reader and central character through the novel, an "esthetic stasis," as Stephen himself would say (P 206), or a kind of parallel relation, as Euclid would put it, where reader and character remain aligned, yet equidistant and never to meet.[27] Such an equidistant relation resembles Stephen's description of the "epical form" in his discussion of aesthetics, in chapter 5 of *A Portrait* (P 214), to which I will return. Nonetheless, much of the critical commentary on the novel in terms of the aesthetic theory it contains makes clear that Stephen's definitions of the lyric and dramatic modes can apply as well to Joyce's techniques of presentation (see P 214–15), that *A Portrait* varies from intense moments when Stephen's lyric subjectivity dominates to moments when the detachment of the indifferent author of the text becomes evident, and that the readers' relation to the text is unstable. These attempts to read *A Portrait* in terms of Stephen's theory suggest that readers of the novel will not be satisfied with the "static" (P 205) view of their relation to Joyce's text, the "parallel postulate." In fact, it might be more accurate to describe the readers' relation to Stephen as "kinetic" (P 205). Joyce's overall strategy is to move his readers gradually away from an initial identification with Stephen as an "everyboy" whose early childhood experiences are universal and toward an increasingly alienated, distant relation to Stephen the young intellectual and artist (presented with increasing irony), who is a highly individual young man, as detached from his community as he is from the readers. In the later portions of *A Portrait* Joyce accomplishes what Walter Benjamin recognized in the "epic theatre" of Bertolt Brecht, in which "hardly any appeal is made to the empathy of the spectators." Like Benjamin's Brecht, what Joyce does by creating "parallels" that diverge, that curve away from an initial point of contact, establishes a non-Euclidean geometry for the readers' relation to his text: "Brecht introduces his art of the drama as non-Aristotelian, just as Riemann introduced a non-Euclidean geometry. . . . Riemann eliminated the parallel postulate; Brecht's drama eliminated the Aristotelian catharsis, the purging of the emotions through empathy with the stirring fate of the hero" (150).

(Benjamin is responding to the alienation effect in Brecht's drama, contemporaneously with Brecht's formulation of the concept and coinage of the term *Verfremdungseffekt* in his "Verfremdungseffekte in der chinesischen Schauspielkunst" [1935]. Brecht appropriated this concept from the formalist critical theory of Victor Shklovsky; his German neologism is his translation of Shklovsky's *Priem Ostrannenija*, usually translated as "the estrangement effect" or "defamiliarization" [Brecht 99]. Shklovsky, in turn, was profoundly influenced by Russian futurism, which in turn was influenced by the development of non-Euclidean geometry [Shklovsky 3–24; Eichenbaum 99–139; Henderson 255–73]. Benjamin's analogy to Riemannian geometry suggests that he was well aware of this chain of associations.)

The parallel relationship between the readers and Stephen Dedalus in *A Portrait* is similarly Riemannian, diverging from the initial point of contact at the novel's opening, as both settle into a story, "Once upon a time" (*P* 7), and increasing in distance toward the book's close, as Stephen becomes a progressively alien figure for the readers and his friends alike: "Dedalus, you're an antisocial being"; "You're a terrible man, Stevie. . . . Always alone" (P 177, 201).[28] Since Riemannian parallels invariably meet, diverging from one point of contact only to reconverge at another point, this geometrical analogy gives a new meaning to the open-endedness of *A Portrait*. Joyce's novel ends with Stephen still remote from the audience's sympathy. The curve back toward an ultimate reunion, a rejoining of the readers and Stephen, however, does not take place in *Ulysses*, as I show in the next chapter. The reciprocal Riemannian parallel, the convergence of once distantly separated lines at an endpoint, is in fact present in *A Portrait*, for its readers do progress toward a union not with Stephen but with the artist in maturity, Joyce himself. (One could argue that this union with the artist is a union with a hypothetical future Stephen only if, as a few critics have maintained, Stephen is the ultimate narrator of *A Portrait*.)[29] Readers of *A Portrait* gradually come to share the author's ironic view of his subject, increasingly empathize with the teller of the tale, and ultimately join with him in their reading of the novel's final words, the tale of its telling: "Dublin 1904/Trieste 1914" (P 253; see figure 6). Joyce's two pictures of Riemannian parallels in the "Ithaca" chapter of *Ulysses* provide apt models for this structural paralleling in *A Portrait*. Stephen Dedalus and Leopold Bloom begin the "Ithaca" episode, as Stephen and the reader begin *A*

Portrait, pursuing "parallel courses. . . . Starting united" (*U* 17.1–2). Toward the end of "Ithaca" Bloom replicates the reader's relation to the invisible creator of *A Portrait* when, gazing at Molly, he "silently recall[s]" her father, the man who created her and whom she evidently resembles. Bloom "reproduce[s] from infinity" the "absent face" of Major Brian Cooper Tweedy, the *author* of Molly, which he recovers by mentally "retreating . . . with constant uniform acceleration, along parallel lines meeting at infinity" (*U* 17.2081, .2085–87). To reinforce this Riemannian parallel, Joyce, who has opened his episode with two "lines" of catechetical questions and answers, "starting united," closes by rejoining these lines that have enclosed an area in the final dot that concludes "Ithaca" (*U* 17.2332), a dot that represents both the geometrical *point* and the "conventional sign" for the Q.E.D. of Euclidean geometry (Gifford, "*Ulysses*" *Annotated* 12; see figure 6).[30]

Joyce's sophisticated use of Riemannian geometry for the form of "Ithaca" seems to be a natural development from his transformation of the Euclidean parallel relationship between the readers and the text in *Dubliners* into the non-Euclidean relation of *A Portrait*. Nevertheless, the influence of non-Euclidean geometry on the form of *A Portrait* resides less in the Riemannian parallel that governs the readers' relation to the text than in the emergence of new conceptions of *n*-dimensional space that resulted from Riemann's elliptic geometry. Hugh Kenner's suggestion that there is some formal resem-

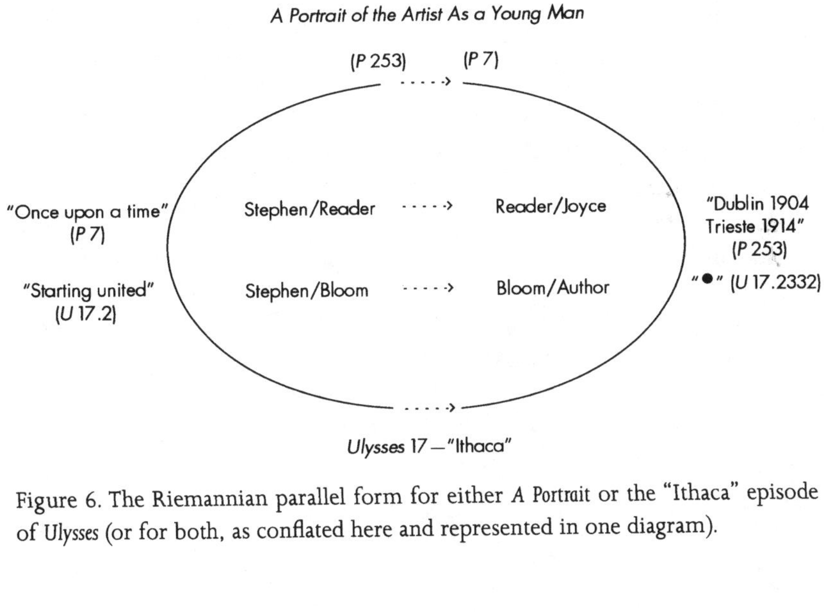

Figure 6. The Riemannian parallel form for either *A Portrait* or the "Ithaca" episode of *Ulysses* (or for both, as conflated here and represented in one diagram).

blance between the novel's "fluid [temporal] transitions" and the techniques of cubism in modern art is right, but for the wrong reasons ("Cubist *Portrait*" 171). Kenner assumes that the cubists conceived space in temporal terms, under the influence of Einstein's fourth dimension of time in the space-time continuum. As Linda Henderson makes clear, however, cubist art responded primarily to the multiple *spatial* dimensions of non-Euclidean geometry; only with rare exceptions, such as Wells's prophetic use of space-time in *The Time Machine*, did time appear as a "dimension" in the popularizations of non-Euclidean geometry prior to the new interest in the space-time continuum of Einstein's theories of relativity among nonscientists in the early 1920s.[31]

The proper analogy between the structure of *A Portrait* and cubist art, then, should pursue the similarities between the multidimensional spatial effects of cubism and both Joyce's multiple perspectives on Stephen's development and his arrangement of his novel into successive narrative "blocks."[32] Joyce's oscillation between external and internal views of his central character, his constant "alternation between scene and psyche" as he moves from passages of third-person description to "narrated monologue," does more than embody the emergence of the artist in the text, "turn[ing] the character into a teller," as John Paul Riquelme has suggested (55, 54, 60); it also does more than provide readers the opportunity to return periodically to the author's ironic vantage point. Joyce's narrative technique in *A Portrait*, his constant shifting "between figure and ground" (Riquelme 48), also intensifies the readers' impression of the novel as a three-dimensional portrait, their spatial sense of Stephen as a figure whom the text "shapes." In the terms of Stephen's own description of the artist's relation to the text in the "dramatic form" in chapter 5 of *A Portrait*, Joyce's "personality . . . passes into the narration itself, flowing round and round the persons and the action," as he shifts from figure to ground, filling Stephen "with such vital force that he . . . assumes a proper and intangible esthetic life" (P 215). Stephen, then, anticipates Leopold Bloom, who achieves three-dimensionality as an "allroundman" in *Ulysses* (10.581), a result of Joyce's continuing spatial approach to his materials. Although Joyce's methods are less complex and less technically advanced in *A Portrait* than in *Ulysses*, we can recognize in this earlier work his movement toward what the artist Frank Budgen describes as a "cubist" approach (*James Joyce* 156) in Joyce's shifts from outer to inner treatments of his characters (91–94) or from external to internal perspectives on events in *Ulysses*: "Every event is a many-sided object. You first state one view of it and then you draw it from another angle . . . , and both aspects lie side by side in the same picture" (156–57).

In a similar fashion Joyce shaped the form of his novel into a series of thematically related scenes spatially juxtaposed in his text as he condensed *Stephen Hero* into *A Portrait of the Artist as a Young Man* in the years between 1907 and 1915. Thus, although the readers proceed linearly through the five chapters of the novel, tracing the steady progress of Stephen's physical, spiritual, and intellectual growth, Joyce's arrangement of scenes in the book encourages these readers to circulate within the text and recombine its elements as they recognize, for example, the patterned repetition of Stephen's encounters with his biological, religious, and artistic "fathers"—Simon Dedalus, the priests, Daedalus—or his recurring encounters with the female other that punctuate the novel's five chapters: "his mother" and Eileen Vance (P 7–8), "E——C——" (P 70; i.e., Emma Clery [SH 65 and passim; P 115]) and the prostitute (P 100–101), his soul (always gendered as feminine), the "strange and beautiful seabird" girl of his seaside epiphany (P 171), and Emma, again, "the temptress of his villanelle" (P 223). Moreover, although Joyce's conception of spatial form in *A Portrait* may anticipate his structural techniques in *Ulysses*, it also foreshadows his appropriation of n-dimensional non-Euclidean geometry in *Finnegans Wake*, for his readers remain aware throughout the novel of the existence of the "artist" of the work, "invisible, refined out of existence" in the three-dimensional universe of the book, yet present in some other spatial dimension "within or behind or beyond or above his handiwork" (P 215). Like the four-dimensional HCE of the *Wake*, the artist is a ghostly presence in his work, "the prisoner of that sacred edifice" (*FW* 100.25), housed in a "worldroom beyond the room world" (*FW* 100.29; *Weltraum* = space [McHugh *Annotations*]), "suggesting" the "canonicity of his existence as a tesseract" by "the gravitational pull" of his irony (*FW* 100.32–35; also see Solomon 119–29).

THE CARTESIAN COORDINATES OF STEPHEN DEDALUS

Stephen progressively alienates himself from the readers of *A Portrait* primarily by his increasing subjectivity as he develops into a highly individual young man. His fellow undergraduate MacCann attacks him as "antisocial" because he realizes what readers already know about Stephen: he is "wrapped up in" himself (P 177). Davin recognizes that Stephen has isolated and insulated himself from others because of imagined slights, "all in your own mind, Stevie" (P 202). Indeed, Stephen's intensifying subjectivity has been apparent almost from the opening of this novel—much of which takes place in his own mind—which is one consequence of Joyce's technique of narrated consciousness but also a result of Stephen's particular mode of consciousness.[33] (It is easy to overlook the fact that many of the dialogues and dramatic "scenes" in *A Portrait* are in fact all in his mind, as *recalled* by Stephen). Readers are less able to empathize with Stephen, in the conversational sense of this term, "to sympathize," because of Stephen's own tendency toward empathy: "the imaginative projection of a subjective state into an object."[34] Unlike the boy in the opening story of *Dubliners*, "The Sisters," whose desire to "look upon" the "deadly work" of paralysis illustrates the Cartesian worldview grounded in Euclidean geometry (*D* 9), the "perceptual model of objective knowledge" (Tiles 50), the schoolboy Stephen assumes that "by *thinking* of things you could understand them" (*P* 43; my emphasis). "To see" no longer means to see for Joyce, although Stephen never recognizes the inescapable subjectivity of the Cartesian *cogito*. Stephen naively assumes that his thought will lead him to an immediate, unmediated reality: "He wanted to meet in the real world the unsubstantial image which his soul so constantly beheld. He did not know where to seek it or how: but a premonition which led him on told him that this image would, without any overt act of his, encounter him" (*P* 65).

Throughout the early chapters Joyce shows Stephen's increasingly futile efforts to encounter his subjectively shaped reality in the real, chronicling the "slight shocks to his boyish conception of the world . . . [that] obscured his mind" (*P* 64) or the changes in his family's "fortune which [were] reshaping the world about him into a vision of squalor and insincerity" (*P* 67). Joyce repeatedly makes his readers aware of Stephen as a detached and "watchful" spectator (*P* 68), yet an unreliable one, projecting his subjectivity into objects observed and as often as not seeing specters of his own creation.[35] Stephen's visions of "goatish creatures with human faces" (*P* 137), of a procession of "masked memories" that pass "quickly before him" (*P* 157), of the "mental spectre of the face of . . . Foxy Campbell" (*P* 161), or of "cloudy shapes and beings" as his "soul" swoons "into some new world, fantastic, dim, uncertain as under sea" (*P* 172) at the conclusion of chapter 4 all emphasize the difference between Stephen's conception of the encounter with reality and what he is actually doing: constructing fantasies.[36] That Stephen's fancies often take form as imaginary figures loosely associates his mental habits with those of the Euclidean geometer, who imagines and constructs figures taken for realities. Ironically, like the geometer, Stephen is most subjective when he thinks of himself as objective—his hysterical visions of his sins, most likely the effect of Fr. Arnall's hellfire sermons, Stephen considers to be the result of his "cold indifferent knowledge of himself" (P 103)—or when he attempts to come to terms with objective realities in his theory of the "beautiful object" (P 209, 212), as I will show. By emphasizing Stephen's subjective "objectivity," Joyce reflects the non-Euclidean realization that Euclidean geometry offers no more than an illusion of objectivity.

Of course, Joyce need not have been directly inspired by the non-Euclidean revolution when he decided to recast *Stephen Hero* as *A Portrait of the* [Subjective] *Artist as a Young Man*. There are any number of prototypes for Joyce's method in nineteenth-century literature and post-Kantian philosophy that could have encouraged him to develop the problematic of subject and object in Stephen. Nevertheless, the full impact of non-Euclidean geometry was to affect "the basic notion of truth itself" (Blumenthal 17), to remove the certainty that *any* objective truth was possible: "*I have created a new universe from nothing*" (Johann Bolyai [qtd. in Bonola 98]). This implication goes well beyond Kant, who used Euclid's axioms as illustrations of the synthetic a priori, models of unquestionable objective truths. The ultimate consequence of non-Euclidean geometry was, furthermore, to undermine the entire empirical, Cartesian worldview, which rested on the confident assumptions that reality can be measured (by geometrical coordinates), analyzed (by analytic geometry), and thus understood, *known*. In his *Science and the Modern World* (1925), for example, Alfred North Whitehead, dismissing the Euclidean "certainty of our geometrical knowledge of the space of the physical universe [as] . . . a delusion which has vitiated much philosophy in the past, and some philosophy in the present" (32), argues that simultaneous developments in mathematics, science, and philosophy (e.g., James's reconception of consciousness and Bergson's "protest against spatialisation" [212]) had fully discredited both Euclidean-Cartesian-Newtonian "scientific materialism and the Cartesian Ego" (205).[37] Moreover, as Gaston Bachelard was to observe more succinctly, the collapse of Cartesianism meant the loss of (the) "point" for geometry, for physics (i.e., the electron), and for the world (*New Scientific Spirit* 129). That Joyce both grasped these implications of the non-Euclidean revolution and rewrote *Stephen Hero* with them in mind is evident for two reasons: (1) he transfers the role of naturalistic, "scientifically" objective spectator from the detached artist, the narrator of most of the *Dubliners* stories and *Stephen Hero*, to Stephen Dedalus, the character within the text whose highly subjective objectivity becomes readily apparent, as I have shown, and (2) he embeds geometry and geometrical imagery in the text of *A Portrait* to emphasize Stephen's misplaced confidence in his Euclidean worldview. Like his namesake, the cunning artificer and geometer Daedalus, Stephen comes to be imprisoned by the structures of his own creation.[38]

Much of *A Portrait* takes place in the mind of Stephen Dedalus, then, a mind dominated, even in early childhood, by the elements of Euclid's geometry, from the lines on the football field at Clongowes (P 8) or the lines of letters and "curves of the capital" in his composition book (P 46) to completed figures such as the notorious "square ditch" (P 10) into which Wells had shouldered him, the "square" itself (the boys' urinal), where strange things happen (P 42–43), or that other kind of square, in the Dublin cityscape, where figures coincide: Simon Dedalus "walk[s] bang into" Fr. Conmee, "just at the corner of the square," and arranges his sons' enrollment at Belvedere College (P 71). Stephen associates his lapses into sin and spirituality, both routinized activities, with the figure of the circle (like the square, a common image in *Dubliners* as well): he approaches "the squalid quarter of the brothels" circuitously, at the beginning of chapter 3, "circling always nearer and nearer in a tremor of fear and joy" (P 102), and later envisions his sins as "goatish creatures . . . mov[ing] in slow circles, circling closer and closer to enclose" him (P 137–38). After his reformation he geometrically "la[ys] out" his "daily life . . . in devotional areas. . . . He drove his soul daily through an increasing circle of works of supererogation. Every part of his day . . . circled about its own centre of spiritual energy" (P 147–48). Even the famous Euclidean conundrum of the quadrature of the circle makes its appearance in the text, once again, as in *Dubliners*, as a symbol of alienation and isolation. Initially Joyce alludes to the problem of squaring the circle to suggest the alien Stephen's approach to the "new and complex sensation" of Dublin, when he attempts to make "a skeleton map of the city *in his mind*" (my emphasis): "In the beginning he contented himself with circling timidly round the neighbouring square" (P 66). Later a somewhat more involuted version of this image of the unsolvable problem comes to represent to Stephen, isolated in his "mild proud sovereignty" (P 168), the irremediable intellectual limitations of his fellow Dubliners: "The grey *block* of Trinity on his left, set heavily in the city's ignorance like a great dull stone set in a cumbrous *ring*, pulled *his mind* downward" (P 180; my emphases). Thus Joyce manages to suggest both that Stephen pictures his reality in Euclidean terms and that Euclidean geometry is itself a form of subjectivity: "The world for all its solid substance and complexity no longer existed for his soul save as a *theorem*" (P 150; my emphasis).

Joyce continues to stress Stephen's Euclidean subjectivity throughout the later pages of *A Portrait*. Lines run on, for example, in Stephen's poetry (P 217–

24), in "Nash's line" ("*Brightness falls from the air*" [P 234]), or in Stephen's view of a flight of birds "in straight and curving lines" (P 224). To Stephen, water forms "diamonds" in the "quadrangle" by the national library, as he distantly and longingly observes girls "holding their umbrellas at cunning angles" (P 216). And circles cycle (from the "cycling" Capuchins [P 155] to those birds again, which Stephen pictures from the library steps "flying from left to right, circling about a temple of air" [P 224]), as he consistently structures the reality he encounters in Euclidean terms. The most intriguing consequence of Stephen's Euclidean worldview, however, appears in his discussion of aesthetics in the fifth chapter (P 204–15). As Stephen and Lynch cross the squares of Dublin (e.g., P 211), Stephen pursues "the line" of his "esthetic theory" (P 209), both joking in Euclidean terms ("You would not write your name in pencil across the hypothenuse of a rightangled triangle" [P 208]) and conflating the Aristotelian/Thomistic idea of forms with the geometrical concept of form.[39] To Stephen, the artistic object is initially seen and apprehended geometrically: "The first phase of apprehension is a bounding line drawn about the object to be apprehended" (P 212). The second stage of this process involves an analysis of form that reads like a digest of the procedures of Euclid's *Elements*, written by Joyce in that "curious droll stylized language, every bit as distinctive in its own way as that of the Authorized Version of the Bible," which "the wording of Euclid's works" had ingrained in the minds of "generations of schoolchildren" (Barrow, *Pi in the Sky* 9): "Then, said Stephen, you pass from point to point, led by its formal lines; you apprehend it as balanced part against part within its limits. . . . In other words the synthesis of immediate perception is followed by the analysis of apprehension. . . . You apprehend [the art object] as complex, multiple, divisible, separable, made up of its parts, the result of its parts and their sum, harmonious" (P 212). Stephen's third stage of apprehension is quite simply an assertion of the Euclidean-Cartesian "perceptual model of objective knowledge" (Tiles 50); the audience discovers the congruence of their mental perceptions of the object with the object in reality, whereas the artist *realizes* his inspiration in the created artifact: "You see that [the art object] is that thing which it is and no other thing. . . . This supreme quality is felt by the artist when the esthetic image is first conceived in his imagination" (P 213). (Joyce emphasizes Stephen's unself-conscious assumption that no active subjectivity works in this process of objective apprehension by having him repeatedly resort to the passive voice throughout his elaboration of his theory.)

Similarly, Stephen's distinction among the lyric, epical, and dramatic forms, which concludes his theory, moves implicitly and then explicitly from the simple to the more complex figures of Euclidean geometry. When Stephen describes the lyrical form as "in fact the simplest verbal vesture of an instant of emotion" (P 214), he clearly has in mind both the geometrical and the poetic lines, lines of verse (P 221) that he compares to rays three times (P 218) when he formulates his own "rhythmical cry" (P 214) into a villanelle a few pages further in the text. Stephen more explicitly identifies "the simplest epical form" as the circle; "the artist," the firm foot of the geometer's compass, "prolongs and broods upon himself as the centre of an epical event and this form progresses till the centre of emotional gravity is equidistant from the artist himself and from others. . . . The personality of the artist passes into the narration itself, flowing round and round the persons and the action like a vital sea" (P 213–14). Finally, Stephen imports both the sphere of solid geometry and the idiom of projective geometry to represent the dramatic form in literature: "The dramatic form is reached when the vitality [of the artist] which has flowed and eddied round each person fills every person with such vital force that he or she assumes a proper [three-dimensional] and intangible esthetic life. . . . The esthetic image in the dramatic form is life purified in and reprojected from the human imagination" (P 215). Stephen's famous removal of the artist from the work, then, is not simply an early expression of the modernist ideal of impersonality but an artful dodge, an avoidance of the more complex figure that *two* centers, two foci, artist and character, might make in the evolution of the dramatic form out of the "circular" epical form. The geometrical form with two foci is the ellipse, or staying with the suggestion of three-dimensionality, the ellipsoid. Had he taken this route, he would be approaching the non-Euclidean terrain of Riemann's elliptic geometry, the geometry of the form of *A Portrait*, which contains two foci, Stephen and Joyce (see figure 7). He misses this turn, however, because his knowledge of ellipses and ellipsoids is limited; Stephen has failed to pay any attention to his physics lecturer, earlier this same day, who distinguishes "between elliptical and ellipsoidal" (P 191), even though the "ellipsoidal balls" of Moynihan's "rude humour" linger in his mind, to reappear, subjectively reappropriated, in the erotic reverie that accompanies his composition of the villanelle: "The earth was like a swinging smoking swaying censer, a ball of incense, an ellipsoidal ball" (P 192, 218).

Possibly Stephen has been inattentively present for an introductory lecture on *n*-dimensional and non-Euclidean geometry in the "physics theatre" (P 184), a discussion springing from the basic Riemannian figure of the

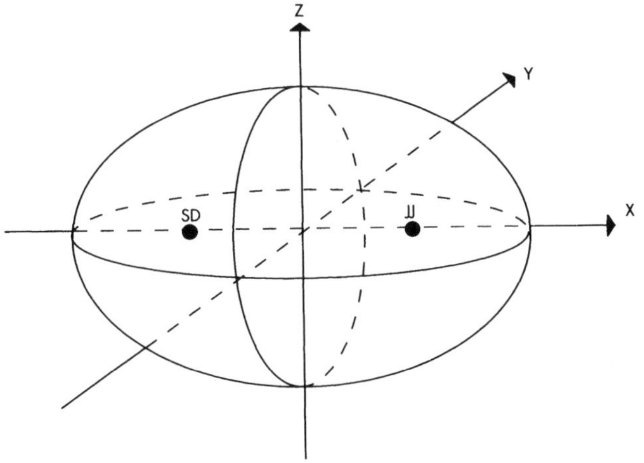

Figure 7. An "ellipsoid of revolution" generated by rotating an ellipse 360° (e.g., fig. 6) about the x-axis of the diagram (Wentworth 256). The points SD and JJ on the x-axis represent the two foci of the original ellipse. (Adapted from George A. Wentworth, *Elements of Analytic Geometry* [1886], 273.)

"ellipsoid" (P 192). Unlike Stephen, Joyce realizes that the world has been changed by the non-Euclidean revolution, that even a discussion of language (e.g., the meaning of "tundish" [P 188]), must now take place in the "theatre of physics." Ironically, most readers of *A Portrait*, too, have been inattentive to the scientific and mathematical emphases of Stephen's education, insofar as they see Stephen in the role of student in the book. In fact, excepting his unfortunate Latin class in the first chapter (when Fr. Dolan pandies Stephen for being a "lazy idle little loafer" [P 50]), the only occasions on which the reader sees Stephen in the classroom in the narrative present (rather than in Stephen's "mind," in his recall of schoolrooms [e.g., P 78–79]) is when he is being instructed in mathematics and science.

Joyce establishes the Cartesian coordinates of Stephen's education from the earliest pages of *A Portrait*, simultaneously illustrating the mathematical and scientific emphasis of the revised *Ratio Studiorum* and Stephen's tendency to subjectivize experience. At Clongowes Stephen, representing the house of York (the white rose), loses "the war of the roses," the math competition, to Jack Lawton (the red rose of Lancaster) in Father Arnall's arithmetic class: "Stephen tried his best but the sum was too hard and he felt confused" (P 12).[40] He rationalizes his loss, turning inward to contemplate beauty at the expense of a mathematical truth: "He could not get out the answer for the sum but it did not matter. White roses and red roses: those were beautiful colours to think of. And the cards for first place and second place and third place were beautiful colours too: pink and cream and lavender. Lavender and cream and pink roses were beautiful to think of" (*P* 12). Joyce juxtaposes Stephen's growing subjectivity and his more advanced mathematical curriculum at Belvedere College, at the beginning of chapter 3 of *A Portrait*, when Stephen once again turns inward to transform an algebraic equation into the fantastic geometry of a fin-de-siècle design:

> The equation on the page of his scribbler began to spread out a widening tail, eyed and starred like a peacock's; and, when the eyes and stars of its indices [i.e., exponents] had been eliminated, began slowly to fold itself together again. The indices appearing and disappearing were eyes opening and closing; the eyes opening and closing were stars being born and being quenched. The vast cycle of starry life bore his weary mind outward to its verge and inward to its centre, a distant music accompanying him outward and inward. (*P* 102–3)

Like Gabriel Conroy's reverie of painting Gretta in "The Dead" ("*Distant Music* he would call the picture" [*D* 210]), Stephen's elaborate fantasy emphasizes his subjective appropriation of a reality, one more interaction with the "outer world" that progressively "obscure[s] his mind" in the course of the novel (*P* 64). Similarly, attending the university physics lecture inattentively in chapter 5, Stephen turns inward and away from the discussion of the difference between ellipses and ellipsoids, and more immediately from Moynihan's crude joking, to a delightful but totally irrelevant extended fancy of a procession of his instructors "ambling and stumbling, tumbling and capering," through "the cloister of [his] mind, . . . in a sabbath of misrule" (*P* 192). Stephen may appropriate the term *ellipsoidal* for his later villanelle reverie (*P* 218), but he has conspicuously failed to realize the relation between what he is being taught and the world he directly confronts: MacAlister's "oblong skull," which he observes twice on the next page (*P* 193), is, in fact, an ellipsoidal form in his immediate experience. And whereas the laughter of his fellow students distracts Stephen from his lesson on the correspondences of non-Euclidean geometry to reality in the physics theater, his own laughter (rare in this novel) seems to prevent him, on an earlier occasion, from recognizing the distance between his ethereal mental life and the ground of the real: "Then a short laugh broke from his lips as he thought of that solitary farmhand in the kitchengardens behind their house whom they had nicknamed the man with the hat. A second laugh, taking rise from the first after a pause, broke from him involuntarily as he thought of how the man with the hat worked, considering in turn the four points of the sky and then regretfully plunging his spade in the earth" (P 162).

Joyce patterns and punctuates Stephen's development, as I have already observed, by his incremental repetition of figures (e.g., "fathers") and events in the novel (e.g., encounters with the feminine other), not to mention the leitmotifs he weaves throughout (water, birds, beasts [cows, sows, and oxen], flowers, etc.). Stephen's sequential encounters with mathematics and science, in which he moves from perplexity to inattention and indifference, create one more element of patterning in *A Portrait*, but they serve more than a structural purpose in the book. That Stephen learns little math, indeed, that Stephen recurrently responds to his lessons with a subjective inward turn, means that he fails to grasp that mathematics is itself a form of subjectivity, an abstraction from concrete reality. Like the man with the hat, Stephen recurrently gazes at the sky, but unlike the solitary farmhand, he never "plung[es] his spade in the earth." Thus he overlooks the fatal flaw in his own attempt to appropriate the figures of Euclidean geometry as objective truths, to picture both his world and his aesthetic. A true Cartesian, he is intensely subjective just when he thinks he is being objective (Caton 130–58 and passim). Joyce's analysis of the inescapable subjectivity of "objectivity" in his portrait of Stephen Dedalus recognizes that same duality and conflict (e.g., between faith and skepticism) that Max Horkheimer was to observe of Cartesianism in "On the Problem of Truth" (1935):

> The doctrine of a solid *res cogitans*, a self-contained ego independent of the body, which . . . is preserved immutable in the metaphysics of Descartes and his idealistic successors, reveals itself as an illusion, corresponding to the situation of the bourgeois individual and present before the inquiry rather than based on it. The independent existence of individual souls, the principle which for Descartes makes the world philosophically intelligible, is no easier to reconcile with the criteria and the whole spirit of the analytic geometry which he himself invented than is his proclamation of empty space as the sole physical substance with the theological dogma of transubstantiation. Complete doubt as to the reality of material truth, the constant emphasis on uncertainty, conditional character and finiteness of all definite knowledge,

> immediately next to ostensible insights into eternal truths and the fetishization of individual categories and modes of being—this duality permeates the Cartesian philosophy. (408–9)

As I show in the next chapter, Stephen remains imprisoned by this subjectivity in *Ulysses* ("Shut your eyes and see" [U 3.9]), and although he has grown more aware of his subjective position "between two roaring worlds" (U 10.824), more conscious of the gap between his mental life and reality ("There all the time without you: and ever shall be, world without end" [U 3.27–28]), he continues to view the world in terms of the Cartesian dualism of self and other.[41]

Although it is tempting to speculate that Stephen's next encounter with a man with a hat, Leopold Bloom, will help him to free himself fully from the bondage of his subjectivity—to recognize that the real exists "without you" (i.e., both outside and independently of the self)—we can be no more certain of this than we can assume that his meeting with Bloom will somehow enable him to free himself from the labyrinth of Dublin. Joyce, however, has clearly escaped both forms of captivity. What he implies in *A Portrait of the Artist as a Young Man* and makes explicit in both *Ulysses* and *Finnegans Wake* is that there is one way out of the dilemma of subjectivity: individuals can escape the subjective, paradoxically, by being objective about their own subjectivity. Joyce's Parisian contemporary, Gaston Bachelard, professor of the philosophy of science at the Sorbonne, was to argue in his formulation of a non-Cartesian epistemology in *The New Scientific Spirit* (1934) that we can dialectically transcend the Cartesian dualism of subject and object "if we practice conceptualizing each in terms of the other, and if we use each to limit the other's application" (93; Bachelard develops this dialectic in the context of the several indeterminacies of the new physics, the dualities of matter and energy, space and time, particle and wave, determinism and probability, etc.).[42] Joyce's reconception of *Stephen Hero* as *A Portrait of the Artist as a Young Man* similarly transcends the dualism of self and other by "conceptualizing each in terms of the other," simultaneously presenting the subjective subject objectively (irony and authorial detachment) and admitting the subjectivity of the purportedly indifferent artist ("A" Portrait, not "The" Portrait). This dialectic is also precisely Joyce's response to the problem of subjectivity in *Ulysses* and *Finnegans Wake*, where he not only approximates Bachelard's thesis but also anticipates the full maturation of this non-Cartesian epistemology evident in two interrelated developments in our contemporary natural and social sciences, chaos theory and complexity. Although Joyce continued to "play" with Euclidean and non-Euclidean geometries—both the "*Elements of Geometry*" (*U* 17.1398) and "*The aliments of jumeantry*" (*FW* 286.L4) function in these last two works to undermine the specious illusions of objectivity—ultimately, as I will show, he turned his attention to the larger issues that multiple geometries raise, the nature of subjectivity itself and the relation of the subjective self to an objective, external, existent, aboriginal reality, "There all the time without you," "what you damn well have to see" (*U* 3.27; 9.86). In doing so, Joyce arrived at the position now occupied by the resurgent movement among scientists and philosophers of science called "scientific realism" (Leplin passim). Thus, although Joyce was very much of his time in *Dubliners* and *A Portrait*, he was so much ahead of his time in *Ulysses* and *Finnegans Wake* that we are only now, in Richard Ellmann's words, "learning to be [his] contemporaries" (*JJII* 3).

In the next two chapters, then, I turn my attention away from Joyce's reflection of contemporary mathematical and scientific thought in his early fiction and toward the ways in which our own cultural context—specifically, the emergent reconception of chaos and complexity in mathematics and science—offers new models for reading Joyce's later fiction, *Ulysses* and *Finnegans Wake*, works that anticipate the contemporary transformation in how we "organiz[e] reality" (Pagels, *Dreams of Reason* 13).

3

ULYSSES, CHAOS, AND COMPLEXITY

Pause. J. J. O'Molloy took out his cigarettecase.

False lull. Something quite ordinary.

Messenger took out his matchbox thoughtfully and lit his cigar.

I have often thought since on looking back over that strange time that it was that small act, trivial in itself, that striking of that match, that determined the whole aftercourse of both our lives. —(U 7.760–65)

This passage from the "Aeolus" episode of *Ulysses*, with its peculiar shifts in time and tone, has provoked its share of commentary, chiefly searches for the source of Joyce's apparent parody of the anachronic conventions of Victorian fiction (in this case a prolepsis, a "flash-forward"). This "Messenger" interpolation, however, has both local and global significance for *Ulysses*, neither of which has received much attention. For example, the fully responsive first-time reader, that ideal creation, would immediately naturalize the narrative's shifts by seeing them as yet another move into Stephen Dedalus's stream of consciousness. Within the passage itself Stephen likewise defends himself against the seductions of rhetoric, first by preparing to hear "something quite ordinary" in O'Molloy's rendering of Bushe's "polished periods" (U 7.747) and then by supplying this something ordinary: a portentous narrative cliché, its banality reinforced by its awkward style. (The second sentence features six *thats*.)

The rereader of this brief sequence, one who has gained the prospective and retrospective vision that the passage itself illustrates, might also notice an emergent pattern in the novel: various "messengers" accost Stephen/Telemachus this morning, such as the milkwoman/Athena of the first episode (a "messenger from the secret morning" [U 1.406]), the sententious Mr. Garrett Deasy, or the *Frauenzimmer* and cocklepickers of "Proteus." This reader will find that Leopold Bloom completes the "messenger" pattern in *Ulysses*. Bloom's "ignited lucifer match" in "Ithaca" comes to seem, in hindsight, as determined and deterministic as Messenger's "striking of that match"; Bloom becomes the latest entry in Stephen's catalog of significant firelighters (U 17.131, .135–47). Nevertheless, responses such as these overlook one of the most important features of the Messenger passage: its absolute content. This textual intrusion reminds the reader of four basic facts of human existence: (1) minute causes can have momentous consequences; (2) events appear to be purely accidental and contingent in the present moment of their occurrence; (3) these same events, once displaced into the past and reviewed "as in a retrospective arrangement" (U 14.1044), seem to have been fully deterministic, to have "determined the whole aftercourse of . . . our lives"; and (4) in the real world, as we know it and as contemporary physics attests, we can establish with *certainty* that determinate effects result from determinative causes, no matter how apparently insignificant (*pace* the postmodernist deconstructions of causality, the "fixed origin," and the metaphysics of "presence" [Derrida, "Structure, Sign, and Play" 278–80 and passim]).

Like Tom Kernan, the genre of the novel has always been "dead nuts" on "*retrospective arrangement*" for its "*trenchant rendering*" of experience (U 6.147–50). Reading, conversely, is prospective; criticism, however, reverses the orientation once again, replicating the retrospective processes of the book's creation. The history of *Ulysses*'s reception, for example, clearly shows the critics' reciprocal retrospective assimilation of the novel's apparently contingent details into deterministic patterns of interpretation. Even more important, the Messenger passage offers a strong correlation between the fundamental premises of chaos theory in contemporary science and our four "basic facts" of real and fictional existence: (1) minute causes may have momentous consequences; (2) everything in the world of the present, as the early Wittgenstein would have it (71), is accidental; (3) the dynamic systems most characteristic of life itself, although driven by the stochastic (random) variables of chance, behave in a deterministic fashion; and (4) it is possible to arrive at "*objective truth about the world*" (Gross and Levitt 52). In *Ulysses* James Joyce uncannily anticipates the perspective of the new scientists of chaos and shares the metaphysical implications of their worldview. Moreover, understanding *Ulysses* in light of chaos theory can substantially refine our sense of how the novel should be read and interpreted.

Chaos theory, quite simply, springs from the discovery that chaos is *ordered*, that a vast array of complex and purportedly random phenomena, studied in sufficient detail, reveal deeply embedded patterns, designs that exist independently of the individual's act of observation.[1] Scientists and mathematicians generally avoid the popularized term "chaos theory," preferring to call their emergent discipline "dynamical systems theory," "nonlinear systems theory," or the like. Whatever we chose to call it, this study of the paradoxical orderly chaos in natural and social phenomena as diverse as weather, commodities markets, earthquakes, evolution, viruses, politics, heart rhythms, populations in ecosystems, and distributions of galaxies (and the list goes on) seems to be a recent development. James Gleick, in his excellent introductory survey *Chaos* (1987), traces "the genealogy of [this] new science" (8) back to the meteorologist Edward Lorenz's construction of a computer weather model in 1960 and his subsequent discovery of the famous "butterfly effect" (9–31), the principle of sensitive dependence in nonlinear systems, to which I will return. Increasingly powerful computer technology has accelerated the emergence of chaos science by enabling scientists to generate and examine vast amounts of data in detail and with speed, but the roots of chaos theory reach back to developments early in this century. As Ian Stewart observes, Jules Henri Poincaré (1854–1912), the greatest mathematician of his era and, as I mention in the previous chapter, an influential popularizer of his discipline (he was the chief proponent of non-Euclidean geometry in France), had already explored the chaotic behavior of certain nonlinear equations by the end of the nineteenth century.[2] Not only did Poincaré, the "last of the great mathematicians . . . capable of working in every area of the subject" (Stewart, *Does God Play Dice* 62), grasp the relation between the behavior of unpredictable dynamical systems in reality and that of nonlinear equations, but he also created a non-Euclidean geometry, topology, to represent the shifting, malleable shapes of reality more accurately.[3]

Poincaré's mathematical models for the study of nonlinearity and topology eventually proved to be essential for the analysis of chaotic dynamic systems. In addition, other developments in mathematics, such as the emergence of the several competing non-Euclidean geometries described in the previous chapter, and in physics, such as Einstein's relativity theories and quantum theory, forced the scientific community to realize that it had misplaced its confidence in the presumably objective, visualizable, rational pictures of reality afforded by Euclid, Descartes, and Newton. The discoveries that parallel lines can meet, that light does not travel in a straight line (or through the medium of ether), or that subatomic matter behaves interchangeably as particles and as waves combined to prepare a community to reconsider its rational conviction that chaos means the absence of order, interest, and information.[4] Orderly chaos appears to be an irrational idea only insofar as reality itself can be seen as a rational order, obedient to the individual's preconception of design. As John Casti remarks, "chaos and common sense go together like oil and water" (93). Casti is correct, not because chaos contradicts reason, but, as is often the case with paradox, because "common sense" does. "The most important and most exciting problems" in the search for an understanding of the phenomenal universe, Karl Popper has argued, "must remain completely invisible to those who confine themselves to analysing ordinary common-sense knowledge" (*Logic* 18).[5]

The full significance of chaos theory resides in another and greater paradox: the study of chaos, although a long-term consequence of the early twentieth-century loss of the Euclidean-Cartesian-Newtonian certainties in mathematics and the physical sciences, reaffirms certainty in the realm of science.[6] By demonstrating that chaos has a deeply embedded design, chaos theory reverses the increasingly skeptical twentieth-century conviction, ascendant in the postmodern moment, that all orders that the individual *discovers* in phenomena are merely ideological *covers* subjectively imposed by the observer, a culturally constructed subject and subjectivity (e.g., Marshall 81–84 and passim). Chaos theory thus restores the realist's picture of a reality that exists "independently of observers. . . . The [scientific] realist assumes that universal laws of Nature exist 'out there' apart from our perception of them, and the thing that is observed makes the main contribution to knowledge, not the observer or the process of observation itself" (Barrow, *World* 12). Casti remarks that "chaos implies truth" in a world of apparent indeterminacy and unprovability, that "the existence of strange attractors [in chaotic systems] allows us to hold out the hope that the gap between proof and truth can at least be narrowed—even if it can never be completely closed" (148–49). The consequences of this restoration of the possibility of "truth," in Casti's terms, will extend beyond the natural and social sciences; chaos theory promises to follow the same directions already taken by the ideology of uncertainty in contemporary culture, ultimately providing both a counterview and a supplement to the indeterminacy of postmodernism that has recently dominated the dynamic systems of literature and criticism.[7]

The importance of chaos theory for contemporary culture, and by extension for the reading of a work of literature like *Ulysses*, is thus its restoration of objective knowledge and determinism to our picture of a complex reality, a paradigm shift that will realize Karl Popper's many-worlds hypothesis in "Indeterminism Is Not Enough" (*Open Universe* 113–30).[8] Popper maintains that both human consciousness and objective knowledge ("Worlds 2 and 3") assimilate and transcend the indeterminism of physical reality ("World 1") to make human freedom possible in a universe that blends determinism and chance: "Our universe is partly causal, partly probabalistic, and partly open: it is emergent" (130; also see Ruelle 26–30). Popper sees the individual, like the characters of *Ulysses*, poised between phenomena that are deterministic in retrospect and unpredictable in prospect: "Popper thus argues that human reason is unlimited with regard to criticism yet limited with regard to its powers of prediction; and shows that both the lack of limitation and the limitation are, in their respective places, necessary for human rationality to exist at all" (Bartley xv). As I will show, Joyce poises the reader, possessed of consciousness and objective knowledge, above and beyond the apparent indeterminism of "World 1," the world of his text of *Ulysses*. Resembling the metaphysical determinist and scientific realist Einstein, Joyce "leaves the possibility open that the world [of *Ulysses*], with everything in it, . . . is completely determined if seen *from without*" (Popper, *Open Universe* 87).

I should clarify both the special sense and the significance of this charged term *determinism*, which I appropriate from chaos science and use in the balance of this chapter. Ian Stewart captures the paradoxical perspective of chaos theory, which allows us to discover *after the event* the determinate causes of unpredictable and apparently chance phenomena, by defining chaos as "stochastic [random] behaviour occurring in a deterministic system" (*Does God Play Dice* 17). We must keep this concept of *stochastic* determinism distinct from the classical, "scientific" determinism of the Newtonian scientific tradition—and the religious doctrine of predetermination that it replaced and essentially replicated (Popper, *Open Universe* 5–6)—and from the Einsteinian conception of "metaphysical" determinism, which it partially recovers. As Popper recounts in *The Open Universe* (29–40), the French astronomer and mathematician Pierre Simon Laplace offered the most famous formulation of scientific determinism (in his *Essai philosophique sur les probabilités* [1819]), his "doctrine," in Popper's words, "that the structure of world is such that *any event can be rationally predicted, with any desired degree of precision, if we are given a sufficiently precise description of past events, together with all the laws of nature*" (1–2). A "superhuman intelligence," therefore, one "capable of ascertaining the complete set of initial conditions of the world system at any one instant of time," in principle could "deduce all future states of the world system" (30). This supreme intelligence, dubbed "Laplace's demon," is "not [the] omniscient God" of traditional religion but "merely a super-scientist" (30). As Popper notes, it is impossible to achieve this supreme intelligence, yet—and here he sounds much like Wittgenstein—it is also impossible to refute Laplace's doctrine "*from within* the world" (87).

The concept of metaphysical determinism continues to maintain that "all events in this world are fixed, or unalterable, or predetermined," but it differs from scientific determinism, slightly but significantly, by asserting that they are not "known to anybody, or predictable by scientific means" within the world. Nonetheless, like scientific determinism, it remains an absolutist principle: metaphysical determinism "asserts that the future is as little changeable as is the past" (*Open Universe* 8). In *The Open Universe* Popper recounts his 1950 discussion with the metaphysical determinist Einstein (the "Parmenides" of an "unchanging" four-dimensional universe [90]), during which he unsettled the physicist by arguing that Einstein's conception of an unchanging script for the universe did not allow for a change in "us" (i.e., the human experience of change) as a change in the world and thus "did not allow for the asymmetry between the past and the future" (92). If Popper could have had available to him the insights of chaos theory, which retains the mechanics of classical, Newtonian science to account for the random, unpredictable, asymmetric future behaviors of a physical system generated by deterministic initial conditions in its past, he might have been able to negotiate the impasse between his and Einstein's worldviews. This Janus-like "furrowards, bagawards" (*FW* 18.32) perspective of chaos theory sees metaphysical determinism in the past history of dynamic systems yet absolute unpredictability in the future history of these systems because of the limits on our capacity for achieving anything remotely close to Laplace's desired degree of precision in our knowledge of the system. This impossibility accounts for our perception of chance and opens the future of the system to our own interaction ("spontaneous activity") (Poincaré 397–98 and Churchland 114; also see Ruelle 29–30).

One might well object that there is little use for this idea of stochastic determinism, which strips away the apparent value of determinism by leaving the future unknowable and unpredictable, that is, by asserting the indeterminism of chance in future phenomena. This objection, however, overlooks the contemporary importance of the chaos scientists' demonstration of the deterministic *origins* of apparently random phenomena, their ability to trace the histories of systems through "retrospective arrangement." The reaffirmation of causality in chaos theory directly subverts the indeterminist view of what has passed or is passing, the ideology of uncertainty in a postmodern culture that has questioned the possibility of reaching such exact knowledge of origin, the assignment of any determinate meaning, and ultimately, the existence of an aboriginal reality. Stochastic determinism may be a determinism with which we can "do nothing" in terms of what is yet to come, but it also reopens the possibility of reaching "objective truth" about the real, as it *is* (Gross and Levitt 52). Chaos theory thus reinforces the conviction that "universal laws of Nature exist 'out there' apart from our perception of them" (Barrow, *World* 12), the fundamental conviction of scientific realism.

In *Dubliners*, as I have already shown, James Joyce employs the "Cartesian-Newtonian" objective narrative techniques of the literary naturalist (and scientific determinist) to present a *scientific* diagnosis of the moral "hemiplegia or paralysis" of his countrymen (*Letters I* 55), at the same time sustaining an imposed, symbolic level of meaning for his stories, maintaining a "Euclidean" parallel to the reality he chronicles. In both his conception of the artist Stephen Dedalus and his manner of telling Stephen's story in *A Portrait of the Artist as a Young Man*, however, Joyce acknowledges the inescapable subjectivity of such acts of imposition for the artist, the scientist, and the geometer alike; this reconception of literary realism, as I have shown, shares some ideological foundations with chaos theory. Moreover, in *Ulysses* and *Finnegans Wake*, while continuing to investigate subjectivity, Joyce contributes to the cultural context that has promoted the emergence of chaos science by legitimating the reader's intuition and disclosing his own intuitive sense that apparently chaotic phenomena possess inherent order. Joyce simultaneously sustains his objective view of the problem of subjectivism from *A Portrait* into *Ulysses* and *Finnegans Wake* while intuitively (subjectively) affirming that an ordered material reality *exists*, apart from our perception and control. Moreover, Joyce's particular version of this scientific realism, as Barrow defines it (*World* 12), although an assertion rather than a "scientific" demonstration, is the realism of the science of chaos.

STOCHASTIC DETERMINISM

The metaphysical implications of chaos theory are considerable. Not only does the new view of chaos reaffirm an element of design in the cosmos, but by demonstrating the order retrospectively discernible in systems that appear to be random because they are inherently unpredictable in prospect, the stochastic determinism of chaos theory achieves a dialectical transcendence of determinism and chance, the many-worlds synthesis of Karl Popper's "open universe," in its pre- and post-, *preposterous* view of dynamic systems.[9] Joyce's conception of *Ulysses* as a retrospective arrangement of the accidental meeting of Leopold Bloom and Stephen Dedalus, of course, anticipates this dialectic by implying that if this chance event, or this novel, has any significance at all, it is because "looking back over that strange time . . . it was that small act, trivial in itself . . . that determined the whole aftercourse of both [their] lives." (Critical readings of *Ulysses* have persisted in seeing the meeting of Stephen and Bloom as having a determining influence on both their futures.)[10] Furthermore, Joyce embodies a dialectic of chance and determinism, analogous to that of chaos theory, in the three principal characters of *Ulysses*. Throughout the novel Stephen expresses a deterministic view of the world, best illustrated by his quotation from Maeterlinck: "*If Socrates leave his house today he will find the sage seated on his doorstep. If Judas go forth tonight it is to Judas his steps will tend*" (U 9.1042–44). Molly Bloom, reading her Tarot cards early in the day or reflecting on the vagaries of chance and luck throughout "Penelope" (e.g., U 18.867–69), confirms her husband's assumption that women "believe in chance because[,] like themselves," it is unpredictable (U 13.808–9). If James Joyce, as has often been observed, stands in a consubstantial relation to Bloom and Stephen—a "holy spirit" presiding over the novel and proceeding out of the bond of the father and the son—within the book Leopold Bloom performs the same function, mediating between the deterministic Stephen and aleatory Molly.

Bloom repeatedly sees himself inhabiting a world where things happen "accidentally by design," caught between fortune (Rudy's conception and death: "Just a chance" [U 6.77]) and fate (Milly's maturation: "Destiny. Ripening now" [U 4.430]). The fortuitous determinism of *coincidence*, the accidental design of experience, intrigues Bloom: "Now that's really a coincidence. . . . Coming events cast their shadows before" (U 8.525–26). In the "Ithaca" episode Bloom muses repeatedly about the intimations of design in the coincidence; his retrospective "reminiscences of coincidences" prospectively "preindicative of the result of the Gold Cup," early in the chapter, lead him to an intuition of the determinism embedded in the chance event of the horse race: he "bear[s] in his arms the secret of the race" in more than one sense (U 17.323–24, .340). Indeed, throughout Joyce's most scientific episode, which opens with the Riemannian coincidence of the "parallel courses" of

Bloom and Stephen, "starting united" (U 17.1–2), Bloom illustrates the chaos scientist's forward-backward, prospective-retrospective view of stochastic determinism, seeing design in past and future chance phenomena, uninfluenced by the individual's act of observation—"the irreparability of the past" (the clown)—and beyond the individual's capacity to foresee—"the imprevidibility of the future" (the coin)—(U 17.975, .979–80). Clearly Joyce himself, building his novel on a fortuitously deterministic coincidence, a chance encounter out of which all the lines of the novel's design emerge, promotes both Bloom's intuition that he beholds "the predestination of a future" as he watches Stephen write (U 17.780) and the reader's realization that this future will contain the retrospective arrangement of the aleatory world of *Ulysses* as a deeply ordered chaotic system.

Although the conflict between those who hold that the world and life itself result from chance and those who see a providential design is a commonplace in Western culture, Joyce and chaos theory share a unique resolution of this antithesis that accepts both fortune and fate, suggesting (Joyce) or showing (chaos theory) that what is unpredictable in prospect will be seen, in retrospect, as the result of deterministic initial conditions. Joyce may have been drawn to consider the conflicting claims of chance and determinism for any number of reasons, including his familiarity with theological debates concerning free will and predestination. It is equally possible, however, that he saw a secular equivalent of this unresolved debate within the scientific community, where the advocates of increasingly statistical, probabilistic experimental methodologies had been contending with the proponents of global explanatory and deterministic theories, from the mid-nineteenth century on; the influence of "probability and its applied cousin, statistics," was pervasive in the development of late nineteenth-century science (Stewart, *Does God Play Dice* 44), whereas, by the beginning of the twentieth century, Ernst Mach's positivism, Poincaré's "conventionalism," and Pierre Duhem's analyses of scientific methodologies had fully exposed the determinism inherent in all theory (Passmore 320–29).

Consider, for example, the contradictory inferences that can be and were drawn from two of the most powerful and influential scientific conceptions of the later nineteenth century, entropy and evolution. Entropy, based on experiments in statistical mechanics, and evolution, a theory postulating a deterministic scheme of development, were and remain widely accepted as truths, yet each apparently offers a direct contradiction to the other. According to the second law of thermodynamics, which holds that entropy (the measure of disorder in a closed system) can only increase with time, it seems impossible for higher orders of creation to evolve and progressively differentiate into a complex order. If shattered crockery never reassembles itself, or if a room never becomes more tidy with time (two common illustrations of entropy), how could random amino acids evolve into highly organized forms of life? A thoughtful individual toward the end of the nineteenth century—H. G. Wells, for instance—might well call down a plague on both the empiricist's and the theorist's houses and question whether either experiment or theory could possibly ascertain truth, as Wells does in his precocious essay "The Rediscovery of the Unique" (1891). Attacking both the scientists' theories and their empirical methods on the ground that even the conception of number is an abstraction, "a purely subjective and illusory reduplication of uniques" (338), Wells ultimately assails "the certainty of all the so-called laws of physics and chemistry" (340). (Wells subsequently attempted to transcend the conflict between entropy and evolution by postulating a long-term devolution of the species and the cosmos in *The Time Machine* [1895], although his solution was no less theoretical and impossible to demonstrate empirically.)[11]

The two most influential scientific formulations of the twentieth century, relativity and quantum theory, reenact this conflict between a deterministic vision of the cosmos and a view of phenomena that rests ultimately on the uncertainties of chance probabilities, a fundamental incompatibility that is best illustrated by Einstein's famous (and frequently misquoted) rejection of the probabilistic Copenhagen interpretation of quantum theory: God "does not play dice." In the winter of 1926–27 Niels Bohr, Werner Heisenberg, and Wolfgang Pauli had combined to formulate their Copenhagen interpretation, countering Erwin Schrödinger's realist conception of the wave function for subatomic quantum phenomena (i.e., "that there is an underlying independent reality that his wave mechanics partly described") with a view based on absolute uncertainty: "This interpretation requires that we accept that we can never 'know' quantum concepts: they are simply beyond human experience" (Baggott 82–83). Einstein's well-known rejection of "the element of chance implied by quantum theory" appeared in his December 1926 letter to Max Born, responding to Born's "probabilistic interpretation of the wave function," one of the foundations of the Copenhagen interpretation (Baggot 29, 82): "Quantum mechanics is very impressive. But an inner voice tells me that it is not yet the real thing. The theory produces a good deal but hardly brings us closer to the secret of the Old One. I am at all events convinced that *He* does not play dice" (qtd. in Baggott 29).[12]

In February 1925, shortly before the formulation of the Copenhagen interpretation, Alfred North Whitehead surveyed the recent developments in contemporary science in his Lowell Lectures at Harvard, published later that year as *Science and the Modern World.* (Whitehead, like Poincaré, had attempted to conceive a post-Euclidean, post-Cartesian, realist mathematics as early as 1906 [Passmore 336–38].) With quantum theory in mind, Whitehead observed that modern scientific thought appears to be going in two opposite directions with, on the one hand, the conception of highly abstract theories and, on the other hand, impressive advances in experimental observation, moving toward increased detail and precision of discrimination (Whitehead 4). Although Whitehead differed from Einstein in seeing the development of quantum mechanics as a promising merger of abstract conceptualization and pragmatic predictive power in a *nondeterministic* theory (219–25), his optimism was ill-founded and might well have foundered had he had Einstein's opportunity to follow the work of Bohr, Heisenberg, and Pauli.[13] As both Ian Stewart (*Does God Play Dice* 65) and James Gleick (52) report, any such "romance between mathematicians and physicists had ended in divorce in the 1930s," and only with the development of chaos theory have theoretical mathematicians and experimental physicists resumed talking with one another. The key difference between chaos and quantum theory is that the scientists of chaos have discovered order at the heart of chaos, whereas the quantum theorists have postulated chaos at the heart of order. Chaos theory emerged from the experimental observation of unpredictable behavior in deterministic phenomena, deeply embedded order creating chaos, whereas quantum theory arose from the hypothesis that deeply embedded uncertainty produces the apparent order of things. Ultimately, chaos theory may offer a more persuasive synthesis of determinism and chance than quantum theory does, the unification of theory and experiment that Whitehead hoped for, because it promises to absorb quantum mechanics, exploring the rule of chaos driving the randomness of quantum phenomena, whereas quantum theory—limited to subatomic behavior—undertakes no explanation of the macrolevel phenomena of chaos.[14] Similarly, a reading of *Ulysses* in light of chaos theory can assimilate and transcend the insights of the literary criticism of indeterminacy, the poststructuralist reading of the novel, by showing that the unpredictability of experience for those who inhabit the dynamic system of the novel (i.e., its characters) is not the condition of those outside the book, who can observe the history of the system retrospectively (i.e., both author and reader). In Popper's words, "indeterminism is not enough" (*Open Universe* 113).

Four important features of chaos theory, all accessible to the nonscientist, have fundamentally altered the study of natural phenomena and offer intriguing applications for the reading and criticism of an orderly chaotic literary work like Joyce's *Ulysses*: (1) the principle of sensitive dependence, (2) the role of feedback in sensitively dependent dynamic systems, (3) the emphasis on scientific explanation rather than prediction, and (4) the concept of design, either innate or emergent, in chaotic systems. These four components move chaos science in the same direction Joyce pursued in his writing of *Ulysses*, toward a more accurate picture of the world in all its complexity and apparent randomness. By recognizing the literary equivalents of these principles in *Ulysses*, we can see that, as chaos theory has effected a paradigm shift in contemporary science, a "chaotic" reading of Joyce's novel shows the necessity for a paradigm shift in both Joyce criticism and postmodern critical theory generally.

SENSITIVE DEPENDENCE

The Cartesian-Newtonian worldview pictures the cosmos as driven by rather simple forces, and nearly three centuries of scientists working in the Cartesian tradition have applied their own version of Occam's razor to their research by assuming that all phenomena can and will ultimately be understood as the results of simple rules, or laws.[15] In literary studies the term *convention* has the same force as the axioms of geometry or the laws of science, so it seems to be no accident that at the same time as the geometer's confidence in Euclid and the scientist's conviction of a lawful cosmos weakened at the turn of the century, the writer's adherence to conventions as *absolutes* began to waver. Stephen Kern has argued that the formal transformations in the arts, parallel to "developments inspired by technology" at the turn of the century, suggest "that a cultural revolution of the broadest scope was taking place, one that involved essential structures of human experience and basic forms of human expression" (6). Reciprocally, Poincaré's influential conventionalist view of mathematics and science maintained that the *laws* of these disciplines are not absolute truths but conceptual systems, "free creation[s] of the human spirit," like the conventions of literary form (Passmore 326). Nonetheless, still generally confident that all events are reducible to the simplicity of law, the working scientist until recently routinely ignored those complex phenomena that seemed to be intractable to mathematical modeling and scientific analysis. For example, consider the entrenched mechanical principle that for every action there is an equal and opposite reaction; two reasonable consequences of this idea are the assumptions that small causes have small effects and that large causes have large effects. (Test this by striking a billiard ball with a "BB" and then with a bowling ball.) One of the most unsettling early emphases of chaos theory, however, was the study of the many events in nature where small causes produce enormous consequences. Often, quite minute differences in the initial conditions of a dynamic system, in fact, lead to vast differences over time, differences both unpredictable and apparently unanalyzable. This is the previously mentioned principle of sensitive dependence on initial conditions, which has been nicknamed the "butterfly effect" from meteorologist Edward Lorenz's description of the dynamics of weather systems in his 1979 paper entitled "Predictability: Does the Flap of a Butterfly's Wings in Brazil Set Off a Tornado in Texas?" (Gleick 322; Lorenz, however, first presented his basic model of unpredictability in the weather, his strange attractor, much earlier, in his 1963 paper entitled "Deterministic Nonperiodic Flow").[16] Unless meteorologists have infinitely precise information for every cubic millimeter of the atmosphere—the exact temperature, wind velocity, atmospheric pressure, and so on—instant by instant, they will be unable to predict the future weather with absolute certainty. Lorenz's numerical weather model (expressed in three nonlinear equations) demonstrates that predictability, the cherished goal of Laplace, if not of Newton, and of generations of scientists since, is as unattainable in global terms as Heisenberg had shown it to be at the subatomic level. No wonder, then, that conventional scientists call these sensitively dependent systems that behave so unpredictably "chaotic."

Actually, Lorenz's "butterfly effect" is not a totally original formulation; Poincaré, the "prophet of chaos" (Peterson 143), had observed something very similar in his study of nonlinear equations, offering a popularized version of his early intuition of the principle of sensitive dependence in his discussion of chance in *Science and Method* (1908):

> A very slight cause, which escapes us, determines a considerable effect which we can not help seeing, and then we say this effect is due to chance. If we could know exactly the laws of nature and the situation of the universe at the initial instant, we should be able to predict exactly the situation of this same universe at a subsequent instant. But even when the natural laws should have no further secret for us, we could know the initial situation only *approximately*. If that permits us to foresee the subsequent situation *with the same degree of approximation*, this is

> all we require, we say the phenomenon has been predicted, that it is ruled by laws. But this is not always the case; it may happen that slight differences in the initial conditions produce very great differences in the final phenomena; a slight error in the former would make an enormous error in the latter. Prediction becomes impossible and we have the fortuitous phenomenon. (397–98)[17]

The nineteenth-century English scientist and founding father of thermodynamics, James Clerk Maxwell, anticipated Joyce's Messenger interpolation in *Ulysses* by using the match to illustrate a similar disproportion between cause and effect: "The match is responsible for the forest fire, but reference to a match does not suffice to understand the fire" (qtd. in Prigogine and Stengers 206).

Lorenz's small act, his formulation of the butterfly effect, is a reiteration of a familiar idea that itself illustrates the principle it concerns, because it has generated, through a series of consequences, a massive reorientation of contemporary thought in the sensitively dependent system of the sciences, a new analytical focus on the complexity, irregularity, and unpredictable muddle of the world as we experience it. Chaos theory moves science toward the description of this real world and indicates that complexity is rooted in the simple in a way very different from the Cartesian-Newtonian conception of simplicity. If Lorenz's "butterfly effect" is an old idea in new terms, then, a computer-assisted demonstration of Poincaré's mathematical insight or of Maxwell's struck match, so also is Stephen's reverie that Messenger's lighting of his cigar, "that small act, trivial in itself, that striking of that match," could determine "the whole aftercourse of both our lives" no profound metaphysical insight; indeed, it sounds very much like a cliché. If it is a cliché, it is because Stephen reflects, through conventionalized narrative style, something often thought and recognized in everyday experience: one's fate sensitively depends on apparently small and accidental initial conditions. Notwithstanding this observation's status as a commonplace, Joyce in fact builds his entire novel on just such a "small act, trivial in itself," the brief encounter of Stephen and Bloom.

In other words, in *Ulysses* Joyce sustains and builds on his conception of the epiphanic significance of the "triviality," the capacity of a "vulgarity of speech or of gesture" or of action to trigger a "sudden spiritual manifestation" wherein the "soul of the commonest" event "seems to us radiant" with meaning: the event "achieves its epiphany" (SH 211, 213). Although

Joyce withdrew this definition of the epiphany from Stephen's discourse on aesthetics when he revised *Stephen Hero*—either because he was no longer satisfied with the idea or, more likely, because he wished to distance himself and his literary convictions from the young man of his *Portrait of the Artist*—the epiphanic moment remains a characteristic feature both in the stories of *Dubliners* and in *A Portrait*. *Ulysses* represents, particularly in "Joyce's use of detail," a "radical extension of [this] epiphanic method" (Gifford, *Notes* xii). A. Walton Litz, for instance, argues that Joyce, "acutely aware of the disintegrating forces in modern European society, . . . turned to the concrete details of place and character as one stable base" in his composition of *Ulysses* (*Art* 24) chiefly because he retained his belief in the epiphanic significance of the commonplace, "the 'showing forth' of character through a seemingly trivial action or detail of appearance" (*Art* 23). Throughout these works and most clearly in *Ulysses*, Joyce's attention to detail joins with his awareness of the enormous sensitive dependence of individual fates on the small, apparently insignificant speech, gesture, act, or event. In the notes he provided Joyce's biographer Richard Ellmann, Stanislaus Joyce describes his brother's fascination with the inconsequentiality that reveals its consequence only in retrospect; Stanislaus recalls Joyce remarking, in an "attempt to explain" his epiphanic "method," "Do you see that man who has just skipped out of the way of the tram? Consider, if he had been run over, how significant every act of his would at once become. I don't mean for the police inspector. I mean for anybody who knew him. And his thoughts, for anybody that could know them. It is my idea of the significance of trivial things that I want to give the two or three unfortunate wretches who may eventually read me" (*JJII* 163).[18] This "significance of trivial things" emerges in the reading of *Ulysses* as a central feature of Joyce's overall conception of his novel—the climactic, anticlimactic chance encounter of Stephen and Bloom—and determines not only "his insatiable desire for concrete details" in "the minutiae of setting" (Litz, *Art* 24), or his plan to invest a day in the commonplace life of a Dublin businessman with Homeric correspondences, but often his handling of style, structure, and motif in his narrative as well. One of Joyce's favorite lines, in defense of his narrative methods, was "Yes. Some of the means I use are trivial—and some are quadrivial" (Budgen, "James Joyce" 347).

This Joycean principle of sensitive dependence operates, in an immediate way, as a basic mechanism in the internal monologue technique of the first several episodes of *Ulysses*, written in what Joyce called the novel's "initial style" (*Letters I* 129). In these early chapters Joyce gives his readers the information they need to negotiate between the external narrative and his characters' internal responses, to recognize that details trigger the flow of his characters' thoughts; Stephen's and Bloom's internal monologues depend sensitively on small external stimuli, such as the touch of an arm (U 1.147, .159) or an advertisement for a "model farm" (U 4.154–58, .191–229). Joyce does this often enough in the first several chapters to convince readers that they can find a logical, causal relation between the external world experienced by his characters and their subjective responses to this world.[19] As the novel proceeds and Joyce's styles vary, in part to suggest the inescapable subjectivity of such acts of reading for character and reader alike, the readers' strategy for naturalizing the eccentricities of the text remains largely the same: seeking the element in a given passage that explains the significance of its headline in "Aeolus," for example, or the detail in the overture of "Sirens" that reappears in the chapter's narrative, or the key words or ideas in the "real" worlds of "Cyclops" or "Circe" that trigger the exaggerated interpolations and hallucinatory episodes in these chapters. Yet though the readers' strategy of negotiating between detail and significance may not change through the book, the challenge to their ingenuity increases exponentially as they contend with the opaque opening paragraphs and chaotic conclusion of "Oxen of the Sun," the convoluted syntax of "Eumaeus," or the sesquipedalian vocabulary, involuted logic, and technical terminology of "Ithaca," "the ugly duckling of the book" (Joyce's phrase for his "favourite" episode; Budgen, *James Joyce* 264). In other words, the readers' response to *Ulysses* replicates the manner of its telling. The straightforward reading of the space between external and internal worlds, a fairly trivial demand on the readers' ability to cope with a text, becomes increasingly problematic as the readers progress toward a greater awareness of the subjective nature of their reading. This awareness of individual subjectivity is a significant dimension of the novel's meaning, as I will show, and it sensitively depends on the small detail of Joyce's early establishment of the readers' confidence in their own objective responses to the text.

The narrative demands of *Ulysses*, as any survey of the criticism of the novel will attest, teach its readers early and well the immense potential significance of even the slightest detail. Consider Joyce's use of the period in *Ulysses*, an apparently perfunctory mark of punctuation, one the least conspicuous and presumably least significant elements of the text, which readers can hardly be expected to notice until they miss its presence in "Penelope," the unpunctuated concluding chapter. The period is nevertheless present, despite its absence as a word or punctuation mark in "Penelope," in the form of Molly Bloom's menstrual *period*, "that thing" which "come[s] on" her during her monologue (U 18.1105). Readers alert to the significance of trivial things can be confident that Joyce intends them to connect these two kinds of periods in "Penelope" because, by doing so, they replicate Leopold Bloom's recognition of the meaning of such minor textual details earlier in the day. Martha Clifford's letter to Bloom, which he reads in "Lotus Eaters," concludes with an erratically punctuated sentence: "Goodbye now, naughty darling, I have such a bad headache. today. and write *by return* to your longing Martha" (U 5.254–57). Bloom repeats Martha's typographical/Freudian slip, "Such a bad headache." and locates the source of this headache in the significant trivial detail of the periods that bracket "today" in her letter: "Has her roses probably" (U 5.285). Furthermore, Bloom, like Molly, Martha, and Gerty MacDowell, too (U 13.561–62), may have his period in the text in the concluding dot of "Ithaca" (U 17.2332); if the rumor be true that as "a finished example of the new womanly man" (U 15.1798–99), Leopold Bloom menstruates (U 12.1658–60), we cannot rule out the possibility that Joyce has used the culminating period of Bloom's day as both a typographical and a physiological symbol. As the readers of *Ulysses* thus come to recognize the significance of such a trivial thing as the period as they move through the book, they may realize that Joyce's larger correlation between biology and style in "Oxen of the Sun" also sensitively depends on the small stimuli of his correlation of physiology and punctuation earlier in the novel.

Joyce fosters the readers' recognition of the importance of trivial things uniformly along the continuum from the small issues of typographical conventions to the large concerns of the novel's meanings, as he prompts their awareness, for example, of the patterns of missing, extra, or inappropriate letters—"ha" for *hat* (U 4.70), "Boom" for *Bloom* (U 16.1260), "world" for *word* (U 5.245), "Eeleven" for *eleven* (U 5.94), or "Nother" for *Mother* (U 3.199)—which may lead to their larger awareness of letters that are missing (e.g., gaps in the text), superfluous (e.g., the catalogs in "Cyclops"), or inappropriate (e.g., Bloom's furtive *correspondence* with Martha Clifford) in the novel. At the next level of magnification, so to speak, at the level of individual words, the readers come to recognize possible significance in Joyce's apparently inconsequential word choices, such as in his patterned repetition of "creak-creaked-creaking" that propagates into those ominous "cracks" that portend, perhaps, like the fissure in Poe's House of Usher, the total collapse of the edifice of the realist-naturalist work of fiction (e.g., see U 4.49, .73, .544; 6.1, .25, .26, .131, .508; 7.177; 8.644; 9.5, .9, .329, .590; 11.337, .433, .761,

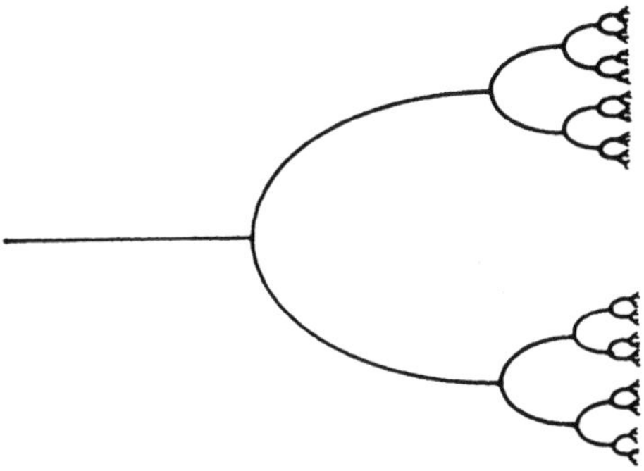

Figure 8. Ian Stewart's "schematic view" of a period-doubling bifurcation pattern. (Reproduced by permission of Blackwell Publishers from Ian Stewart, *Does God Play Dice?* 163, fig. 66.)

.965; 14.408, .424; 17.2061). Furthermore, as I have already shown at the level of style and structure, Joyce promotes the readers' awareness that the significance of trivial things operates in his moves from external narrative into internal monologue, in the relations of parts to wholes in entire episodes, and in the correspondence between the experiences of the typical Leopold Bloom and the archetypal Odysseus.

Any trivial detail in the text of *Ulysses*, the readers come to believe, offers such possibilities for larger meaning or, in terms of chaotic dynamics, may function as a bifurcation point beyond which the behaviors of a system multiply (literally a case of "period doubling" when the meaning of the period doubles; see figure 8).[20] Joyce would no doubt approve this analogy between periodic bifurcation in dynamic systems and his method for exposing the "significance of trivial things" because, as he knew and pointed out to Frank Budgen, the act of bifurcation, splitting into two, lies at the root of the word trivial: "meaning litterally [sic]—carrefour—where three roads meet" (Hart, Introduction xvii).[21]

By emphasizing the sensitive dependence of meaning on the trivial in *Ulysses*, Joyce reciprocates Stephen's linear and deterministic reading of history, which isolates as "possible" only those events "which came to pass"—"they are lodged in the room of the infinite possibilities they have ousted" (*U* 2.50–52)—by introducing the nonlinearity of a dynamic reality that balances determinism with chance, offering the possibility of multiple significances in every moment, multiple histories arising and read retrospectively from every bifurcation point in his text. Of course, to say that Joyce would approve of an analogy between the idea of bifurcation and the radical meaning of trivial, or that he recognized the phenomenon of sensitive dependence in the significance of trivial things, does not mean that he was our first authentic mathematician and scientist of chaos; it does mean that by intuitively recognizing the complex dynamics of reality and seeking to represent this complexity in *Ulysses*, Joyce anticipated in art a similar focus on complex systems in later twentieth-century science.

FEEDBACK AND DESCRIPTION

The reader, likewise, need be neither a mathematician nor a scientist to understand the Messenger passage in "Aeolus," because everyone at one time or another has thought back through a series of events and wondered, "looking back over that strange time" (U 7.763), something like the following: if I had not dropped off my dry cleaning, then I would have been driving on the freeway; and if I had been driving on the freeway, I would have taken the Second Street exit; and then and then and then, on to some calamity or good fortune met or missed. In a similar vein, in "Circe" Bloom remarks, "If I had passed Truelock's window that day two minutes later would have been shot" (U 15.645–46). Such a reflection is simply the retrospective arrangement of a chain of multiplying effects emerging from a single ultimate cause. Through this chain some effect resulting from a prior cause "feeds" into the next causal link, leading to the next effect, which in turn feeds back into the next link. Indeed, this principle of *feedback* characterizes all sensitively dependent phenomena, vastly intensifying the effects of even the most humble of causes.

A graph of the relation of action and reaction in a dynamic system featuring such feedback would not produce the diagonal straight line of a classic Newtonian system, where equivalent causes create equivalent effects; hence, scientists call such systems "nonlinear." Our lives, our world, and "just about everything else of interest," as Heinz Pagels remarks, are resolutely nonlinear (*Dreams of Reason* 73). In the often quoted words of the mathematician Benoit Mandelbrot, "Clouds are not spheres, mountains are not cones, coastlines are not circles, and bark is not smooth, nor does lightning travel in a straight line" (1). (Mandelbrot's fractal geometry, which makes the representation and pictorial description of chaos possible, is the most exciting recent development in the history of non-Euclidean geometries, traced in the previous chapter; for an extended discussion of fractal geometry and its usefulness for describing the irregular structure of a chaotic novel, see Rice, "Iris Murdoch" 213–15 and passim.)

A classic example of a nonlinear system characterized by feedback is the erratic fluctuation of populations in ecosystems. A variety of circumstances will affect the growth and decline of a population of, say, insects in a particular environment: reproductive rates, available food supply, populations of predators, and so on. One of the most important of these conditions, obviously, is the population of the previous generation of the same insects, the parents of the next generation. Population biologists use a formula called the Verhulst equation to project growth rates; the Verhulst equation includes a factor that feeds back the estimate of the present population. This equation is so sensitively dependent that an error of only "one part in ten quadrillion (a one followed by sixteen zeros)" in the estimate of the number of bugs in a pond will make the calculation of the population, after fifty cycles (or iterations of the equation), totally unreliable (Peat, *Philosopher's Stone* 198). To ascertain the likely growth or decline of the population over several years, the scientist would have to have an impossibly exact figure for the initial population; any error will feed back every time the equation is recalculated (iterated) for a subsequent generational cycle. So, if the margin of error can be no greater than 1×10^{-16}, an accuracy vastly beyond human capacity, why should the scientist even attempt prediction in analyzing the behavior of such nonlinear systems? One obvious answer is that these systems are, after all, most characteristic of life as humans know it; science cannot simply abandon the study of nonlinearity. Nonetheless, if scientists cannot project its behavior, what should their objective be in examining a nonlinear system? This is precisely the question addressed by chaos theory and by the larger emerging discipline of which it is a subset, what Pagels calls the "sciences of complexity" in his *Dreams of Reason* (1988). One of the most important consequences of the paradigm shift toward complexity research is that scientists have recognized that they are in the business not of *prediction* but of *explanation*. John Holland, for example, one of the founders of the Santa Fe Institute for the Study of Complexity, responds to the central questions facing scientists of complexity, "How [can] you predict anything? How [can] you have a science?" by arguing, from the example of meteorology, "We can understand how [weather features] interact to produce weather on a local and regional scale. In short, we have a real science of weather—without full prediction. And we can do it because prediction isn't the essence of science. The essence is comprehension and explanation. And that's precisely what Santa Fe could hope to do with economics and other social sciences" (qtd. in Waldrop 255). Prospectively, then, much in the cosmos is unpredictable and accidental, yet in explanation, in description by a kind of retrospective arrangement, we can see that this cosmos is designed and determined. In a word, in Joyce's word from *Finnegans Wake*, the scientists of complexity have found a "chaosmos" in the cosmos (*FW* 118.21).

In *Ulysses* James Joyce employs strategies of textual circulation and recirculation that, by their effects, resemble the intensifying nonlinear feedback of many physical systems. In a straightforward (linear) sense of the term, Stephen, Leopold, and Molly both feed back and "feed on" their memories of recent and remote experiences throughout the day, recycling their pasts. (This seems to be the only feeding Stephen does in the book.) Bloom's most poignant moment of such linear feedback, his memory of his and Molly's first lovemaking "under wild ferns on Howth" (*U* 8.900), occurs to him while he feeds, in "Lestrygonians." Moreover, Joyce surrounds Bloom's retrospective feedback in this episode, his self-absorption, with analogous acts of self-consumption: the feedback of Nosey Flynn, for example, who periodically snuffles up the "dewdrop" descending from his nose (*U* 8.804–5, .836, .983), or of "one of those Habsburgs . . . [who] used to eat the scruff off his own head" (*U* 8.872–73), or of the street "loafer" who "gnaw[s] a crusted knuckle" (*U* 8.1066–67), or of the "ravenous terrier" that "choke[s] up a sick knuckly cud" of vomit and recycles it, "lapp[ing] it with new zest" (*U* 8.1031–32). (No wonder so many in Dublin suffer, like Tom Rochford [*U* 8.1012] and Denis Breen, from "indiges"-tion [*U* 8.252].)

As the novel progresses into its later episodes, however, and even within Joyce's most extended illustration of the linear circulation of his Dubliners in "Wandering Rocks," the readers begin to see something more nearly resembling the nonlinear feedback of dynamic systems, wherein the reiteration of the earlier products of the system's iteration vastly intensifies its chaotic behavior. The text's self-quotation in the crossover interpolations among the mini-episodes of "Wandering Rocks" leads to the increasing feedback of "Sirens," when the lines of the episode's overture return, or when the opening words of "Calypso" resurface ("As said before," "Bloom ate liv as said before" [*U* 11.519, .569]), or when Stephen's thoughts of Shakespeare in "Scylla and Charybdis" (*U* 9.651–53) reappear ("In Gerard's rosery of Fetter lane he walks, greyedauburn. One life is all. One body. Do. But do" [*U* 11.907–8]).

As *Ulysses* becomes increasingly chaotic, it often does so by an expansive feeding back into the text of elements already present in earlier "states" of its text. This is particularly striking in the hallucinatory passages of "Circe"—in which the novel's entire cast through the first fourteen episodes, the earlier states of the system, reiterates—and in the manner in which these passages "act out" the various facets of Bloom's psyche (guilt, desire for recognition, masochism, etc.) and interests (the theater itself), which are known to the readers from events and thoughts earlier in Bloom's day. In addition "Circe's" companion episodes in the novel's later stages emerge similarly from the intensifying feedback of earlier elements of the text: "Sirens" involves a kind of parody of the feeding reverie of "Lestrygonians" and an expansion of Bloom's musical interests; the gigantic interpolations of "Cyclops" exponentially intensify Bloom's own antic fancies in "Hades" ("Bom! Upset. A coffin bumped out on to the road. Burst open. Paddy Dignam shot out" [U 6.421–22]); "Nausicaa" recycles, expands, and compensates for Bloom's anticlimactic voyeurism in "Lotus Eaters" (U 5.98–132); Stephen's literary-historical pathography of Shakespeare in "Scylla and Charybdis" feeds back into the historio-linguistic paradigm of "Oxen in the Sun"; Bloom's characteristic evasions of the idea and person of Boylan emerge as the painfully hesitant manner and circumlocutory style of "Eumaeus"; his scattered ruminations on science and technology similarly key the emergent scientific catechism of "Ithaca"; and Martha Clifford's letter in "Lotus Eaters" (U 5.241–59), sufficiently reiterated, seems to be the initial condition for Molly's monologue in "Penelope."

Although these comparisons between the feedback phenomenon and the increasingly chaotic behavior of the later episodes of *Ulysses* are fairly loose, there is an even more precise analogy between each reader's experience of this novel, or of any work of literature, and the feedback that makes the behavior of dynamic systems both unpredictable and apparently hopelessly complex. In the act of reading, the individual reader's response alters the behavior of the "system," the book, with each "iteration," or reading. The same and many additional readers perform subsequent iterations/readings; in all cases the products of the experience will differ, often subtly, but sometimes with unpredictably vast shifts in the results (e.g., the most recent "new critical insight"). Joyce's own, often noted behavior as a reader of his own work, feeding back his prior experience of the text into the text, clearly intensified the chaotic complexity of *Ulysses*, as any examination of the successive manuscripts, typescripts, placards, and page proofs of the novel will confirm. The exponential growth of *Ulysses* from its earliest state as a short story intended for *Dubliners* and Joyce's well-documented incremental methods of composi-

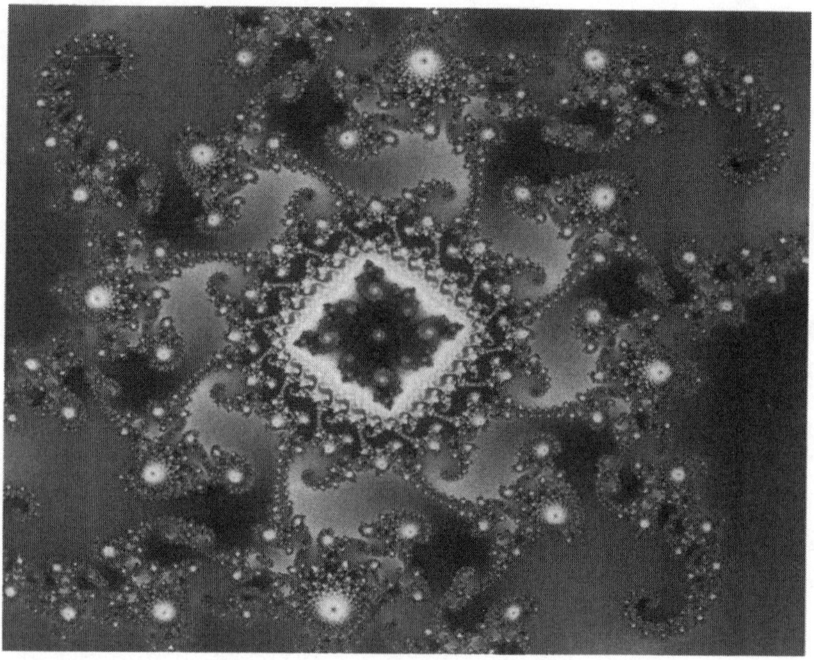

a. "The Crown"

Figure 9. Two representative magnifications of sectors of the Mandelbrot set—"the most complex object in mathematics"—illustrating the rich "complication across scales" generated by a simple initial determinant: "a full description of the set . . .

tion for both *Ulysses* and *Finnegans Wake* strongly parallel the feedback behavior of nonlinear dynamic systems bordering on chaotic turbulence. The apparently simple initial conditions of the Joycean text approach and maintain a tenuous balance on the so-called edge of chaos, that region where the greatest diversity and creativity reside in nature, that fertile realm from which life itself very possibly originated out of a "primordial soup" of random amino acids (Waldrop 123).[22] This edge of chaos, now being examined by the scientists of complexity, is the region Joyce's critics have long inhabited in literary study.

The new emphasis on description rather than prediction as the goal of the sciences of chaos and complexity, their turn away from Laplace's dream of solving the mysteries of the universal machine to accept the long-term unpredictability of any future behavior generated by feedback in a nonlinear

b. *Untitled, #29*

requires just a few dozen characters" of computer code (Gleick 221). (Reproduced in black and white from Krueger and Wolf, *The Fractal Art of Uwe Krueger and Heinz Wolf*, by permission of the creators.)

chaotic system, means, among other things, that the arts and sciences are once again treading on a common ground, or sharing a cup of cocoa under the same roof, like "the artistic" Stephen Dedalus and "the scientific" Leopold Bloom (U 17.560). On the one hand, description has always been the business of the literary and visual arts. On the other hand, computer-generated portraits of chaos—the "Mandelbrot set," for example, a graphic representation of the behavior of a very simple reiterated nonlinear equation—have become a new art form, adorning book jackets, T-shirts, and posters (see figure 9); the success of coffee-table volumes featuring such "portraits of chaos" suggests that the line between computer-generated and nonrepresentational art is thin indeed. Theoretical physicists, such as Stephen Hawking in his *Brief History of Time* (1988), foresee the reunification of physics and metaphysics in the near future; already scientists such as Fritjof Capra (*The Tao of Physics*

[3d ed., 1991]) and Richard Healy (*The Philosophy of Quantum Mechanics* [1989]) are writing about theology and philosophy, while philosophers such as Paul Churchland (*The Engine of Reason* [1995]), Daniel Dennett (*Consciousness Explained* [1991]), and Stephen Kellert (*In the Wake of Chaos* [1993]) are assessing the impact of recent developments in science. (John Passmore sees this interaction between physics and metaphysics—"natural scientists turn philosophers"—as a major trend in twentieth-century philosophy from the beginning of the century [320–42].) The researchers at the Santa Fe Institute for the Study of Complexity approach their subject in much the same way as some critics approach the analysis of literature. This is not entirely coincidental, since one of the founders of the Santa Fe Institute is Murray Gell-Mann, who turned to *Finnegans Wake* to find a name for an elementary particle in quantum physics, the "quark."[23] But note that the methods of the Santa Fe Institute resemble those of some rather than all literary critics, for the similarity extends solely to those who accept the presence of inherent design in art, as the chaos scientists have accepted it in nature.

INDETERMINISM IS NOT ENOUGH

Chaos theory shows that an apparently simple nonlinear dynamic system can generate phenomena of extraordinary complexity, but the reverse also holds: the simple roots of extremely complex phenomena may be discovered by a painstakingly detailed analysis, for chaos has a deeply embedded design. "Chaos is exciting," Ian Stewart writes, "because it opens up the possibility of simplifying complicated phenomena. . . . The great discovery of chaotic dynamics is that apparently patternless behaviour may become simple and comprehensible if you look at the right picture" ("Portraits" 44, 58). Robin Henig describes a fascinating recent example of this new model of scientific simplification, this search for what could be called the *algorithm* of a particularly complex phenomenon, in the ongoing study of the "bizarre, totally unpredictable changes" in the "genetic arrangement" of the influenza virus that lead to flu pandemics (31). Virologists, Henig reports, have discovered that such mutations are neither purely arbitrary events nor the predictable results of annual RNA gene replication (which ordinarily makes immunization effective) but the consequence of the genetic "reassortment" that takes place in the intestines of birds—especially ducks—and swine that live together and in close proximity to, or cohabit with, humans (55). One region where "integrated pig-duck farming" is indigenous and where pandemic influenza "has historically originated" is the Orient, particularly China (64; also see Morse).

The virologists' discovery that "apparently patternless behaviour may become simple and comprehensible if you look at the right picture" is but one illustration of the growing awareness that chaos arises from deterministic initial conditions. Pictures of chaos made possible by advances in technology, by computers that can reiterate nonlinear equations hundreds of thousands of times in a few hours to generate portraits of extraordinarily patterned complexity, gave scientists the first indications that chaos might be orderly. The stunning patterns of the Mandelbrot set (fig. 9), "the most complex mathematical shape ever invented" (Stewart, *Does God Play Dice* 237), seem designed, not random. Erratic statistics such as population distributions or the unpredictable mutations of viruses, which until recently could be studied only a few cycles at a time, similarly seem to be intricately ordered when the scientist can examine a few millennia of data. Chaos theory's most remarkable implication for contemporary culture has been this reaffirmation of the concept of design in natural phenomena, either a Platonic immanent design (Gleick) or an anti-entropic, self-organizational dynamic in nature (Prigogine and Stenger), but in either case a design that is independent of the individual's act of observation. This last point is crucial, because it marks the fundamental difference between chaos theory and the postmodern ideology of uncertainty that has sought its validation in the Copenhagen interpretation of quantum theory.

Ulysses, a novel that many first-time readers perceive as chaotic and incomprehensible, nicely illustrates the distinction between immanent and emergent design in a nonlinear system; more than this, it also exposes the differences between the worldviews of "quantum" postmodernism and complexity science in both its characters and its readers. As is well known, Joyce himself embedded a number of organizational structures in his novel: the Homeric myth, the *Hamlet* allusions, the Gilbert-Linati schemas, and so on. These represent the immanent design of the novel, the deterministic structures of the creator, the lawgiver, which David White calls the novel's "principles of stability" (127). The emergent structure of *Ulysses*, however, comprises random features of the novel, such as messengers or firelighters, marks of punctuation or migrating letters, and patterns of feedback, each of them apparently innocent of intent. Nevertheless, these ostensibly incidental, gradually emerging details progressively combine into a community of behavior as the novel takes on a mind and life of its own. (This impression that *Ulysses* in some sense takes on a "life of its own"—Joyce has, after all, given the novel an anatomy in his schemas—especially characterizes studies of the emergent, evolving styles of the book, those features that Karen Lawrence, for example, describes as "narrative behavior" [55], whereas Michael Groden suggests that "*Ulysses* itself becomes one great 'character'" [55].)[24] Only at rare moments does Stephen dimly intuit that he inhabits the ordered system of a novel: "Who watches me here? Who ever anywhere will read these written words?" (U 3.414–15). Bloom has no idea that he recapitulates the wanderings of Ulysses. Neither Bloom nor Stephen recognizes that his speech and thoughts, for a part of the evening of 16 June, model the embryonic development of the English language. Similarly, no brain neuron has any "idea" that it is acting collectively with other neurons, providing another entity with the much larger and more complex experience of an *idea*.[25] The consumer in the late 1970s who purchased a VHS video recorder rather than a Beta machine had no idea that this simple action might determine the future of an industry through the nonlinear phenomenon of "increasing returns" in the "complex adaptive system" of the economy.[26] Indeed, no consumer can possibly predict how a decision to purchase some product will affect the future "behavior" of the stock market, a complex living structure subject, evidently, to "moods."

Living within a system, such as a novel, Stephen and Bloom and all the other characters of the book cannot grasp the design that contains them. Contemporaneous with Joyce's completion of *Ulysses*, Ludwig Wittgenstein succinctly stated the case in proposition 6.41 of his *Tractatus Logico-Philosophicus* (1921):

> The sense of the world must lie outside the world. In the world everything is as it is, and everything happens as it does happen: *in* it no value exists—and if it did exist, it would have no value.
>
> If there is any value that does have value, it must lie outside the whole sphere of what happens and is the case. For all that happens and is the case is accidental.
>
> What makes it non-accidental cannot lie *within* the world, since if it did it would itself be accidental.
>
> It must lie outside the world. (71)[27]

From Stephen's limited viewpoint, then, it may seem perfectly legitimate to consider any design, any pattern he might perceive in his experience as the creation of his own imagination, as "a conscious rational reagent," "ineluctably construct[ing meaning] upon the incertitude of the void" (U 17.1013–15). Thus the Stephen Dedalus of *Ulysses* is no less subjective than the Stephen of *A Portrait*; he has simply grown more conscious and defensive of his subjectivity. Joyce counterpoints the artistically subjective Stephen, however a creative "reagent," to the scientifically objective Bloom, "a conscious reactor against the void of incertitude" (U 17.2210–11) who, like the contemporary chaos scientist, (1) holds in one conception—coincidence—the unity of chance and determinism; (2) rejects the reduction of complex phenomena to the half-truths of simplicity, for example, to the Citizen's fury in "Cyclops"; (3) accepts the reality of immanent and emergent design, that is, of both cosmic codes, such as "Roygbiv" (U 13.1075–76), and self-organizing systems, such as "find M.C." (U 17.1842); and (4) recognizes that even the infidelity of his wife, the most complex and assuredly *nonlinear* dynamic system in his experience, is "as natural as any and every natural act" by a sensitively dependent, complex adaptive system in the process "of adaptation to altered conditions of existence" (U 17.2178, .2191).

Stephen's "quantum" view of reality as the product of the individual's act of observation, understandable perhaps for a literary character inside the world of the book, is less acceptable for the reader and critic who exist outside the system, where all that happens and is the case is not accidental but, in the terms of chaos theory, the result of immanent and emergent design. One has to ask, then, whether the extreme subjectivism of much poststructuralist criticism risks too "close" a reading of *Ulysses*, celebrating the dislocation of the signifier from the signified and "forc[ing] the reader to see [the text] as artificially produced and resisting identification with any absolute origin in the real world" (McGee 99). Such reading inhabits the limited, subjectivist worldview of the purblind Stephen Dedalus ("Must get glasses" [U 15.3628]) and misses the glimpse of the complexity that is based in an aboriginal reality and expressed through Leopold Bloom. Joyce's critics should start reading *Finnegans Wake*, too, with an eye toward complexity, rather than carry over from *Ulysses* only Stephen's "quantum" view of reality to argue against the metaphysics of presence.[28]

The history of Anglo-American literary theory in our century roughly parallels the developments in the sciences, their paradigm shifts, with a chronological "red shift," a lag of several decades between the scientific theory and its assimilation by the literary academy. (Ironically, artists themselves have often been more timely in their responses: witness Joyce's rather casual and superficial allusions to relativity and quantum theory in *Finnegans Wake* [Duszenko; Langdon; Purdy].) The ascendant "New Criticism" of the 1930s, tracing the generic laws of literature in the model work—the analytic "geometry of meaning" (Todorov 14)—resembles the isolated study of physical systems in ideal states, the methodology of Euclidean-Cartesian-Newtonian science, an approach already three decades out of date. Pursuing this analogy, the formalist and structuralist enterprises that, in the Anglo-American world, grew out of the New Criticism, like Einstein's theories of special and general relativity, do not abandon the deterministic concept of law but see the structures of literature as contingent rather than absolute. The intense subjectivity of poststructuralism seeks its antecedent in the Copenhagen interpretation of quantum theory, which, advancing through the 1920s and taking Einstein further than he was willing to go, argues against origin or aboriginal reality altogether, saying, in effect, that the observer creates "reality" in the act of the observation.[29] Finally, the contemporary return to the study of literature in all its contexts, often called "new historicism" or "cultural studies," which views the work of literature not only in terms of itself and its readers but also in terms of its relations to the complex multiple realities of history, popular culture, politics, and so on, has closed the temporal gap, sharing the fundamental assumptions of chaos theory and the broader, emerging field of the sciences of complexity. Jennifer Wicke, for example, in her recent appeal "for greater rigor" in the study of "mass culture . . . in all its dialectical and internal complexity" (595), sounds very much like the contemporary complexity scientist when she discusses literary consumption "as a complex behavior" (601) or the "textures of modernity" (607) found in "the multivalent complexity" of modern texts (604).[30] Conversely, with only a modest adjustment of terms, Heinz Pagels's description of the emergent sciences of complexity in *The Dreams of Reason* could apply to the most positive directions in contemporary literary study:

> Science has explored the microcosmos and the macrocosmos; we have a good sense of the lay of the land. The great unexplored frontier is complexity. Complex systems include the body and its organs, especially the brain, the economy, population and evolutionary systems, animal behavior, large molecules—all complicated things. . . . Scientists, in a new interdisciplinary effort, have begun to meet the challenge of complex systems and, remarkably, are understanding how complexity can emerge from simplicity. . . . All of existence may be viewed as a complex system built out of simple components.
>
> Some of the themes of the new sciences of complexity . . . [such as]

> the importance of nonlinear dynamics and selective systems [and] the new understanding of chaos . . . portend a new synthesis of science that will overturn our traditional way of organizing reality. (12–13)

Literary work, too, springs from a simple conception, a "struck match," but it grows into a complex system, like the forest fire or the weather—or better yet, like those "complex adaptive systems" such as the stock market or the international community, where the human mind, butterfly wings of a sort, can generate even more unpredictable fluctuations in behavior. A nonlinear dynamic novel like *Ulysses* feeds back on itself, adapting to and affecting its several contexts, and assimilates the reader into its complexity, the reader who feeds on and feeds back into the work and its world. No random phenomenon, *Ulysses* nevertheless strays from the ordered and static world of the stable system, not into chaos, but to the borderline of complexity, the edge of chaos, where small causes have large effects and where both life itself and great works of literature are found.

4

FINNEGANS *WAKE*: THE COMPLEXITY OF ARTIFICIAL LIFE

I shall try to fly by those nets.—(P 203)

Let us leave theories there and return to here's here.—(FW 76.10)

To Joyce reality was a paradigm, an illustration of a possibly unstatable rule.
—*Samuel Beckett* (JJII 551)

[The scientists of complexity study] self-organization in complex systems, . . . the emergence of patterns in evolutionary models that mimic patterns in nature. They're suggesting that living systems, as complex dynamical systems, are driven to these same patterns. They're saying there is a deep theory to the order we see in nature.—*Roger Lewin* (181)

Richard Ellmann begins his 1959 biography of Joyce by stating, "We are still learning to be James Joyce's contemporaries, to understand our interpreter" (*JJI* 1). His 1982 revised edition of the biography repeats this opening verbatim (*JJII* 3), suggesting either that no progress toward this necessary contemporaneity has occurred or that becoming Joyce's contemporaries is an ongoing process, a pursuit of an ever-receding goal. When he asserts that we have not yet understood our "interpreter," Ellmann presumably is alluding to what might be called "the *Finnegans Wake* problem," more explicitly formulated in 1964 by Walton Litz: "Perhaps, as more aids to explication are produced, the *Wake* will—like the once 'unreadable' *Ulysses*—become widely understood" (*Art* 126). By the early 1970s, however, distinguished readers of *Finnegans Wake* such as Fritz Senn, Michael Begnal, and Margot Norris were urging Joyce scholars to move beyond the production of such microcosmic "aids to explication" and on to the macrocosmic reading of *Finnegans Wake* in the hope of achieving "an integrated, theoretical understanding of the whole work" (Norris, "*Conceptual Guide*" 116).[1] Several studies of the *Wake* have answered their call, but (in the terms of Joyce's favorite metaphor for his composition of the book), it seems that these who have been "boring into [the] mountain" of *Finnegans Wake* from the top down, analyzing its grand themes and meaning, have yet to meet those who have tunneled into the novel from the bottom up, examining the book's allusions, motifs, microstructure, and origins and development (Budgen, "Further Recollections" 356).[2] This meeting at the middle of the mountain of the *Wake* may never take place unless Joyce's critics achieve some broader grasp of the full nature of the project they face. (I use the terms "top down" and "bottom up" throughout this chapter, rather than the traditional terms "deductive" and "inductive," both because they are the common usage in complexity studies and because they emphasize the *hierarchical* nature of these reciprocal approaches to a problem, approaches that the sciences of complexity interrogate.)

To date, readers of *Finnegans Wake* have operated like the blind examining the elephant, the common metaphor used by the *Wake*'s readers—if not its author—for the challenge the book offers to all attempts at this "broader grasp." Chief among the limitations in *Wake* criticism have been the largely unquestioned assumptions that *Finnegans Wake* is a work sui generis, that the difficulties in achieving an integrated view of the novel are unique, that the only frame of reference available is the *Wake* itself ("*Finnegans Wake* is about *Finnegans Wake*"), and that "many of the most basic questions (especially that nagging all-inclusive one . . . 'But what is it all about exactly?')" can well "remain unanswered."[3] Several recent and convergent developments in the natural and social sciences, however, responding to similarly daunting challenges to interpretation, suggest that both *Finnegans Wake* and the assumptions that have governed its study are far from unique. These so-called sciences of complexity offer several strategies for reassessing such assumptions and for reading information in (presumably) hopelessly complicated systems.[4] Certainly one of the things that *Finnegans Wake* is about is complexity, although until recently this observation would have seemed neither insightful nor promising for critical discussion. The emergent sciences of complexity, however, may now provide the external frame of reference that can support an ultimate solution of the *Finnegans Wake* "problem," making a local and a global grasp of the *Wake* possible in terms of the nature, function, and significance of complication per se.[5]

Finnegans Wake, it now appears, is but one representative in a "parallel" network of highly individual works produced between the world wars, works that themselves constitute a complex system across a variety of disciplines, that similarly record an increased contemporary awareness of complexity in physical and social systems, and that share a common determinant: each is a largely intuitive reaction to the "complexification of what appeared to be simple" in, for example, the highly publicized mysteries of modern physics, such as Einstein's relativity theories or the new quantum theory, or in the unpredictable, uncontrollable, and apparently incomprehensible nature of public events, such as World War I itself and the subsequent rise of fascism (Bachelard, *New Scientific Spirit* 45; "parallel" rather than "serial" connections are a basic feature of complex networks [Casti 171–211]). Indeed, an Einsteinian recognition of the complex convertibility of mass and motion links such diverse writers as, for example, Antonio Gramsci, who, while imprisoned by fascists, defined political hegemony and the historical bloc as dynamic systems ("reality itself in movement" [193]); Elias Canetti, who, having escaped Hitler's tyranny, pictured the crowd, the mass in motion, as a self-organizing autocatalytic system; Gaston Bachelard, who, writing in Joyce's Paris of the 1930s, called for a new non-Cartesian epistemology based on the "sort of perpetual structural exchange" confirmed by relativity theory (*New Scientific Spirit* 67); or James Joyce, who, sharing the same space and time as these others, created the model, the simulacrum of complexity, that is *Finnegans Wake*.[6]

Although clearly "our century's greatest artistic expression of the sense of a changed world science has given us" (Purdy 216), Joyce's altered view of reality in his notoriously complex book has also been one of many stimuli, one perturbation among many in the sensitively dependent systems of contemporary culture that have culminated in the emergence of the sciences of complexity. As Philip Kuberski has recently remarked, the *Wake* both "assimilates the philosophic consequences of twentieth-century physics and prognosticates several [recent] scientific hypotheses that seek to transcend the objectivist categories of Cartesian thought" (5). Here chaos theory, with its emphasis on the large potential consequences of small stimuli, forces us to adjust our overly linear view of cultural influence as merely a direct matter of proportional action and reaction, linear cause and effect—as I note in the introduction—and helps us to recognize that we cannot finally distinguish Joyce's anticipation or prognostication of recent scientific hypotheses from his possible long-term contributory influence on their formulation in a sensitively dependent cultural field. In other words, *Finnegans Wake* has given more than the "quark" to contemporary culture (see appendix B ["The Field" and "The Quark"]). And if Joyce, together with a number of his contemporaries across a range of disciplines, contributed to the broad cultural field that has generated and legitimated the reexamination of complexity itself among natural and social scientists, the new focus of the sciences of complexity can return the favor by providing a more dynamic perspective on the complex cultural artifact. Complexity flourishes in similar ways in physical and social systems, including the cultural system of literature. If we can transcend the disciplinary boundaries that mute our recognition of the intricate networks of interrelations among natural and human phenomena—one of the chief themes of the sciences of complexity—we may indeed become Joyce's contemporaries.

The sciences of complexity themselves illustrate such an interdisciplinary approach, cutting across the separate provinces of physics, chemistry, and biology, the earth sciences, and the social sciences (especially economics), arguing that all these disciplines, in large part because they are isolated as "disciplines," suffer from the same limitation that plagues the reading of *Finnegans Wake*: "causal decoupling," or the inability to connect an understanding of small-scale phenomena with a grasp of global phenomena. In his *Dreams of Reason* (1988), Heinz Pagels observes that the most successful example of causal *coupling* in the sciences to date has been in the study of genetics. Whereas classical geneticists, observing "regularities of discrete characteristics in living organisms" globally, "postulated genes and their laws of combination," the material existence of genes was confirmed only after the interdisciplinary research of biochemists, working on the molecular scale, could establish the chemical processes of protein synthesis by nucleic acids (DNA and RNA): "The previously discovered genetic laws could now be put on the firm basis of molecular interaction" (198).[7] Perhaps this success story in the sciences encouraged the textual critics of L'Institut des Textes et Manuscrits Modernes, and most particularly David Hayman in his study of the evolution of *Finnegans Wake*, to describe their approach to manuscript research as "genetic" (7). Nevertheless, the present understanding of *Finnegans Wake* more nearly resembles the current state of cognition studies. Pagels describes the unresolved impasse between "the two main approaches to the study of the brain . . . the 'top-down' approach of the cognitive and behavioral psychologists and the 'bottom-up' approach of neuroscientists," using the same metaphor for causal coupling that Joyce favored for his composition of the *Wake*: if "this effort to find a scientific theory of the mind" is to be successful, Pagels writes, psychologists and neuroscientists must join "in the middle of the mountain," like "two tunnel digging crews" (*Dreams of Reason* 195, 197–98). (Pagels seems to be undisturbed by the visual skewing caused by his tunnel metaphor—tunnels usually run from one side of a mountain to the other rather than from the top to the bottom. As I will show, the confusion created by Pagels's tunnel metaphor demonstrates the inappropriateness of applying hierarchical schema, as too often happens in criticism, to the complex nonlinear structures ["webs" or "networks"] Joyce generates in the *Wake*.)

In the years immediately following Pagels's survey of the complex-systems approach to cognition studies in *The Dreams of Reason*, neuroscientists and neurophilosophers made significant advances toward the causal coupling that a "scientific theory of the mind" requires, attempting to explain, from the bottom up, the brain's most complex behaviors: perception, intelligence, creativity, and consciousness itself. What is particularly intriguing about these attempts is that the emerging theories invoke the example of Joyce's fiction as an explanatory model for consciousness, as Daniel Dennett does in his *Consciousness Explained* (1991), and offer an explanatory model for his most complex fiction, *Finnegans Wake*, as Paul Churchland does in *The Engine of Reason* (1995). A brief overview of this complexity-based approach to the study of the brain will help us to grasp the particular problems raised by the analogous study of the complexity of the *Wake*, and a consideration of Dennett's and Churchland's conflicting models for consciousness will give us yet another perspective for viewing the *Wake*'s relations to traditional fiction and to Joyce's own earlier works.

Neuroscience focuses on the intricately networked architecture of the "roughly . . . 100 *billion* neurons," or nerve cells, of the human brain, "one of the most complex systems in the evolution of nature" (Churchland 7; Mainzer 117). The complexity of this system lies not in the sheer number of neurons involved but in the particular kind of structure they assume: contemporary neuroscience has thoroughly established that "the architecture of the brain is that of a massively parallel computing system" (Churchland 264). Unlike a serial system (such as the familiar computer that operates in a linear sequence of discrete steps—its program—to generate output), the parallel network, instead of linking the 100 billion neurons in a long chain, cross-connects these neurons into incredibly intricate meshes, cluster on cluster. This parallel network allows the brain to perform multiple tasks simultaneously (you can walk and chew gum at the same time), but it also can and will assign the same task to several neuron clusters, a multiplication of effort called "*parallel distributed processing*, or PDP for short" (Churchland 11). One obvious advantage of PDP is that the brain can continue to function, sometimes quite normally, as neurologists have often observed, despite the injury to, or total loss of, some portion of its neurons. A serial system, however, like old-fashioned strings of Christmas tree lights or new-fashioned desktop computers, will "crash" with the loss of a single circuit. Parallel distributed processing also generates three additional, increasingly important features of the brain's behavior: (1) The multiple connections (pathways) among neurons allow information to move in many directions, making both a feeding forward and a feeding back of information possible, indeed commonplace, within the system (the "recurrent network" [Churchland 97–121]). As I mention in chapter 3, such feedback is the fundamental dynamic that determines the vast increase of complexity in chaotic systems; accordingly, contemporary neuroscience pictures the brain as a *nonlinear* complex system (Mainzer 117–43).[8] (2) Such feedback seems to be at the root of the brain's abilities to retain, store, and recover information (memory), to learn, and to think creatively, all activities that result, from the perspective of complexity theory, from "process[es] of network self-organization" (Mainzer 138; see also Churchland 97–121 and passim). (3) Most important, as I discuss in the concluding pages of chapter 3, a nonlinear complex system like the brain is capable of manifesting globally a "behavior"—the phenomenon of *emergence*—that is not attributable to any single element of the system acting in isolation: "An important insight of the complex system approach discloses that emergent effects of the whole system are system effects which cannot be reduced to single elements. Philosophically, the whole is more than the sum of its parts" (Mainzer 118).[9] In short, we can view consciousness itself as analogous to emergent phenomena like the complex adaptive system of the economy or the complex "behaviors" of the novel *Ulysses*, parallel illustrations of emergence I discuss at the close of chapter 3. If *Ulysses* "behaves" like the complex, nonlinear, emergent phenomenon of consciousness, however, what does contemporary neuroscience offer for our picture of *Finnegans Wake*? The traditional assumption among Joyce's critics, to which I return at the end of this chapter, has been that the *Wake* represents the unconscious mind, to complement *Ulysses*'s portrayal of consciousness. The complex-system research of contemporary neuroscience, however, has largely erased this conventional distinction between the unconscious and consciousness (Churchland 182–83, 220–22), to present us another and better model for the relations between these two books, a model that emerges from Daniel Dennett's and Paul Churchland's competing theories of the mind.

In *Consciousness Explained* (1991), one of the most provocative attempts yet to achieve a scientific theory of the mind, philosopher Daniel Dennett fully deploys the concepts of complexity—and the interdisciplinary expertise of "a student of neuroscience, linguistics, artificial intelligence, computer science, and psychology" (Marvin Minsky, qtd. in Brockman 188)—to argue that human consciousness is an emergent phenomenon. Dennett wants to determine what in the human brain convinces us "cognitively conatively cogitabundantly," like HCE in *Finnegans Wake*, that both we and "the audible-visible-gnosible-edible world" exist (*FW* 88.6–8). Simply put, Dennett pictures the brain as an enormously complex, parallel-processing computer that runs a serial "software" we call consciousness.

Western humankind, at least since Descartes and Leibniz, has persisted in conceiving the mind in terms of the machines that its minds have created (see Franchi and Güzeldere, "Mindless Mechanisms"). It should come as no surprise, then, that the neuroscientists and neurophilosophers of our own generation have adopted the most influential contemporary machine, the computer, as their model for the mind. What makes this model doubly inevitable is that the father of the computer, John von Neumann, in a further illustration of this synergy of creation and self-creation, based the architecture of his machine in the early 1940s on then current theories of the human brain's serial operations (I return to this later). Much of the research in artificial intelligence (AI), from the formation of "the new scientific community of AI" at the 1956 Dartmouth Conference to the present, has been an extension of von Neumann's original premise (Mainzer 174), and one of the most promising future directions for AI research will be a complexity-based endeavor to assimilate the new perspective of neuroscience and replicate the massively parallel networks of the brain by developing a nondigital and nonserial computer technology (perhaps a "quantum-computer" or a "neural and synergetic computer" based on laser technology; see Mainzer 180–226). Physicists (such as Roger Penrose) and neurophilosophers (such as Paul Churchland, Daniel Dennett, and John Searle) reciprocate the AI community's modeling of mental processes on the computer by invoking the computer as their machine model for the mind. (Even Searle's rejection of the model works within the model.)[10]

Dennett's conception of consciousness as a serial program, or a kind of "software" that runs on the "hardware" of the brain's parallel neural circuitry (210–18), seems to offer a powerful mechanical analogy for the mind's relation to the brain in terms of contemporary neuroscience, an analogy he pursues by characterizing most cognitive processes as serial activities related to language and narrative: "not just spoken language but writing plays a major role, I suspect, in the development and elaboration of the [serial] machines most of us run most of the time in our brains" (220). This distinction between a serial structure for the mind and a parallel architecture for the brain also offers us an apt metaphor for describing the relation between conventional (serial) narrative—the novel as "mind"—and the innovative, intricate linguistic networks and webs that constitute the unique (parallel) form of *Finnegans Wake*: the novel as "brain." Arguing for this correlation between serial thought and traditional narrative, and more in homage to the early than the late works of James Joyce, Dennett calls his model of consciousness a "virtual machine—the Joycean machine" (220). (A "virtual" machine is a "special-purpose" machine, with a "specifically disciplined" architecture, within a general-purpose machine [211–12]; think of a user-friendly computer interface, such as a pull-down menu program, or perhaps the liquid crystal display in some digital watches that emulates the movements of the hands of an analog watch face.)

By characterizing human consciousness as a Joycean virtual machine, Dennett differentiates "what William James dubbed the stream of consciousness, the meandering sequence of conscious mental contents famously depicted by James Joyce in his novels," from the *real* machine of the brain: "The architecture of the brain, in contrast, is massively parallel, with millions of simultaneously active channels of operation" (214). He might well have called this fundamental real machine a "*Wakean* machine," for the picture of the mind created by a neurophilosopher of complexity like Dennett, up to the level of consciousness but as yet unself-conscious, is remarkably similar, as I will argue, to the picture of the "underlying cognitive activities" of the brain created by *Finnegans Wake* (Churchland 182). To further appropriate Dennett's terms, we could argue that among Joyce's works the *Wake* represents the "hardware," the massive, complex, parallel system underlying the virtual machine of consciousness, the Joycean machine so aptly portrayed, as Dennett acknowledges, in *Dubliners*, *A Portrait of the Artist as a Young Man*, and *Ulysses*.

The reader may have already recognized a serious limitation, however, in Dennett's conception of consciousness as a serial system, like language or narrative, driven by the nonlinear dynamics of the brain. As I have already shown, nonlinearity invariably generates escalating complexity toward the edge of chaos, not simplicity. Moreover, were consciousness merely serial, as Dennett maintains, we would not be able to distinguish language from life, nor could we recognize serial narrative *as fiction*. As Paul Churchland makes clear, by establishing the serial processes of language and narrative as his "prototype[s] for cognitive activity" (265), Dennett's theory fails entirely to account for *any* of the complex, multidimensional features of consciousness:

> There exists a different way, a much more natural and effective way, of accounting for the well-behaved temporal unfolding of consciousness, and it has nothing essential to do with serial computers or language-like processing. The alternative lies in the dynamical behavior of real (not virtual) *recurrent* [feedback] networks, with their dramatic ability to generate complex representations with a continuously unfolding temporal dimension. . . . Dennett's account of consciousness is skewed in favor of a tiny subset of the contents of consciousness: those that are broadly language-like. Human consciousness, however, also contains visual sequences, musical sequences, tactile sequences, motor sequences, visceral sequences, social sequences, and so on. A virtual serial machine has no especially promising explanatory resources for any of these things. A recurrent parallel network does. (267, 269)[11]

As I show in the previous chapter, even the relatively linear narrative of *Ulysses* portrays the nonlinearity of mental phenomena, the tendency of small stimuli like the touch of an arm (*U* 1.147) or a punctuation mark (the period) to generate large consequences through the recurrent flow of information, through feedback, for character and reader alike: this is the Joycean "significance of trivial things" (*JJII* 163).

Churchland maintains that consciousness is a classic illustration of the emergent phenomenon in a complex system, a phase transition toward self-organization in a dynamic system that inevitably occurs, Stuart Kauffman argues, whenever the ratio of the number of connections among the individual components of the system (e.g., the axons in the brain) to the number of components (e.g., the neurons) passes a certain threshold (approximately .5, or a ratio of one connection to every two nodes) (*At Home* 54–62). In the brain the ratio of axons to neurons far exceeds this critical threshold (there are, in fact, several axons for every neuron). Not only do the dense feed-forward and feedback (recurrent) networks *constitute* the physical complexity of the brain, but as Churchland convincingly demonstrates, they *generate* the emergent global behaviors, the complex cognitive phenomena of the mind. Recent advances in neuroscience and experiments both in the computer modeling of neural networks (e.g., for pattern recognition and speech synthesis) and in solid-state technology (the silicon retina), which Churchland summarizes (35–55, 84–91, 236–44), have made clear that the cognitive phenomena of the mind are direct consequences of the physical structure of the brain: "mental phenomena just *are* brain phenomena" (212).

In *The Engine of Reason* Churchland identifies the seven defining features of consciousness, all produced by the recurrent network structure of the brain: a short-term memory, an ability to think independently of external stimuli, a steerable attention, a capacity to recognize ambiguity, a tendency to disappear (loss of consciousness, as in sleep), a tendency to reappear in "muted" form (dreaming), and a tendency to conflate "the several basic sensory modalities within a *single unified experience*" (213–14). This last, most intriguing element of consciousness is where we locate our awareness of self. This sense of selfhood, which we experience as a unitary, holistic conception, is an emergent phenomenon resulting from the interconnection of our multiple and multidimensional sensory processes. Churchland, in fact, describes the emergent self in terms eerily reminiscent of Joyce's representation of consciousness in *Finnegans Wake*: "But who . . . can be *watching* this . . . show [of consciousness]? The answer is straightforward: no one. There is no distinct 'self' in there, beyond the brain as a whole. On the other hand, almost every part of the brain is being 'watched' by some other part of the brain, often by several other parts at once" (8).

Churchland, however, stops short of explaining the final piece of "the puzzle of consciousness" (187): the final phase transition to self-awareness, to the emergence of self-consciousness, self-reflection, and self-reflexive behavior, all of which are clearly consequences of the brain's recurrent network structure, its "capacity for self-representation" (225), its ability to view and review itself. In the end Churchland comes close to agreeing with Dennett's metaphor of the Joycean machine for consciousness, although *only* insofar as we represent ourselves to ourselves, by "suggest[ing] that, where consciousness and other mental phenomena are concerned, we are all characters in our own ironic story" (225). Given the nonlinear nature of these phenomena, we inhabit an "ironic story" very like James Joyce's *Ulysses*. Were this final emergent phenomenon of self-awareness stripped away, not yet evolved, or given over to another—say a reader of, rather than a character within, this "ironic story"—we would be left with the spectacle of those massively parallel "underlying cognitive activities" of the brain, which "are exceedingly unlikely to have . . . a sentence-like and inference-like structure" (182). We would be left with *Finnegans Wake*.

Both Daniel Dennett and Paul Churchland freely admit that their scientific theories of the mind remain incomplete. Churchland has quite clearly shown the limitations of Dennett's model for consciousness (as have several of Dennett's colleagues and most constructive critics, such as Nicholas Humphrey, Francisco Varela, and Steven Pinker [qtd. in Brockman 190–97 and passim]). But even if his "explanation . . . is far from complete," Dennett writes, "it *is* a beginning, because it breaks the spell of the enchanted circle of ideas that made explaining consciousness seem impossible" (455). Churchland similarly confesses that he has stopped far short of the causal coupling necessary to achieve Pagels's "scientific theory of the mind": "I do not know, and you should not believe, that the preceding account is the correct account of consciousness. There is a remote chance, perhaps, that it is. Much more likely, it is only a small and still tangled part of the true account. . . . What is central to my purpose is that the story just told is a logically *possible* neurocomputational account of the phenomenon of consciousness" (223). The great importance of work like Dennett's and Churchland's for my present purposes, then, is less their final resolutions of the mind-body problem than their illustration of the prototypical question they and other complexity scientists seek to answer: how do small-scale phenomena interact to complete the vast, complex, global networks of reality? In reaction to the cheerful certainty among some theoretical physicists, such as Stephen Hawking, that science has achieved a relatively complete understanding of physical phenomena, down to the infinitesimally small realm of still mysterious quantum events and up to the ultimate boundaries of the universe, complexity theory argues that what equally baffles the scientist is how to connect all those phenomena that lie between the very small and the very large. Since this is the same question Joyce's readers ask of the *Wake*, the sciences of complexity, too, have a "*Finnegans Wake* problem."

Complexity theory involves a way of looking at phenomenal reality that is familiar but, paradoxically, difficult to define, precisely because it is complex.[12] In his analysis of scientific techniques of problem solving, *Tools for Thought*, C. H. Waddington laments that "no one has yet succeeded in giving a definition of 'complexity' which is meaningful enough to enable one to measure exactly how complex a given system is" (30), an observation as true today, despite Waddington's own attempts, as it was in 1977. This perhaps insurmountable difficulty in definition, however, is less a discouragement than a confirmation of one of the central recognitions of complexity science: a reductive definition of complexity would itself violate a basic premise of the theory by imposing a simplifying schema on complicated phenomena. So, rather than pursue a capsule definition of complexity here, in the balance of this chapter I present overviews of (1) the first principles of complexity science, (2) the perspective on existential reality that has both stimulated and been fostered by complexity theory, and (3) the central importance of the evolutionary model in complexity studies, before considering the bases for regarding *Finnegans Wake* as *the* literary model of complexity. This chapter, then, is a prolegomenon for the study of the *Wake* as a complex literary system, not itself a full reading of Joyce's work in terms of complexity, which would demand another book altogether.

FIRST PRINCIPLES

Complexity theory recognizes the basic fact that not only the brain but virtually all systems occurring in nature and society are complex networks of mutually interacting forces: "Think of the quadrillions of chemically reacting proteins, lipids, and nucleic acids that make up the living cell, or the billions of interconnected neurons that make up the brain, or the millions of mutually interdependent individuals who make up a human society" (Waldrop 11). Complex systems inhabit a continuum between, on the one hand, the simplicity of idealized structures—the pure geometrical shapes of Euclid, for instance, or the simple dynamics of Galileo's pendulum and Newton's solar system, or the model hierarchies of social theory, such as the Marxist paradigm of base and superstructure, or even the idealized structures of cultural systems, such as the genres of literature—and, on the other hand, absolute randomness, "classical" chaos (as distinguished from the "chaos" of chaos theory, which reveals deep structure and pattern). By the turn of the century the scientific community and to some extent the general public were becoming increasingly aware of the vast middle ground occupied by nonlinear phenomena that were undermining the idealized pictures of reality offered by Euclidean geometry, classical mechanics, the conventions of literature, and any number of other logical and coherent structures humans have traditionally imposed on reality. As I have argued, Joyce's recognition of the subjectivity of such purportedly objective linear structures for reality distinguishes *A Portrait of the Artist as a Young Man* both from its earlier incarnation, *Stephen Hero*, and from *Dubliners*. I also have argued that Joyce's unconventional (or anticonventional) novel *Ulysses* possesses many of the features of the nonlinear dynamic systems studied by chaos scientists. The sciences of complexity, which subsume chaos theory by examining how numerous nonlinear systems interact to create a field—an extended horizontal network of interrelated systems—provide both a broader view of complicated phenomena and several formal analogues for Joyce's even more unconventional novel *Finnegans Wake* (e.g., the novel as "brain"). Complexity does more than this, however; it also offers a model approach for the analysis of the complex system: although a "phenomenon is sometimes observed from the 'top down,'" it is "ultimately understood from the 'bottom up'" (Pagels, *Dreams of Reason* 198).

Of course, this approach is notoriously difficult. Most humans, and literary critics especially, have a strong preference for the top-down direction, if for no other reason than it is the most "convenient" way to achieve a sense of mastery over complex phenomena. (Poincaré uses his favorite term, *commode*, "convenient," throughout his discussions of this mode of "conventionalism" [x and passim].) Humankind has always organized phenomenal reality for its convenience by superimposing simplifying patterns of meaning—cultural and institutional paradigms that generate "conventions" of interpretation—and although this recognition was central to Kant's phenomenology, only in our own century have both the arts and the natural and social sciences realized the full implications of this subjectivism through their gradual assimilation of the critique of subjectivity implicit in the post-Cartesian revolution. Horkheimer and Adorno, for example, import the dialectical relation of subject and object into their social and political critique in *Dialectic of Enlightenment* (1944) by observing that from age to age one generation may reject the subjectivism of the previous generation's mediation of reality, progressing to a more "enlightened" perception of what is actually the case, but with each transformation the goal of objectivity recedes from its grasp, because these progressively enlightened perceptions are invariably ideological. To paraphrase Adorno, even the concept of objectivity is subjective, and we must be objective about this ("Subject and Object" 497–511). For the "ordinary people" however, the most recent stage in this dialectic, which began in the era still known as the "Age of Enlightenment," conditions their everyday perceptions of the world; that is, they continue to live by the Cartesian illusion that the individual can stand alone, outside the system observed, and attain an empirical grasp of reality. Ironically, the very scientific advances that were themselves made possible by empirical research—most significantly the theories of relativity and quantum physics—and that have destroyed the Cartesian dualism of self and other in many fields of thought have gradually begun to destabilize such everyday, common-sense perceptions of "simple" reality. (Horkheimer and Adorno anticipate complexity theorists by comparing this event to the demise of the Ptolemaic cosmos following the Copernican revolution [91 and passim].)[13]

Such paradigm shifts in the general perception of reality do not occur suddenly or globally in a population; Gramsci, noting that emergent phenomena like "moral and intellectual renewal [do] not develop simultaneously in all of the social strata," observes that "on the contrary, it is worth repeating that even today many people are Ptolemaic and not Copernican" (396–97). Nevertheless, one clear illustration of a changing perception of the world in recent years, a "Copernican" decentering of the autonomous self, has been the heightening public awareness that humanity exists in an ecosystem; people no longer feel comfortable with the conception of nature as separate from the self, solely for their domination and exploitation. Rather, they have grown aware that humanity exists in a complex symbiotic relationship with the environment, affected by their effects on it. Similarly, the end of the cold war between West and East, a parallel dissolution of the dichotomous view of self versus other, has prepared individuals to see the unpredicted events of 1989 in Eastern Europe not as a simple revolution or as a conspiracy of nations but as a "phase transition" in a sensitively dependent political system responding globally to a complex of local but mutually interdependent causes. Most reasonably intelligent observers recognize that the "fall of communism," a model illustration of the complex phenomenon, was neither planned nor accidental but something between the ordered and the chaotic. Recent perspectives on at least two important components of reality, nature and politics, thus have clearly changed to reject reductive schemas of explanation, recognizing their subjective and ideological bases, and to embrace the complex over the simple.

Such transformed awareness, the development of what we might call "complexity consciousness," is the flip side of another common response to the collapse of Cartesianism: the celebration of subjectivity. The move from structuralism to poststructuralism in modern French and Anglo-American thought—paralleling the move from relativity to the Copenhagen interpretation of quantum theory in twentieth-century physics (see appendix B)—is merely a transition from the recognition of humanity's natural tendency to order reality to the claim that *all* order is the product of the individual's mediation. As a consequence, postmodernist readings of *Finnegans Wake* insist on the absence of "origin," or a grounded narrative reality for the text (e.g.,

Heath 61; Rabaté, "Lapsus" 97–98).[14] Nevertheless, although "heavily fetishized by deconstructionists" (Hayman 10), Joyce's book has recently begun to receive more attention among critics for its reflections of "social reality."[15] Such readings of reality in the complexity of *Finnegans Wake* illustrate the secondary response to the collapse of Cartesianism that I have called complexity consciousness—a response already implicit in Wittgenstein's *Tractatus* of 1921, as I mention in chapter 3—by admitting the possibility of an ordered reality independent of the observation of the individual, who is necessarily a part of that which is observed. Chaos theory has confirmed this possibility, demonstrating the existence of orders beyond the unaided observer's range of perception in phenomena that Cartesian science had dismissed as hopelessly complex, random, or chaotic.

The sciences of complexity, emerging from the studies of chaos, maintain that a vast majority of natural and social phenomena exists in a borderland between simple order and pure randomness, the so-called edge of chaos, the realm of intricately ordered complexity. Mitchell Waldrop, for example, extends his observation that the complex dynamic systems studied by chaos scientists "have somehow acquired the ability to bring order and chaos into a special kind of balance" to describe the behavior of complex *social* systems:

> This balance point—often called *the edge of chaos*—is where the components of a system never quite lock into place, and yet never quite dissolve into turbulence, either. The edge of chaos is where life has enough stability to sustain itself and enough creativity to deserve the name of life. The edge of chaos is where new ideas and innovative genotypes are forever nibbling away at the edges of the status quo, and where even the most entrenched old guard will eventually be overthrown. The edge of chaos is where centuries of slavery and segregation suddenly give way to the civil rights movement of the 1950s and 1960s; where seventy years of Soviet communism suddenly give way to political turmoil and ferment; where eons of evolutionary stability suddenly give way to wholesale species transformation. The edge of chaos is the constantly shifting battle zone between stagnation and anarchy, the one place where a complex system can be spontaneous, adaptive, and alive. (12)[16]

One of the startling results of complexity theory is that its premises and procedures apply with equal force to physical and social phenomena. "General laws may govern the evolution of complex entities," Stuart Kauffman concludes, "whether they are works of nature or works of man" (*At Home* 206).

"Human societies," Klaus Mainzer writes, "are governed by the nonlinear laws of complexity like atomic groups, molecular mixtures, cellular organisms, or ecological populations" (273–74). These claims will not surprise those who remember that social philosophers from Plato to the present have assimilated contemporary scientific models into their accounts of human phenomena: Thomas Hobbes, for example, bases his "mechanistic [political] model of modern society" presented in *Leviathan* (1651) on Galileo's physics, the eighteenth-century French "physiocratic school" assimilates the "mechanistic clockwork" of Descartes's worldview into its economic system, Adam Smith applies Newton's celestial mechanics to ethics and economics in *The Wealth of Nations* (1776)—as do David Ricardo and John Stuart Mill into the nineteenth century—and John Maynard Keynes assimilates a version of Poincaré's conventionalism into his economic theories in our own century (Mainzer 241–42, 246–50). Stuart Kauffman's extension of his concept of the edge of chaos for a complex-systems analysis of our "emerging global civilization" in *At Home in the Universe* (273–304), to cite one contemporary illustration, joins with this rich tradition of social theory. Kauffman stresses that endogenous (internal) factors generate the same phenomena from the bottom up in physical and social systems, from nonlinearity (the sensitive dependence on the individual act) to emergence (self-organization) and "self-organized criticality" (e.g., the extinction events caused by cultural collision) (*At Home* 28–29, 301–2).

In *Thinking in Complexity* Klaus Mainzer emphasizes the revolutionary implications of this complex-systems approach to social and cultural phenomena. The sciences of complexity simply erase the traditional distinction that social scientists and humanists have made "between biological evolution and the history of human cultures," a distinction based on the assumption "that the development of nations and cultures is obviously guided by the intentional behavior of humans with their attitudes, emotions, plans, and ideals, while systems in biological evolution are assumed to be driven by unintended self-organization" (266). Complexity scientists, on the contrary, have opened to study those unintended global social and cultural phenomena that emerge from the butterfly effect of individual intentions and desires (including catastrophically chaotic phenomena—as both Kauffman and Mainzer warn—that may result despite the individual's best intentions): "the crucial point of the complex system approach is that from a macroscopic point of view the development of political, social, or cultural order is not only the sum of single intentions, but the collective result of nonlinear interactions" (Mainzer 266).[17] Complexity theory thus sees both natural and cultural phenomena as "systems" rich in information and recognizes that the information content of phenomena approaches the maximum as the system nears the edge of chaos. Ultimately, by studying the complex behaviors of "information-rich sequences . . . generated spontaneously by a dynamical system" (Nicolis and Prigogine 186), complexity science offers an approach to another complex, information-rich, *cultural* phenomenon, *Finnegans Wake*. Dynamic systems thus can be considered "'messages' or 'texts' containing information" (Nicolis and Prigogine 186); in this study I reciprocate this insight by maintaining that we can view a text like *Finnegans Wake*, situated "halfway between pure order and pure chaos" and generating the maximum information content possible in a message, in terms of its symbolic dynamics (Connor 826).[18]

THE EVOLUTIONARY MODEL

A second, startling result of complexity science has been the accelerated development of dynamic evolutionary models for research. The new awareness of the value of operational models that grow, change, adapt to altered circumstances, and even reproduce their own components and the recognition of the obvious applicability of such models to complexly evolving real-world systems are equally indebted to the computer modeling of chaos scientists (e.g., Lorenz's weather model), to the realization that modeling, as much as calculation, is "one of [the computer's] primary applications as a research instrument" (Pagels, *Dreams of Reason* 89), and ultimately to the early modern reconception of theoretical models for reality, such as the *Gedanken* experiments of quantum physics or a thought experiment like *Finnegans Wake*. The recent and interrelated developments of computer technology, chaos theory, and complexity science have transformed the scientific sense of the word *model* to privilege *becoming* over *being*, to change into a transitive verb and into an activity what had been a noun, a substantive thing of some sort: an apparatus, a manikin, a paradigm (Kuipers; Ubbink). Mathematicians and scientists, from the classical era to the twentieth century, had traditionally conceived models as objective representations of a given reality, from Euclid's triangles to Ernest Rutherford's "picture of the atom" (1911)—"a little solar system with the nucleus as the sun and the electrons as the planets" (Pagels, *Cosmic Code* 52)—and equally often constructed models as objects (e.g., the orrery).[19]

By the late 1940s, however, John von Neumann (1903–57), "the man who thought up the computer" (Heppenheimer 8), was already exploring the possibilities for modeling the dynamics of intelligence, behavior, and even self-reproduction on the computer through the creation of evolving "cellular automata." Von Neumann's recognition of an analogy between the electrical activity of neural networks and the binary function of computer circuits (both neurons and circuits are either "on" or "off") prompted him to see the computer's potential for replicating the activity of the human brain. His brilliant insight in the late 1930s has become a commonplace today, largely through von Neumann's influence on the logical structure of computers in the developing field of computer science in the 1940s, his many papers on computing, his stimulus to the entire field of artificial intelligence, and his last book, *The Computer and the Brain* (1958) (Heppenheimer 8–16; Aspray 173–212). (As I noted earlier, von Neumann based his architecture for the computer on the current neuroscientific conception of a linear, serial brain rather than the massive parallel network of recent neuroscience: "All [his] brilliant developments are mainly ruled by principles of linearity" [Mainzer 254]. Most of the recent research in AI, to simulate the parallel networks of the brain, employs "virtual" parallel-processing machines [programs] that run on the real machine of the von Neumanesque serial computer [Dennett 217–18].) Joining a tradition extending at least from the fourth-century A.D. mechanical gadgets of Hero of Alexandria and running through the clockwork automata of Renaissance engineers, von Neumann, long before the technology was available, considered the ultimate possibility of replicating life itself, of simulating lifelike behavior from the bottom up, by arraying computer circuits in "cells"; he even showed the feasibility of creating cellular automata capable of self-reproduction (see his posthumously published *Theory of Self-Reproducing Automata* [1966]).[20]

To visualize cellular automata, picture an electronic message board that is not governed by a global program (e.g., the message the lights must spell) but within which each "lightbulb," or automaton (actually a cluster of circuits), has its individual program, codes that will tell it how to act based on the behavior of neighboring automata. "Imagine an infinitely large grid of squares, like endless graph paper," Roger Lewin suggests. "Each of the squares, or cells," behaves in a particular fashion, "depending on the activity of neighboring cells. . . . Complex, dynamic patterns develop and roam across the entire grid, the nature of which is influenced but not tightly determined in detail, according to activity rules. Notice that global structure emerges from local activity rules, a characteristic of complex systems" (46–47). Von Neumann offered his classical description of cellular automata in his 1953 Vanuxem Lectures at Princeton:

> Von Neumann called these structures "crystalline regularities" but also "cellular automata," using modern terminology. They are homogeneous, two-dimensional arrays of square cells, each containing the same twenty-nine-state finite automaton. Any cell can assume at a given time the unexcitable state . . . , one of twenty quiescent states . . . , or one of eight sensitized (excited) states. Quiescent cells can respond to ordinary stimuli from adjacent cells; unexcitable cells respond only to special stimuli, which initiate the construction or growth of new cells. The state of a given cell at a given time is determined, according to a set of transition rules, by the states of that cell and its four nondiagonal neighbors at some fixed earlier time. (Aspray 203)

In an influential *Scientific American* article (1955), John Kemeny reported on von Neumann's theory of cellular automata presented in these lectures—expanded and published in *Theory of Self-Reproducing Automata*—stimulating further development of automata (e.g., cellular automata research has enlarged his five-cell array, called the "von Neumann neighborhood," to include the four diagonal neighbors of the given cell in a nine-cell array, the Moore neighborhood, which also behaves according to von Neumann's "transition rules" [Casti 214–29]). Although von Neumann conceived of his cellular automata as analogous to neural networks, the information processor of the human brain, his two-dimensional arrays were also ideally suited for graphic representation by the pixels of the still undeveloped computer monitor. Thus cellular automata are widely used today in computer modeling to produce a wide range of community activities on the computer screen (e.g., "artificial life"), all made possible by von Neumann's recognition that a limited number of program elements and transition rules can generate enormously complex behaviors: "It is amazing to see how [the] handful of simple rules" in John Conway's cellular automata called the Game of Life "can generate such complexity," observes Pagels. "Likewise, it is impressive how the rules of atomic combinations in the real world can generate the complexity of living things—the real game of life" (*Dreams of Reason* 102).

Pagels's comparison of computer-generated and real-world complexity points indirectly to the crucial difference between, for instance, Chris Langton's "artificial life" project at the Santa Fe Institute, his attempt to model life itself on the computer screen, and the Promethean ambition of, say, Mary Shelley's Dr. Frankenstein to create life. Conway's and Langton's cellular automata do not produce life; they only present what *looks like life*. The distinction resides in the scientists' recognition that the model is only an emulation, a reproduction of the productions of reality.[21] It is the classical model that does greater violence to the real by imposing the observer's preconception of structure on a complex reality, a short step from the attempt to fashion reality in one's own image and likeness. With cellular automata, however, the programmer takes a few basic elements of the real that are encoded in selected activity rules, or "algorithms," that seem to characterize some local behavior (e.g., consumer preferences) in some global system under study (e.g., an economy), sets them into action, waits a bit, and sees what happens. Often the result is little information and less interest: the computer screen goes dead, quickly coalesces into "a set of static blobs," or produces totally random, chaotic behavior, "universality classes" I, II, and III for cellular automata, in Stephen Wolfram's terms (Waldrop 225). Occasionally, however, the modeler stumbles on a set of rules that can generate class IV phenomena on a computer monitor, behavior at the edge of chaos: "coherent structures that propagated, grew, split apart, and recombined in a wonderfully complex way. They essentially never settled down. In that sense they were all very much like the most famous member of Class IV, the Game of Life" (Waldrop 226).

Cellular automata, then, do not "represent" any given reality; rather, they simulate information-rich patterns of complexity that may, in turn, provide reasonable approximations, simulacra, of the complexity of real-world dynamic systems. The chief purpose for generating such operational models is to see whether the pictures created will roughly match observed phenomena, to operate "the model by manipulation of its elements . . . in order to see how it reacts (and by analogy how the real world should react)" (Waddington 206).[22] If the pictures do match, if birdlike clusters of pixels flock and fly across the monitor screen, as birds do across the sky, if simulated rivers flood and flow as their real-world counterparts do when observed from satellites, if sectors of the screen prosper and decline as sections of a city do, then perhaps the rules that generate their behavior in the model can provide some of the underlying, simple codes that propagate complex real-world phenomena: "the emergence of patterns in evolutionary models . . . [suggests] that living systems, as complex dynamical systems, are driven to these same patterns" (Lewin 181). Thus models in complexity science—not all of which are cellular automata (Gell-Mann 307–25)—are not embodiments of a top-down, preconceived reading of a simplified reality but rather bottom-up attempts to generate a simulation of the complex real. In conception and execution the models of complexity science are similar (a "match" of a matchmaking methodology) to James Joyce's *Finnegans Wake*, which, like cellular automata, is less a representation of reality than an evolutionary model of the complex real.

Most literary works can be described as classical models, representing relatively simple systems governed by the natural laws, the rules or conventions of their genre, and consoling their readership with a generally high degree of predictability. (This generalization is meant not to dismiss premodern literature as lacking in complication or "complexity" in the usual sense but to distinguish the complex model of *Finnegans Wake*, a work of many degrees of freedom, from the relatively conventional work that admits few degrees of freedom into its system. In short, "complicatedness" differs from the algorithmic, physical, and logical forms of complexity described in the next section.) The unpredictable element of fiction, its modest degree of complexity, is usually a rather simple hierarchy of cause and effect, whereas the complexity of poetry is often a rather simple hierarchy of signification. By concentrating on either the diachronic or the synchronic dimension of the traditional literary work, the reader experiences the satisfaction of mastering its complications. Modern and postmodern literature, of course, deny such immediate satisfactions, presenting the reader with works that violate these laws of genre, as *Ulysses* and *Finnegans Wake* do, and that require the reader simultaneously to proceed both diachronically and synchronically. Joyce's novels destabilize the conventional hierarchies of their genre for the sake of their structural complement, the *network*. As I will show shortly, the measure of complexity in a system is directly proportional to the precedence of the network (the parallel system) over the hierarchy (the serial system) in its structure (Pagels, *Dreams of Reason* 50–70). Networking complicates the reader's task in *Ulysses*, whereas the networked, "proteiform graph" of *Finnegans Wake* (*FW* 107.8) virtually eliminates hierarchies for the sake of a "geodetic" structure (*FW* 114.15) that generates progressively higher degrees of complexity, complexity that apparently defeats mastery. It is a commonplace in Joyce criticism that the primary structural model for *Finnegans Wake* is the web, or network; the *Wake* demands a reading strategy that abandons "sequential progression along the printed line" in favor of reading as "sortilege" (Bishop 305), a strategy that *Ulysses* merely invites. One fundamental difference between Joyce's two last works, then, is that *Ulysses* remains, despite its technical and stylistic complications, generally obedient to narrative demands, still privileging, like most conventional fiction, hierarchical reading: the novel's plot "line" remains visible, its superstructure discernible, its contact with consensual represented "reality" close. Any of these components can function as keys for reductive simplification or interpretation. *Finnegans Wake* provides fewer of these accessible keys. In terms of complexity theory, the decreasing availability of keys for the *Wake* is a measure of the increase in the "algorithmic complexity" of Joyce's fiction.

MEASURES OF COMPLEXITY

One of the standard (albeit competing) strategies for measuring complexity is to determine the degree of algorithmic complexity present in a system.[23] An algorithm is the mathematical term for either a simple instruction that invariably generates the same complex result, working from the bottom up (e.g., the Mandelbrot set), or conversely, an instruction that simplifies complexity, working from the top down (e.g., the "lowest common denominator"). The number 10101010101010101010 has several algorithms: "repeat '10' ten times," or "write a one followed by a zero ten times," and so on. Even a million-digit number can possess a simple algorithm: "repeat '10' 500,000 times." A system that can be described by a simple algorithm possesses low algorithmic complexity. On the other hand, staying with mathematics, some rather easily generated numbers have no simple algorithm: take a six-sided die and roll it 100 times, writing down the digit for each roll. Each time you do so, you will produce a different complex number, the simplest description of which can only be the complete written form of the number. The algorithm of this number, the instruction that will always give the same complex result, then, will likely be exactly as long as the number itself. This is the highest degree of algorithmic complexity, indicating pure numerical randomness, or classical chaos, which can never be reduced to a simple principle of order. There exist extraordinarily complex numbers, however, midway between the simple ten-times-ten and the random digits of the rolled die, that have algorithms of relatively low complexity. The number 3.14159265 . . . (the digits go on forever) has the simple, one-letter algorithm π (as in "poi" [*FW* 295.32]; strictly speaking, π is a *symbol* for the following algorithmic statement: "the ratio of the circumference of a circle to its diameter"). The number 12357111317 . . . is simply described by the algorithm "write the prime numbers in consecutive order."

In these terms the search for keys to the interpretation of *Finnegans Wake* has been a top-down quest for the algorithms of the complex phenomena that appear on the printed page. Conversely, the "genetic" study of *Finnegans Wake*'s evolution has been a bottom-up exploration of how Joyce has created complexity out of essentially simple algorithms: a few narrative nodes, a limited cast of characters (for which he interestingly enough adopted pseudo-mathematical symbols, or sigla: "The Doodles Family" [*FW* 299.F4]), and "activity rules" for their interaction (the motifs of the book).[24] Such are "The keys to. Given!" us (*FW* 628.15), out of which he generated the complex network of the finished novel. Joyce's writing process strongly resembles the behavior of a sensitively dependent, nonlinear dynamic system that propagates enormous degrees of complexity out of rather simple initial conditions, as modeled in cellular automata such as the Game of Life, which behave according to a limited number of von Neumann's transition rules: " 'If there is any difficulty in reading what I write it is because of the material I use. In my case the thought is always simple' " (Budgen, *James Joyce* 291).[25] Since Joyce's initial algorithms are now "givens," available in his manuscript materials and elsewhere, the algorithmic complexity of *Finnegans Wake* is in the low to moderate range. By two other standards for measuring complexity, however, "physical complexity" and "logical complexity," *Finnegans Wake* is complex indeed.

Physical complexity might best be understood by remaining with the concept of algorithmic complexity a bit longer. Notice that there is a fundamental difference between those algorithms that generate textual complexity in *Finnegans Wake* and those that facilitate simplification in *Ulysses*. A. Walton Litz, in his ground-breaking study of Joyce's compositional processes, sees the writing of *Finnegans Wake* as an extension of the top-down approach of *Ulysses*: "the ultimate form of the book was fixed in his mind, and—as in the last stages of writing *Ulysses*—he elaborated like a mosaic worker upon a predetermined pattern" (*Art* 92). It might be more accurate, however, to say that the later stages of Joyce's composition of *Ulysses* show him moving away from the predetermined pattern of the novel's hierarchical superstructure and toward the networking strategies fully realized in *Finnegans Wake*. With the later novel Joyce reversed his writing procedures from *Ulysses*, taking a few seeds of inspiration and allowing them to grow, mutate, and intertwine, whereas in the earlier novel he created superstructures by and within which his novel would achieve order and meaning, for author and reader alike.[26] (The basic unit of Joyce's text, the *word*, which evolves into the complexity of the portmanteau, illustrates this process microcosmically.) The distinction is between Joyce's top-down method of composition for *Ulysses* and his bottom-up method for *Finnegans Wake*. Joyce's readers, too, can approach his works from both of these directions, analogous to the schoolboy Stephen

Dedalus's two ways of reading what "he had written" on the flyleaf of his geography text:

Stephen Dedalus
Class of Elements
Clongowes Wood College
Sallins
County Kildare
Ireland
Europe
The World
The Universe
(P 15)

Mirroring Joyce's reversal of compositional approaches from *Ulysses* to *Finnegans Wake*, Stephen as reader first proceeds from the macrocosmic to the microcosmic, from the top of the hierarchy, the universe, down to himself: "he read the flyleaf from the bottom to the top till he came to his own name. That was he." Stephen then reverses the direction: "he read down the page again. What was after the universe? Nothing" (P 16). Notice that Stephen does not, in the first case, read this list in the order that the reader of *A Portrait* does; Joyce already seems to be encouraging reading as the act of both ante- and anticomposition and promoting the boustrophedonic "furrowards, bagawards" (*FW* 18.32) movement of both text and reader characteristic of *Finnegans Wake* (Riquelme 16–23). Complexity theory similarly undermines the most prevalent way in which observers have traditionally ordered and read reality, as Stephen does in his first reading of his schema—from the bottom of the page, it is true, but more important, from the top of the hierarchy down.

Joyce's text in *A Portrait* forces on the reader the reverse process, reading from the base of the structure to its pinnacle, and the reverse again by presenting Stephen's first reading from the top down, and the reverse once more in Stephen's second reading, either to thoroughly confuse top and bottom or to suggest that the hierarchy itself is an arbitrary structure, deficient in its narrowing of reality, its lack of horizontal breadth, its failure to account for the complex labyrinths of reality that enmesh Stephen and from which he will later attempt to escape through art: "I shall try to fly by those nets" (P 203). The second principal measure of complexity in a system, "physical complexity," is the ratio of just such networked or horizontal interaction among the components of a system to the hierarchical structures present in the system. The greater this horizontal interaction, the more difficult is the job of connecting the bottom and the top of the hierarchies.

The "Night Lessons" chapter of *Finnegans Wake* (II.2), probably the most notorious example of Joyce's formal play with networked versus hierarchical relations in the book, provides a clear illustration of the physical complexity of the *Wake*. Parodying the typographical conventions of an old-fashioned academic textbook, appropriately in an episode concerning the children's homework assignments, Joyce provides marginal glosses (the comments of the twins) and footnotes (Issy's contributions) that require the readers to refocus their attention from the text in three additional directions: two lateral directions, to the left and right margins, and one vertical, to the foot of the pages. One thing that becomes clear in an otherwise very perplexing portion of the book, "the most difficult of all" the parts of the work, as Joyce recognized (*Letters* I 406), is that the marginalia provided by Shem and Shaun are consistently relevant to the text they gloss and, as most readers would recognize even if Joyce had not pointed it out to Frank Budgen, they enact a sort of story of their own ("the twins . . . change sides at half time" [*Letters* I 406]). Shem's glosses are all slangy irreverence ("*Bet you fippence, anythesious, there's no puggatory, are yous game?*" [*FW* 266.L1]), while Shaun's are all latinate sobriety ("THE PART PLAYED BY BELLETRISTICKS IN THE BELLUM-PAX-BELLUM" [*FW* 281.R1]), and although the typography of the chapter remains uniform (lowercase italic on the left margin, capitalized roman on the right), the respective "voices" of Shem and Shaun clearly switch sides on page 293. Unlike the twins' marginalia, however, Issy's footnotes rarely suggest any plausible connection to the text they annotate, although they do remain consistently in her voice throughout. Joyce, then, both systematically frustrates his readers' expectation that they will find the illumination or clarification usually provided by the footnote in its hierarchical relationship with a text and reinforces his readers' realization that greater meaning may be found on his text's lateral axis, in the networked relations of its parts. In terms of the measurements of complexity, Joyce's privileging of boustrophedonic/lateral interactions of the components of his text over hierarchical/vertical interactions, a most apparent feature of the "Night Lessons" chapter but also a characteristic of the book as a whole, greatly intensifies the physical complexity of *Finnegans Wake*.

The readers of the *Wake* find Issy's annotations particularly frustrating because individuals seem to have a strong preference for top-down, hierarchical patterns of order, such as Stephen Dedalus's chain of being in *A Portrait*, and are accustomed to subjectively imposing such patterns on phenomena. For instance, it is easy for readers of *A Portrait* to assume that the universe has an impact on Stephen and difficult to imagine Stephen having any influence on the universe; Stephen's later assertion in *Ulysses* that "Ireland must be important because it belongs to me" (U 16.1164–65), then, strikes both Joyce's readers and "Mr Bloom [,] bending, fancying he was perhaps under some misapprehension," as a preposterous inversion of the normal order of things: "in a quandary . . . he couldn't tell exactly what construction to put on [belongs] . . . which sounded rather a far cry" (U 16.1166–67, .1173–74). Chaos theory, with its pre-post-erous emphasis on the massive consequences of minuscule causes, has helped to reorient contemporary perspectives here by enhancing the recognition of the immense, intricate network of phenomena generated by the simplest of initial conditions. This weblike structure of complex phenomena, the logical complement to hierarchical structure in its emphasis on horizontal chains of interaction rather than vertical chains of cause and effect, is something people intuitively recognize but find extraordinarily difficult to pin down; it seems that the mind's peripheral vision is less well developed than its depth perception. This difficulty represents the third principal measurement of complexity in a system, "logical complexity," which is a measure of how difficult it is to understand a networked system from the bottom up, "how hard it is to put something together starting from elementary pieces" (Pagels, *Dreams of Reason* 67). Since such a networked system is the closest model for the structure of *Finnegans Wake*, the problem of interpreting Joyce's novel is attributable, technically speaking, to its high logical complexity. Clive Hart aptly describes the challenge, and frustration, of the reader's attempts to master the logical complexity of the *Wake*: "The relationship of parts, the concatenation of metaphor and image, the details of argument in *Finnegans Wake* are often very subtle and extremely difficult to grasp fully. This is never so apparent to the reader as when he embarks on a short *explication de texte* of some more or less self-contained passage. No matter how thorough the linguistic analysis, no matter how many of the referential loose ends may be gathered together, the difficulties usually fail to disperse" (*Structure* 35).

ARTIFICIAL LIFE

Joyce uses every available strategy to intensify the logical complexity in his text, frustrating the readers' tendencies toward hierarchical reading by accentuating the *Wake*'s labyrinthine webs of lateral associations: rejecting the linearity of cause and effect ("plot") for the sake of multiple interaction; abandoning stable characters who possess histories and "develop" and replacing them with what may be one constantly mutating, preemergent consciousness (the neural mesh of von Neumann's cellular automata or the "underlying cognitive activities" of the brain [Churchland 182]); supplanting temporal succession with an infinite "*noughttime*" (*FW* 349.06); dissolving space in a novel that occurs nowhere and everywhere; and so on. The greatest and most startling contribution complexity theory offers for coming to terms with these sorts of complication is the recognition that *Finnegans Wake*, from this point of view, generates artificial reality, a dynamic representation of the real itself. The *Wake*, no less than the Game of Life, *models* an aboriginal reality, "a sequentiality of improbable possibles" (*FW* 110.15), which, since unmediated by a intervening, self-conscious observer and thus lacking a fully emerged consciousness, has never 'taken person': "utterly impossible as are all these events they are probably as like those which may have taken place as any others which never took person at all are ever likely to be" (*FW* 110.19–21).

Finnegans Wake, a complex book about a "complex" (Hayman 109), a work that takes the concept of imitative form to the absolute limit (Hart, *Structure* 14), compels reader and writer alike to contend with complexity: "It is a bewildering business. . . . Complications to the right of me, complications to the left of me, complex on the page before me, perplex in the pen beside me, duplex in the meandering eyes of me, stuplex on the face that reads me. And from time to time I lie back and listen to my hair growing white" (*Letters* I 222). Yet *Finnegans Wake* also takes the premise of formal realism in the novel to its logical limit, ironically fulfilling the most basic definition of the genre it so conspicuously and consistently violates, by generating a representation of the real in all its complexity and demanding the same strategies for reading that physical and social phenomena demand of the scientists of complexity. This is one answer to the question "What is it all about exactly?" (Benstock, *Joyce-Again's Wake* 3).[27]

Of course, this contention vies with one of the earliest and most persistent assumptions about *Finnegans Wake*: its status as a dream. Joyce, it is true, seems to have supported those who used the idea of the dream as "an explanatory strategy," as Attridge observes, but there is actually "very little evidence to suggest that he associated his laborious project with the night, sleep, or dreams" ("*Finnegans Wake*" 17–18). To Attridge, the oneiric reading of the *Wake* seems to have arisen more from "American critical ingenuity" (22) than from Joyce's definite intention. Joyce, in fact, was characteristically evasive and often contradictory about his intentions for "Work in Progress."[28]

The strongest evidence Ellmann, for example, can give to support his discussion of Joyce's adoption of "the esthetic of the dream" (*JJII* 546) is Harriet Weaver's "impression," expressed in a letter she wrote to J. S. Atherton in 1954, that Joyce used the "dream form . . . 'as a convenient device,' because of its 'shiftings and changes and chances . . . allowing the freest scope to introduce any material he wished—and suited to a night-piece' " (*JJII* 544). Ellmann conveniently omits Weaver's statement, earlier in this same letter, that the "ascription of the whole thing to a dream of HCE seems to me nonsensical" (Atherton, *Books* 17).[29] Joyce seems to have viewed his novel interchangeably as a dream work ("I have put the language to sleep" [*JJII* 546]) and as a representation of "waking" reality, as a typical 1926 letter to Weaver suggests: "Will you let me know whether the 'plot' begins to emerge from it all? Between the close of Δ [Anna Livia Plurabelle, I.8] and Λa [the first 'watch' of Shaun, III.1] there are three or four other episodes, the children's games, night studies, a scene in the 'public,' and a 'lights out in the village' [II.1–4]" (*Letters* I 241).

Joyce may have supported both approaches to the *Wake* because he conceived of the dream not in Freudian terms, as overdetermined by consciousness,[30] but as analogous to a reality possessing an immanent design as yet unformed by a mediating consciousness, the immediate "reality" perceived by Dennett's "real machine" of the brain (210–18) or processed by Churchland's model of the "underlying cognitive activities" of the mind (182): "How does one know that . . . what occurs to one as a jumble of disarranged impressions is not just that: a jumble of disarranged impressions, perhaps concealing a secret structure of its own . . . upon which one imposes a coherent narrative structure after the fact in order to make logical sense of it?" (Bishop 9). In other words, Joyce may have viewed the dream analogy for his novel as no more than a convenient device for a picture of reality that, in Beckett's words, he conceived of as "a paradigm, an illustration of a possibly unstatable rule" (*JJII* 551). Joyce appears to have conceived of reality as an intricately complex system that continually intimates patterns of design, the order of an other, and to have reflected this conception in *Finnegans Wake*, his model of complexity. (The presence of Joyce, then, originator and designer of his own fiction, confounds those who argue against "origin" in his text.) If this is so, Joyce anticipates the view of natural and social phenomena in the emergent sciences of complexity that George Cowan, founder of the Sante Fe Institute for the Study of Complexity, has called "the sciences of the twenty-first century" (qtd. in Waldrop 13).

Perhaps *anticipates* is not the right word, however. Actually, Joyce's objective analyses of subjectivity in *A Portrait* and *Ulysses*, his experiments with fictional convention in the later stages of *Ulysses*, and his remarkable technical innovations in *Finnegans Wake*, rejecting both the dualism and the hierarchical structures of Cartesianism to generate a complexly emergent text from the bottom up, were progressively more influential contributions to the "sensitively dependent" cultural context, the cultural "field," from which contemporary complexity consciousness has emerged. *Finnegans Wake* is not the sui generis work it has been taken to be. Rather, Joyce's final work not only "emerges" out of his earlier fiction but represents one of several, highly individual contemporary reactions against Cartesianism that reject both imposed orders and, their logical antithesis, chaos to demonstrate an intuitive recognition of the "deep theory to the order we see in nature" (Lewin 181), simplicity at the root of complexity: "Sink deep or touch not the Cartesian spring" (*FW* 301.24–25). We must see *Finnegans Wake* as part of a larger cultural context embracing the glimpses of complexity found in Antonio Gramsci's rejection of the Marxist base/superstructure system in his concept of political and social hegemony, Theodor Adorno's similar rejection of the Hegelian dialectical hierarchy in his emergent *Negative Dialektik* (1966), Elias Canetti's rejection of the hierarchical Freudian paradigm of the individual psyche in his analyses of group psychology and mass behavior (*Masse und Macht* [1960]), or Gaston Bachelard's rejection of the progressivist history of science for the sake of a constructivist view of mutating epistemes in the community of scientists (*Le Nouvel Espirit scientifique* [1934] and *La Formation de l'espirit scientifique* [1938]).[31] The methodology of the sciences of complexity, which are now attacking the problems of causal decoupling in the physical and social sciences, may ultimately provide models for a holistic understanding of the evolution from simple origins of densely integrated, recurrent networks of mutually interacting components in a given system. If we can widen the boundaries of our own hierarchical system, the discipline of literature, to learn from what our contemporaries are doing with complex systems in the natural and social sciences—as this study has sought to do—perhaps we too can finally attack the difficulties of negotiating the distance between a genetic, bottom-up study of *Finnegans Wake* and a broadly interpretive, top-down analysis of the novel's "meanings." If successful, if and when we truly become Joyce's contemporaries, we may well master the physical and logical complexity of his final achievement.

APPENDIX A: JOYCE, MATHEMATICS, AND SCIENCE

The standard sources of information about Joyce's education—Ellmann's *James Joyce* (1959, 1982), Kevin Sullivan's *Joyce among the Jesuits* (1958), and Fr. Bruce Bradley's *James Joyce's Schooldays* (1982)—comment little on his mathematical and scientific training even though, as Sullivan notes (73), the revised Jesuit curricula of 1832 emphasized instruction in mathematics and science. Bradley, however, does reproduce the "Results of Examinations" tables for the "Intermediate Examination" that report Joyce's examination totals for 1894, 1895, 1897, 1898 (110–11, 116–17, 130–31, and 140–41; Joyce did not take the examination in 1896); of the possible 600 points for the Euclid section of the exam for these years, Joyce scored 230, 175, 180, and 40, respectively, certainly undistinguished totals but sufficient in each case for him to win exhibition prizes. Joyce also stood examinations during these years, with comparable results, in algebra, arithmetic, "natural philosophy" (physics), chemistry, and plane trigonometry.

Despite the relevance of Euclidean and non-Euclidean geometries for *Dubliners* and *A Portrait of the Artist as a Young Man*—as I demonstrate in this study—Joyce's early fiction has invited little commentary on its mathematical or scientific backgrounds, with the exception of my own earlier article "The Geometry of Meaning in *Dubliners*" (incorporated into chapter 1 of this study) and scattered studies of Joyce's figurative use of the "gnomon" in *Dubliners* (Albert; Weir) or throughout his work (Herring 3–5, 10–14).

The case is quite different with *Ulysses* and *Finnegans Wake*, both of which have provoked substantial attention for their uses of mathematics and science. Much of this discussion of *Ulysses* concentrates on Joyce's "scientific" episode, the seventeenth chapter of the novel, "Ithaca" (Fleishman; Madtes 24–32 and passim; Marre; Watson; Weinstein), although there have also been significant commentaries on his understanding and use of astronomy in the novel as a whole (for example, DiBernard; Heusel; Littman and Schweighauser). Robert M. Adams's 1962 survey of what he sees as Joyce's accidental computational errors in "Ithaca" (*Surface and Symbol* 182–84) had the unintended effect of raising the possibility that Joyce's critics had underestimated his mathematical skills, a direction pursued in general by Salvadori and Schwartzman and specifically in terms of his use of non-Euclidean geometry by McCarthy, who argues that Joyce's errors were for the most part deliberate and demonstrate his considerable grasp of mathematics, and by Wilcox, who suggests that Joyce highlighted the mathematical challenge posed by non-Euclidean geometry to heighten his readers' awareness of "the difficulty of creating an 'axiomatic' system of reading" *Ulysses* (646). (For Joyce's principal allusions to geometry in "Ithaca," see *U* 17.1–10, .690–91, .1071–72, .1397–1407, .1696–97, .2085–89, .2312–16, .2328, .2332, and for his notes on mathematics and science, made in preparation for the writing of "Ithaca," see his *"Ulysses" Notesheets* 415–89 passim.)

When the French critic Valéry Larbaud compared Joyce's new celebrity to Einstein's in December 1921, two months before the book publication of *Ulysses* (*JJII* 522), he probably intended no more than a superficial parallel between two men who had become suddenly famous. Later critics have been less cautious, however, and comparisons between the novelties of Joyce's literary experiments in *Ulysses* and the revolutions in the new physics of the first quarter of this century have become commonplace in Joyce criticism and the literary history of modernism. Following the early lead of Wyndham Lewis, in his "Analysis of the Mind of James Joyce" in *Time and Western Man* (1927), and Edmund Wilson (191–236), in his essay on Joyce in *Axel's Castle* (1931), critics of *Ulysses* have routinely studded their discussions with rather loose correlations to an often misrepresented version of Einstein's theories of relativity (see, e.g., Eco 55–56 and passim; Fleishman; French 5, 12, and passim). French makes a confusing move from casual references to Einsteinian relativity to the terminology of quantum mechanics, primarily concentrating on a Heisenbergian "incertitude" in her reading of *Ulysses* (17) and illustrating what Perlis describes as the chief danger in the overly "facile" application of scientific terminology to *Ulysses* (196). (Eco slips similarly into quantum terms, 55–56.) The most thorough argument for a reading of

Ulysses in terms of relativity and quantum theory is Booker's "Joyce, Planck, Einstein, and Heisenberg: A Relativistic Quantum Mechanical Discussion of *Ulysses*," although a recent general study of the fiction, Phillip Herring's *Joyce's Uncertainty Principle* (1987), loosely appropriates one of the central precepts of quantum theory, Heisenberg's uncertainty principle, to describe Joyce's working methods. (For discussions of the uncertainty principle and its common misappropriation in contemporary culture, see Gross and Levitt; Hofstadter, "Heisenberg's Uncertainty Principle"; and appendix B.) For the best recent discussions of Joyce's general relations to modern science in *Ulysses*, see Perlis and Friedman. For the only study of *Ulysses* in relation to the new paradigms of chaos and complexity science, see the earlier version of chapter 3 of this book (Rice, "*Ulysses*").

The best examination of Joyce's understanding and use of mathematics in *Finnegans Wake* is Solomon's *Eternal Geomater* (1969), an excellent overview of the geometries of the book that remains a standard reference. There have also been numerous studies of *Finnegans Wake* in light of developments in twentieth-century science—focusing on the influences of the relativity and quantum theories—including one book-length publication, Duszenko's *The Joyce of Science: New Physics in "Finnegans Wake"* (1989); articles by Duszenko ("Relativity Theory"), Hassan, Langdon, Mink, Overstreet, and Purdy; and several suggestive comments both by John Bishop in *Joyce's Book of the Dark: "Finnegans Wake"* (43–48, 146–58, 188–90, 253, and passim) and by Clive Hart in *Structure and Motif in "Finnegans Wake"* (65–66 and passim). S. B. Purdy offers both the most skeptical and the most reasonable view of the relations between the new theories and Joyce's work: "No twentieth-century science provides more than a superficial source for the book" (216). A recent work, *Chaosmos: Literature, Science, and Theory* (1994), by Philip Kuberski, contains the first consideration of the challenges of reading *Finnegans Wake* in terms of chaos theory (49–97). Although Kuberski explores concerns rather different from mine in his discussion of the *Wake* (examining Joyce's experimentation with language), he argues, as I do, both that *Finnegans Wake* reflects Joyce's "critique of the fundamental humanist values which have come down to us from the Enlightenment" (53; e.g., Cartesian empiricism) and that theories of interpretation based on the pseudo-uncertainty principle, as applied to the *Wake*, fail "to transcend the objectivist categories of Cartesian thought" (5). Like me, then, Kuberski recognizes that the "scientific hypotheses" of chaos science establish a truly new and genuinely postmodern scientific paradigm; the literature and criticism of indeterminism, based on the mid-1920s

Copenhagen interpretation of quantum theory and usually labeled *postmodern*, are "not sufficiently 'after' or 'other' to warrant the prefix" (3). The only attempt to relate the central conceptions of complexity theory—which Kuberski does not discuss—to the complex dynamic system of *Finnegans Wake* is the earlier version of chapter 4 of this study (Rice, "Complexity").

APPENDIX B: MODERN PHYSICS

Mentally strained from reading work on German physics.—(FW 543.24–25)

I think it is safe to say that no one understands quantum mechanics.
—Richard Feynman (qtd. in Pagels, COSMIC CODE 113)

I have provided accounts of Euclidean and non-Euclidean geometry, chaos theory, and the sciences of complexity in the body of this study. For the sake of those readers unfamiliar with several other important developments in twentieth-century science that I allude to at various points in this study, or discuss with a minimum of contextual clarification, I offer here brief histories and nontechnical explanations of the concept of the field, Einstein's relativity theories, quantum theory, the Copenhagen interpretation of quantum theory, Werner Heisenberg's uncertainty principle, and the quark of contemporary high-energy physics. The various sources I cite in these brief sections are good works to consult for more extensive and informative discussions of these scientific concepts.

THE FIELD

To visualize the (invisible) phenomenon of the field, first think of an intricate mesh or web—say, a spider's web—where each thread represents a "line of force" within the field. A body in this field, the spider, will create tension in the strands of the web that will act, over the distance of the web's filaments, on any other body (a fly) that the web contacts. This is a crude mechanical model of gravitational attraction, the action at a distance of Isaac Newton's theories, which Joseph Lagrange formulated in 1773 as "a force-field filling the whole of space in a continuous manner" (Barrow, *World* 87).

By the mid-nineteenth century Michael Faraday's recognition that "both electrical and magnetic forces existed and exhibited very similar action-at-a-distance effects to the gravitational force" led to James Clerk Maxwell's unification of these two forces (the electromagnetic field), just as Faraday's experiments with field lines created by iron filings acted on by a magnet led to Maxwell's formulation of the wave model to explain the force field of electromagnetism (Barrow, *World* 90–92). Maxwell further "concluded that electromagnetic waves were a form of light, which was also known to exhibit the behaviour characteristic of a wave phenomenon, and as a consequence unseen forms of light must exist" (i.e., electromagnetic radiation) (Barrow, *World* 94). So scrap the spiderweb model for the force field and substitute a picture of a field of waves—say, on the surface of a body of water, or better yet, on an ultrathin plastic sheet, stretched taut—through which energy (force) travels in wave motion. (Drop a stone in the water or on the sheet, and you will observe how an event in one sector of the field will generate response—via waves—in objects located in other sections of the field: a floating cork will bob in the water, or a coin, perhaps, placed elsewhere on the sheet, will bounce.) This conception of energy moving as waves through a field led the physicists of the later nineteenth century to postulate that light travels through some unknown medium, a fluid called "ether." Einstein's 1905 theory of special relativity showed that, "if he was right," ether "was a superfluous concept. Electromagnetic fields needed no medium in which to propagate" (Pagels, *Perfect Symmetry* 186). Einstein thus moved physics beyond our ability to create easily visualized, material metaphors for the field concept.

Both relativity theory and quantum theory, which I turn to later, nevertheless retain something akin to "the classical concept of a continuous 'field' of force," the wave field of electromagnetism, as a convenient visual model for describing the behavior of "the four known forces on Nature": gravitation, electromagnetism, the weak nuclear force, and the strong nuclear force (Barrow, *World* 177). The two most important components that I have appropriated from this field concept in my use of it as a metaphor for cultural phenomena are that all elements within a field are invisibly interconnected, even though widely distant from one another, and that events in the field will generate responses elsewhere because of this connectivity.

RELATIVITY

During 1905 Albert Einstein, then employed in the Swiss patent office in Bern, received his doctorate in physics from the University of Zürich and published three revolutionary papers in the *Annalen der Physik* (Pagels, *Cosmic Code* 12–23). The first of these, on the subject of statistical mechanics, confirms the hypothesis that atoms are elementary particles of matter by analyzing the phenomenon of "Brownian motion" (e.g., the fluttering movements of dust motes in still air). The second paper, on the photoelectric effect, argues that light, although wavelike in behavior (see the previous section), is actually a stream of electrically charged particles (electrons) called quanta. (Max Planck had introduced the concept of the "quantum" in 1900.) Ironically Einstein received his Nobel Prize in 1922 for this "light quantum hypothesis, not for his greatest work, the relativity theory"; the existence of the light quantum, called the "photon," was confirmed experimentally in 1923–24 (Pagels, *Cosmic Code* 16).

Einstein's third paper in 1905, his *annus mirabilis*, formulated the *special* theory of relativity, which, as its fundamental intuitions were experimentally confirmed, "changed forever the way we think about space and time" (Pagels, *Cosmic Code* 16). (Einstein's paper offered his famous deduction of the equivalence of mass and energy, his contention that light "has a certain mass associated with it" and that energy is a form of mass [$E = mc^2$], in a brief postscript to this paper [Calder 11–13].) Albert Michelson and Edward Morley had "measured the speed of light," the *c* of Einstein's equation, "with unprecedented accuracy" in the 1880s and concluded through numerous measurements that this speed seemed to be unchanging, but Einstein was the first to intuit that the speed of light is a constant, approximately 186,000 miles per second; it was the "first great inference in relativity theory" (Calder 105). All objects in the phenomenal universe are in various degrees of motion, and all objects move at (vastly) slower speeds than this absolute speed of light. Thus any measurement we might make of space or of time is *relative* to the degree of our movement. "Using these postulates," and a few thought experiments, "Einstein mathematically deduced the laws that related space and time measurements made by one observer to the same measurements made by another observer moving uniformly relative to the first" (Pagels, *Cosmic Code* 18). Two observers moving uniformly but at different speeds relative to one another would arrive at different measurements for either space, time, or both. These measurements and the laws of nature that we base on them, therefore, represent not absolute truths but only relative perceptions. "The concept of length does not have any absolute meaning," and "there is no absolute standard of time"; "strange as these concepts of space and time are, they are confirmed daily in physics experiments the world over" (Barrow, *World* 103–4). Moreover, although Einstein destroyed "the notion of a universal concept of space and time that is independent of the observer" in his special theory of relativity, he simultaneously affirmed the possibility of certitude in science: "The principles of special relativity are statements of *invariances* in Nature. They are laws about laws" (Barrow, *World* 105). Einstein remained a scientific realist, and as I point out in the introduction, his relativity theory provides no license for relativism. He always resisted the indeterminism of quantum theory, seeing indeterminism as the condition of the observer's relative position, not of the phenomena observed.

In his 1916 paper on *general* relativity Einstein tackled those phenomena that result from nonuniform changing speed or direction, concluding, for example, "that it is impossible to distinguish the effect of gravity from a nonuniform motion" (Pagels, *Cosmic Code* 25). The "gravitational field . . . has a relative existence," Einstein concluded as early as 1907 (qtd. in Pagels, *Cosmic Code* 27), a thesis that makes sense if we conduct a simple experiment: first, drop a rock off a cliff and observe how it speeds away from you, standing there at apparent rest (nonuniform motion); second, jump from the cliff just as you drop the rock and observe how both you and the rock seem to be at rest, or in constant uniform motion; you have no sensation of gravity (until you and the rock feel its effect when you reach the bottom of the ravine): "*for an observer in free fall . . . there exists, during his fall, no gravitational field*" (Einstein's italics; qtd. in Pagels, *Cosmic Code* 27).

Once Einstein had dismissed gravity as "a superfluous concept," he was in a position to reach the great intuition of general relativity. If gravity is merely the effect of nonuniform motion (e.g., acceleration), one would assume that light (which, remember, has mass) must be exempt from its effects, since the speed of light is constant. Rather than make this assumption, Einstein, who had become intrigued with Riemann's non-Euclidean geometry (discussed in chapter 2), theorized that light does indeed curve as it travels through space, not as a result of gravitational attraction, but because space is itself a curved four-dimensional field. Light, a geodesic ray, travels in a straight line through a space that is curved by the masses it contains (much as a rock sitting on a taut plastic sheet—my previously adduced field model—will curve the sheet). Put another way, "Gravity is the curvature of space. . . . The old idea—going back to Newton—was that matter, like the earth, produces a gravitational field that attracts other matter to it. This idea is now replaced by Einstein's idea that matter changes the geometry of space from flat to curved in its vicinity" (Pagels, *Cosmic Code* 32).

Einstein suggested three experiments that could confirm his theory, the first of which (observing the sun's curvature of passing light rays from distant stars during a solar eclipse) gave results, in 1919, that agreed with his predictions. In addition, numerous trials—made possible by increasingly sophisticated technology—of his other two experiments, one concerning the orbit of Mercury and one theorizing that clocks run more slowly under the effect of gravity (and consequently that time is much the same as the three spatial dimensions), have further confirmed Einstein's theory of general relativity (Pagels, *Cosmic Code* 33–37). Most of the cosmic theories that we have developed through the twentieth century have emerged as logical consequences of Einstein's initial premises (e.g., the expanding universe and black holes).

Einstein's conception of relativity, then, both special and general, is quite distinct from the "popular notion that [he] says that 'everything is relative.'" John Barrow concludes his account of Einstein's work and influence by cautioning us that a

> little reflection reveals this journalistic catch-phrase to be meaningless. . . . *Relativity* is an appropriate term to describe the character of things observed in space and time: their lengths, lifetimes, and masses are measurable concepts which are meaningful only by reference to a particular class of observers, who are defined by their motion relative to the object whose properties are being measured. But the reason different observers have different measures of length and time is because two things are *not* relative: the speed of light is measured to have the same value no matter what the state of motion of the observer, and the laws of physics are the same in all laboratories moving with respect to one another at a constant speed. That is, they are *invariant* under a particular type of change. The relativistic laws of Nature are arrived at on the assumption that Nature adheres to certain invariance principles.
>
> Ideally a description of how Nature operates should not depend upon the describer. (*World* 111)

QUANTUM THEORY

Evolving from 1900 to 1926, and initially the creation of Danish physicist Niels Bohr, quantum theory offered a new conception of the atom and its behavior. Bohr was dissatisfied with Ernest Rutherford's (1911) Newtonian picture of the atom as a miniature solar system (a nucleus/sun with orbiting electrons/planets), which defied the laws of classical physics (the virtually massless electron remains in orbit instead of spiraling into the massive nucleus). Bohr simply assumed that the deterministic rules of Newtonian (and Einsteinian) physics do not apply at the subatomic level (Pagels, *Cosmic Code* 53) and then accounted for the stability and behavior of electrons by appropriating Max Planck's and Albert Einstein's notion (ca. 1900–1905) that matter "at its ultimate level . . . exists in the form of tiny, discrete packages" of energy called quanta (Peat, *Einstein's Moon* 28); according to Bohr's model, electrons either remain in their orbits around the nucleus or ascend to higher and descend to lower orbits by the absorption and emission of these discrete amounts of energy (quantum jumps).

What particularly troubled Einstein in this model was Bohr's inability to explain what causes electrons to jump or exchange orbits, to predict when the jump will take place, or to predict what direction the energy emitted in the jump will follow (Pagels, *Cosmic Code* 54). In the late 1910s and into the early 1920s, several physicists combined to study these questions of electron behavior, arriving at the basic premises of quantum theory. These premises share an often counterintuitive nature and a resistance to simple, readily visualizable models: "the visual conventions we adopt from the world of ordinary objects do not apply to quantum objects" (Pagels, *Cosmic Code* 47).

One central illustration of these difficulties (which Pagels calls "quantum weirdness" [*Cosmic Code* 65 and passim]) is the famous wave-particle duality of quantum physics. Into the early 1920s Bohr and associated physicists, including Werner Heisenberg, Max Born, Wolfgang Pauli, and Paul Dirac, developed a mathematical picture of atomic behavior ("matrix mechanics") based on the assumption that matter at its ultimate level is particulate. In 1923, however, Louis de Broglie, with Einstein's support, suggested that the electron could "sometimes behave like a wave" (Pagels, *Cosmic Code* 61). The Austrian physicist Erwin Schrödinger, pursuing this lead, formulated a wave mechanics for quantum phenomena based on his conviction that the "particle idea" for the electron is "wrong or only approximate" (Pagels, *Cosmic Code* 62). In June 1926 Max Born fully moved quantum mechanics toward its unique status as a nondeterministic theory by arguing that Schrödinger's wave functions do not describe the nature of the electron; rather, they describe the probability of locating an electron "at some point in space. Born realized the waves are not *material*, as Schrödinger wrongly supposed; they are waves of *probability*, rather like actuarial statistics for the creation of individual particles that can change from point to point in space and time. This description of the motion of quantum particles is inherently statistical—it is impossible to track them precisely. The best physicists could do was to establish the probable motion of a particle" (Pagels, *Cosmic Code* 63). Einstein's rejection of Born's thesis is the origin of his famous claim that God "does not play dice" (Baggott 29). What Einstein specifically rejected was Born's contention that there exist "physical events that [are] forever unknowable and unpredictable" (Pagels, *Cosmic Code* 65).

But the wave-particle duality is more than a theoretical dispute that Born finessed with his revision of Schrödinger's wave mechanics. A variety of experiments have demonstrated that elementary matter in fact behaves *both* as particles and waves: "the electron has a dual, schizophrenic existence: Design an experiment that looks for particlelike behavior, and the electron behaves like a particle. Design one that looks for waves, and it behaves like a wave!" (Peat, *Einstein's Moon* 12; also see Barrow, *World* 132–37). This is consistent with the most startling and influential implication that quantum theory has contributed to contemporary culture: at the subatomic level the very act of observation, by the means available to us, will affect the nature of what we observe. Any device sensitive enough to determine the location of an electron, for example, will necessarily disturb the electron and change its location (Pagels, *Cosmic Code* 74). It is "meaningless to talk about the physical properties of quantum objects," Pagels observes, "without precisely specifying the experimental arrangement by which you intend to measure them. Quantum reality is in part an observer-created reality" (*Cosmic Code* 76). The cultural misappropriation of this conception of an observer-created reality, however, the extension to large-scale phenomena of this assumption that reality exists solely as a mental construct, ignores the qualification that this picture of quantum reality applies only to subatomic phenomena. There is no contradiction between quantum physics and the laws of classical physics at the macrocosmic levels of human observation. "We live in [a] world," John Barrow writes, "where things . . . are too big for their quantum ambiguity to be perceptible" (*World* 161).

THE COPENHAGEN INTERPRETATION

Formulated in 1927 by Bohr, Heisenberg, and Pauli, the Copenhagen interpretation of quantum theory "maintains that there is no deep reality for us to discover in the traditional sense, only a description of it. The reality that we observe is determined by the act of observation. It really exists when it has been measured—it is not an illusion—but there is no sense in which we can say that it exists in the absence of an act of observation" (Barrow, *World* 150). I have already discussed two components of the Copenhagen interpretation: Max Born's probabilistic interpretation of Schrödinger's wave function and the wave-particle duality of subatomic matter. (Bohr's "idea of complementarity" maintains that "although the wave picture and the particle picture are mutually exclusive, they are not contradictory, but complementary" [Baggott 85–86].) The third, most famous element of the Copenhagen interpretation is Werner Heisenberg's formulation of the "uncertainty principle," to which I turn shortly.

As Krips makes clear, it is not necessary to accept the "transcendental idealism implicit in Bohr's views of the relation between science . . . and the world" in the Copenhagen interpretation, his insistence on the Kantian notion that our ability to know the world is "predetermined by the categories of the understanding (and ultimately by the categories of perception) rather than developing out of the world as it is" (Krips 127), that is, his assertion that the only reality we can know "is determined by the act of observation" (Barrow, *World* 150; also see 140–41). Both Born and Heisenberg resisted Bohr's impulse to turn quantum theory into a "transcendental philosophy" (see Honner 71–107). Krips (126–33) offers a succinct argument for a contrary "realist interpretation" of quantum theory (QT): "QT is true [in] that the objects QT refers to (electrons, protons, etc.) exist, that the properties it refers to are 'real,' and in particular that the physical quantities it refers to are 'real'; in short [this] also means that we can interpret QT 'literally' in the sense that we can take all its referential terms as genuinely referring and not just as convenient fictions or metaphors for the real" (126; Michael Redhead's *From Physics to Metaphysics* [1995] offers a similar argument for a metaphysical realism in quantum theory).

THE UNCERTAINTY PRINCIPLE

As I already noted, at the subatomic level the act of observation, by the means available to us, will affect the nature of what we observe. Any device sensitive enough to determine the location of an electron will necessarily disturb the electron and change its location (Pagels, *Cosmic Code* 74). Heisenberg thus theorized that the experimenter could never measure "simultaneously" the "exact position and momentum of a quantum particle" (Baggott 32), because the most sensitive instrument imaginable for measuring either position or momentum of this particle—say, an electron microscope, which can "see" a particle only by bouncing electrons off of it—will necessarily change the target's momentum and position by striking it. Although Bohr wished to extend Heisenberg's principle to make it a metaphysical statement about the possibility of knowledge, Heisenberg was more cautious: "He concluded that . . . the uncertainty principle . . . tells us that there are limits on what is *measurable* and it is impossible to do anything other than speculate on what is not measurable" (Baggott 33).

The cultural misappropriation of Heisenberg's principle through "careless paraphrases," as Douglas Hofstadter notes (e.g., "The observer always interferes with the phenomenon under observation"), results from both a misunderstanding of precisely what the principle states and a misapplication of the "quantum-mechanical uncertainty principle . . . to everyday phenomena" ("Heisenberg's Uncertainty Principle" 455–57). Heisenberg's principle is not a statement of a metaphysical condition of incertitude; in fact, his principle affirms certitude: "accurate measurement of *either* position *or* momentum" of an electron "is possible; you just can't get *both*" at the same time (Hofstadter, "Heisenberg's Uncertainty Principle" 464). Moreover, Heisenberg's mathematical statement of the principle (expressed as a mathematical inequality) contains no reference whatever to "the notion of an *observer* disturbing the thing under observation. . . . In short, it is a total misinterpretation of Heisenberg's uncertainty principle to suppose that it applies to macroscopic observers making macroscopic measurements" (Hofstadter, "Heisenberg's Uncertainty Principle" 463–64).

THE QUARK

The history of high-energy physics from the 1920s to the present is largely a story of the search for the fundamental building blocks of matter. Rutherford's standard model of the atom—a nucleus with orbiting electrons—seemed to be confirmed by his own discovery of the proton in 1919 and James Chadwick's discovery of the neutron in 1932 (Morris 6; the number of positively charged protons in a stable atom must equal the number of negatively charged electrons [this is the atomic number of the given element]; the difference between the atomic number and the unit atomic *weight* of the atom gives you the number of uncharged neutrons in the nucleus).

Carl Anderson's discovery, also in 1932, of the first antiparticle, the positively charged anti-electron, which he called the "positron," immediately challenged this standard model (Morris 6–7). Anderson's subsequent discovery of the muon—a moderately heavy electron—in 1936 added to the complexity of the standard model, and over the next three decades physicists described scores of new short-lived particles or created new classifications for the elementary particles: baryons, mesons, neutrinos, pions, leptons, hadrons, and so on (Morris 8–12).

In 1964 Murray Gell-Mann (with George Zweig) proposed a new model for the elementary building blocks of subatomic matter. Accepting the current classification of electronlike particles (as six varieties of leptons), Gell-Mann and Zweig proposed a mathematical description for all the heavy atomic particles, the hadrons—protons, neutrons, baryons, and mesons—that pictures each of these particles as composed of some combination of three *quarks* ("up," "down," and "strange"; three more kinds of quark—"charm," "bottom," and "top"—have joined the list, bringing the total number to six) (Morris 13–17). Gell-Mann chose the term *quark* from the opening of the twelfth chapter of *Finnegans Wake* (II.4: "*Three quarks for Muster Mark!*" [383.01]) and selected deliberately nonreferential names for the kinds of quark because he initially "considered the quarks to be nothing more than useful mathematical fictions, not particles that had a real physical existence" (Morris 14). Ironically, from 1968 on, a series of high-energy experiments confirmed that quarks, with the characteristics Gell-Mann postulated, are "apparently very real after all" (Morris 15).

Gell-Mann, incidentally, now tells a slightly different and rather confused version of his choice of the name for the quark in *The Quark and the Jaguar,* claiming that he came on Joyce's use of the word only afterward, "in one of my occasional perusals of *Finnegans Wake*" (180).

NOTES

INTRODUCTION

1 For the best introductions to chaos and complexity, respectively, see Gleick's *Chaos* and Pagels's *Dreams of Reason*. Chapters 3 and 4 of this study provide concise discussions of the concepts of chaos and complexity that I allude to in this chapter—nonlinearity, sensitive dependence, emergence, and the evolutionary model.

2 Although it is not the main object of my study, I touch again on this "chaotic" view of cultural influence, particularly in chapters 3 and 4. Two small illustrations of specifically Joycean infiltrations in recent scientific thought are Murray Gell-Mann's coinage of the term *quark* in quantum physics (from *FW* 383.1) and Daniel Dennett's model for consciousness, the "Joycean machine," in neuroscience. I return to Gell-Mann and Dennett in chapters 3 and 4, respectively; see also appendix B ("The Quark").

3 For more extensive descriptions of the concept of the field in the physical sciences, quantum theory, and the Copenhagen interpretation of quantum theory, which I refer to here and in the next several paragraphs, consult appendix B.

4 Gross and Levitt also devote a section of their chapter on postmodern criticism to Katherine Hayles, not for her appropriation of the field concept for the discussion of the cultural relations of literature and science in *The Cosmic Web* (1984), but for her serious distortions of chaos theory in her subsequent book, *Chaos Bound* (1990). Unlike me, Hayles sees chaos theory as an affirmation rather than a contradiction of her poststructuralist reading of literature, and this perhaps accounts for her inability to find much writing that accords with her premises. Hayles "is committed to the idea that chaos theory is somehow paradigmatic of the postmodern condition, . . . arguing for deep parallels and assonances

between the mathematics of chaos and the theoretical practices of textual critics loyal to the tenets of postmodernism. . . . Her recent book, *Chaos Bound*, is devoted to promulgating this odd hypothesis. Hayles's underlying assumptions seem curiously Hegelian. The cultural moment, she reasons, has brought forth chaos theory simultaneously with Derrida's *Of Grammatology* and de Man's *Allegories of Reading*, and hence, some unspecified mechanism of the zeitgeist must be responsible for both developments. This is a bizarre thesis" (98–99).

5 For example, in a review of Phillip Herring's *Joyce's Uncertainty Principle*, Joseph Valente writes, "Heisenberg hypothesized that the very existence and activity of the observer necessarily altered the character of the phenomena to be observed, that the instruments of scientific measure could not but skew the measurements: in sum, that abstract conclusions were invariably distorted by the material relations that produced them" (506). This is simply wrong; Heisenberg's uncertainty principle neither says nor implies any of Valente's paraphrase (see appendix B). Gross and Levitt also describe the poststructuralist critic's equally common misunderstanding and misappropriation of Gödel's incompleteness theorem to argue that "modern science supposedly generates insights that confirm their own view of the universe" (78); see also D. Thomas.

6 See Zola; for Joyce's experience as "an unsuccessful medical student" in Dublin and Paris (1902–3), see Lyons 18–37.

7 For a good overview of the current status of realism in the philosophy of science, see Leplin's *Scientific Realism*.

8 See Dewey's *Experience and Nature* and *The Quest for Certainty*; see also Hacking.

9 For representative discussions of the early twentieth-century sense of living in an era of rapid and radical scientific and technological change, in "high" culture and "mass" culture, respectively, see Kern's *Culture of Time and Space* and Hynes's *Edwardian Turn of Mind* (132–71 and passim).

10 See Kuhn's response to his critics in his "Postscript—1969," added to the second edition of his *Structure of Scientific Revolutions* (174–210 [205–7 especially]); see also appendix B ("Relativity").

CHAPTER 1: THE ELEMENTS OF GEOMETRY IN DUBLINERS

1 See Bradley 110–11, 116–17, 130–31, and 140–41; McCarthy; Wilcox; and Solomon 113–29 and passim; see also appendix A.

2 See also Salvadori and Schwartzman 340.

3 For an account of the early and sustained relationship between Cartesianism and religious belief, see Butterfield 171–86.

4 For Joyce's derivative understanding of Aquinas and selective use of his ideas, see Noon 2–17 and passim.

5 Only thirteen of the books of the *Stoicheia* are indisputably Euclid's; two late sections, books 13 and 14, were probably composed by Hypsicles of Alexan-

dria, about 160 B.C. (Seyffert 227); for a good brief history of the origins of Euclidean geometry, see Kline, *Mathematics in Culture* 40–59.

6 For the origins of geometry in ritual, see Barrow, *Pi in the Sky* 73–81; Solomon notes Joyce's familiarity with ritual geometry (145, n. 40).

7 Joyce's familiarity with Plato's *Timaeus* can be inferred from his otherwise cryptic lines "body, matter, property of . . . contained in / described in Δ," among his notes on geometry for "Ithaca" (*"Ulysses" Notesheets* 451); see also Atherton, *Books* 272–73, and Solomon 108.

8 For surveys of Bacon's importance for medieval science, see Copleston, *Medieval* 2:168–70, and Peterson 277–84.

9 See also Peat's full discussion of the rise and fall of the Cartesian perceptual model (*Philosopher's Stone* 22–34).

10 For Descartes's debts to Scholastic thought, see N. Wells.

11 See also Caton's discussion of the "optical bias of Cartesian physics" in his *Origin of Subjectivity* (74–77).

12 The educational changes "effected in the revised *Ratio* of 1832," the curriculum guide for Jesuit schools, were particularly notable for their "promotion of mathematics and science," and although "it was not until the eighties that the full effect of the revised *Ratio* made itself felt" in Ireland, this full implementation of the math-science curriculum coincided with Joyce's education at Clongowes Wood and Belvedere College (1888–91, 1893–98) (Sullivan 73). Richards's *Mathematical Visions* is the most thorough study of the importance of geometry in British education in the nineteenth century, stressing both the fundamental "link between geometrical knowledge and the knowledge developed in scientific fields" and the deep enmeshment of "the study of mathematics . . . in a whole tangle of broader intellectual and cultural issues" (8).

13 For an overview of the transmission of Euclid's *Elements*, from the third century B.C. to the beginning of the twentieth century, see T. Smith 56–87.

14 Bloom's volume of geometry may not be the "largest in bulk" in his library (U 17.1415), but it certainly has the longest title entry: "*Short but yet Plain Elements of Geometry* written in French by F. Ignat. Pardies and rendered into Englifh by John Harris D.D. London, printed for R. Knaplock at the Bifhop's Head, MDCCXI, with dedicatory epiftle to his worthy friend Charles Cox, efquire, Member of Parliament for the burgh of Southwark" (U 17.1398–1402). The British Museum lists Pardies's *Geometry* (1701) but no edition for 1711 (Thornton 476).

15 Ellmann, *Consciousness* 6, 111. Although Joyce composed "Ithaca" in Paris between February and October 1921 and had no access to Hall and Stevens (which he left behind in Trieste the previous year [6]), he prepared for its composition much earlier. His notesheets for "Ithaca" contain numerous references to his Euclidean material (*"Ulysses" Notesheets* 432–44, 450–51, 453, 462, 470, 475, 485–89); see also Madtes 7 and passim.

16 See, for example, Stone and Walzl.

17 For the dangers in associating Stephen's aesthetic with Joyce's, see Scholes and Litz's "Epiphanies and Epicleti" (253–56).

18 See also Brown's discussion of "the artist as passive observer" (13–23), which in effect describes the narrator's assumption of the Cartesian perceptual model in *Dubliners.*

19 Hart reproduces Leonardo's *Proporzioni del corpo umano* as the frontispiece for his *Structure and Motif in "Finnegans Wake"*; see also note 36 to this chapter.

20 For a good discussion of the synthetic a priori in Kant, see Copleston, *Modern Philosophy: Kant* 16–19, 33–36.

21 For more discussion of Kant's "visual geometry," see Hopkins and Kline, *Loss of Certainty* 75–78.

22 Gifford argues that Joyce based the three-part structure of *Ulysses* similarly on the syllogism and sees the concluding dot on the last page of "Ithaca," the most mathematical episode of the novel, as representing the "conventional sign" for Euclid's *Q.E.D.* (*"Ulysses" Annotated* 12).

23 For a discussion of the three-part structure of "The Dead," see Burke.

24 In 1905–6 Joyce added two stories to his original twelve, placing "Two Gallants" among the stories of adolescence and "A Little Cloud" among the stories of maturity. He wrote "The Dead" in the spring of 1907, well after his conception of his arrangement for the collection in 1905–6, and never specified whether it should be viewed as a fourth story of public life, as Kenner (*Dublin's Joyce* 53) and Kershner assume (117), or as a kind of coda or "epilogue" for the collection, in a separate category altogether (Litz, *James Joyce* 53), a more common assumption among Joyce critics; see also note 33 to this chapter. For the composition history of *Dubliners*, see Scholes, "Some Observations" and "Further Observations."

25 Joyce probably also dropped the definite article from his title for "Clay" and switched the story's position in the collection with "Counterparts," either at this stage or shortly afterward, in June–July 1906, when he made additional revisions (Gabler, Preface xxx).

26 For summaries of Joyce's tortuous negotiations with Richards, George Roberts of the Dublin firm of Maunsel and Co., and Richards again, see JJII passim; Gorman, *James Joyce* 145–58, 202–23; and Scholes and Litz 257–93.

27 Ellmann writes, "when Gorman's biography duly reached him in proofs during the summer [of 1939], it proved to be what he expected, but Joyce could not resist the opportunity to ventriloquize a little" (JJII 725; see also 631–32, 665–66, 723–26, and passim). As late as June 1939 Joyce still teased Gorman with the possibility that he could promote his book as the "authorized" biography, reminding Gorman, corresponding in the voice of his secretary, Paul Léon, that "Mr Joyce . . . has always been willing to give you all assistance in his power [and] has made a number of rectifications on many pages of the typescript" (*Letters III* 445). Kevin Dettmar describes Joyce as "an enthusiastic and energetic, if cleverly disguised, amateur advertiser," skilled in using his admirers for the

"surreptitious" marketing of his works (795); concentrating on Joyce's promotion of *Ulysses*, Dettmar describes Joyce's contemplated use of Gorman (along with Stuart Gilbert and Frank Budgen) to market *Ulysses* (800–801) and his involvement in "orchestrating the first apologia for *Finnegans Wake*" (801; also see Beckett). Morton Levitt suggests that Joyce was also indirectly involved in James Laughlin's commissioning Harry Levin's introductory study of Joyce (90).

28 The immediate impact of Gorman's publication of the letters to Richards on Joyce scholarship was, as Robert Scholes notes, the result as much of their portrait of the young artist as martyr as of their value for criticism: "When Herbert Gorman revealed the full details of Joyce's writing difficulties in his 'official' biography (1939) many readers found this sensational story of the misunderstood artist more interesting than *Dubliners*, and for a number of years Joyce's problems with publisher and printer were more frequently discussed than the stories themselves" (Scholes and Litz 298).

29 In *Dublin's Joyce* (1956) Hugh Kenner begins his chapter on *Dubliners* by quoting from two letters, 15 October 1905 and 5 May 1906 (48–49), also cited by Levin (40), giving Gorman as his source, and organizes his comments on the individual stories in terms of "The Plan" (53–61). In the same year Brewster Ghiselin quoted both the Richards correspondence and Levin to argue his view of the collection as "both a group of short stories and a novel" in his essay "The Unity of Joyce's *Dubliners*" (318). In 1966 alone three distinguished Joyceans similarly stressed the four-part organization in their overviews of Joyce's literary achievement: A. Walton Litz, discussing "the design of *Dubliners*" in his Twayne introduction (*James Joyce* 49–53), Robert M. Adams, concluding his critical overview of *Dubliners* in his *James Joyce: Common Sense and Beyond* (90), and James S. Atherton, describing Joyce's discovery of his "technique" in "The Joyce of *Dubliners*" (44). Among prominent recent commentaries I need cite only John Paul Riquelme's *Teller and Tale in Joyce's Fiction* (1983) (97), Bernard Benstock's *James Joyce* (1985) (26–27), and the chapter/division titles of both C. H. Peake's *James Joyce: The Citizen and the Artist* (1977) and R. B. Kershner's *Joyce, Bakhtin, and Popular Literature* (1989).

30 Tindall, however, does allude to two letters to Grant Richards, 15 October 1905 and 5 May 1906, in his first study of Joyce (*James Joyce* 6); for a search for the thematic "patterns" that link "the stories inseparably together and [lock] them in significant order" (297), apparently performed with no knowledge of Joyce's intended arrangement, see Wigginton.

31 Both Adams and Atherton indicate their own sense of the apparent illogic of Joyce's announced design, worrying about the tendency of Joyce's critics to "impose a mechanical form on the stories" (Adams, *James Joyce* 86), although Atherton admits that we should not dismiss either "Joyce's original plan" or some of the more extravagant patterns critics have found in *Dubliners* on the "grounds that [they are] oversubtle or farfetched" ("Joyce" 44–45).

32 Although Joyce's use of the word *quincunx* captures the attention of most crit-

ics of "Grace," few have attempted to find special significance in the term; the exception is Lobner, who explores the numerological pattern (2 + 1 + 2) in the story. Kenner asserts that Joyce's quincunx is an allusion to Dante's arrangement of the souls of the "courageous . . . in the fifth heaven" in the form of a Greek cross in *Paradiso* (*Dublin's Joyce* 61–62), a dubious assumption both Beck (298) and Niemeyer (199) accept without question (see canto 14:97–108 [Dante 3:204–6]). As I argue later, Joyce could have found a clearer and more geometrical source for his use of the quincunx in Dante's final canto, which would have the added advantage of paralleling the conclusion of "Grace" with the last lines of the *Commedia*; see also note 36 to this chapter. It is tempting to speculate that, if the term *quincunx* reminds the reader of the strange words in the opening paragraph of "The Sisters," Joyce might himself have been inspired to introduce these terms into his first story by his equally inspired, earlier choice of the word *quincunx* for the seating arrangement of his characters in "Grace"; as I will demonstrate shortly, there is a particularly direct connection between a quincunx and a gnomon.

33 Hence, *quincunx* can also refer to a cruciform reliquary. The original meaning of *quincunx* is the fraction five-twelfths; I presume that it came to mean the arrangement of five points, as Joyce employs it, because of the design of the number five in the duodecimal system of playing dice (both the five die and any combination of two dice that totals five—if superimposed—form a quincunx). I leave the possibility that Joyce intended some allusion to the duodecimal system in his original twelve-story arrangement for *Dubliners*, by this implication in his use of the quincunx, to more imaginative critics than I.

A more likely possibility for relating the quincunx design to the final arrangement of *Dubliners* is that Joyce's use of the quincunx in "Grace" in late 1905 may have lingered in his mind as a model for the place of "The Dead" in the final form of the collection when he began planning his last story in 1906 (Scholes and Litz 500). Although Joyce never specified the place of his latest-written story in his arrangement for *Dubliners* (see note 24 to this chapter), he may have conceived of its position—"bring[ing] the themes of all the other stories into vital relationship with each other" (Litz, *James Joyce* 55)—as analogous to the position of the central point in the quincunx, which stands in a "vital," equidistant relation to the four remaining parts of the design.

34 Gifford notes that "Euclid defines a gnomon as what is left of a parallelogram when a similar parallelogram containing one of its corners is removed" (*Joyce Annotated* 29); the gnomon, as presented in the *Elements* (Euclid 31) and as I represent it in figure 1, may inhabit a square (i.e., a rectangular parallelogram); see also Simson 43. Kain suggests that " 'Grace' is a *gnomon*, an indicator or exposé, of *paralysis* and *simony*" (" 'Grace' " 135), but does not pursue this insight far (or see a connection to the quincunx design); see also note 44 to this chapter.

35 For various "Dantean" readings of "Grace," see Boyle; Kenner, *Dublin's Joyce* 61–62; Kain, " 'Grace' " 146–50; Niemeyer; and Reynolds 158–64.

36 See Sinclair's concluding note on canto 33 (Dante 3:487–92). Joyce's subsequent fascination with the unsolvable problem of "the quadrature of the circle" (U 17.1696), which he occasionally inverts into "circling the square" (*FW* 186.12; see also P 66), might well have stemmed from his seeing this most notorious inscription problem in geometry as a model for the alienation that the individual "figures" in "Ivy Day in the Committee Room" and "A Mother," and most particularly Mr. Kernan in "Grace," suffer in their failure to achieve a full integration with the society that surrounds and constrains them; see also *Letters* I 251; U 15.2399–2401 and 17.1070–72; Kenner, *"Ulysses"* 166–67; McCarthy 611–12; and note 32 to this chapter. Gerard Pendrick has identified Joyce's reference to one classic attempt to square the circle—by Antiphon (fifth century B.C.)—in the *"Ulysses" Notesheets* (450). Clive Hart discusses Joyce's connection of the quincunx design with the quadrature of the circle throughout *Finnegans Wake* (*Structure* 134–42), a visual association he shares with Leonardo da Vinci: "in a celebrated drawing by Leonardo, genitals and navel are the centres of the square and circle which circumscribe the human figure drawn in two superimposed attitudes, approximating a *tau* cross and a quincunx respectively. . . . This drawing of Leonardo's is an illustration to the *De Architectura*, III, i, of Vitruvius, whom Joyce names in acknowledgment at 255.20" of the *Wake* (*Structure* 137); see also note 19 to this chapter.

37 Boyle's essay explores "a four-level treatment of ['Grace'] analogous to the four-level treatment Dante describes in his letter to Can Grande" (11); Dante's letter to Can Grande illustrates in Dante criticism, I should add, an even more celebrated example of the "infiltrative powers" of an author's "self-representations" than the case of Joyce's letters to Richards (Hardwick 85). For a somewhat idiosyncratic application of the "four aspects [that] all good myths have" to *Ulysses*, see Ellmann's *"Ulysses" on the Liffey* (xii and passim).

38 Aristotle distinguishes among the "material," "formal," "efficient," and "final" causes in his *Physics* (W. D. Ross 74–78), a work Euclid undoubtedly assimilated into his schema for geometry, although he was principally indebted to Aristotle's *Posterior Analytics* for the organization of, and as a logical model for, his *Elements* (W. D. Ross 47–48).

39 Thus, reading *Dubliners* ahistorically, Rabaté misses Joyce's reflection of the fundamental assumption of Euclid's "scriptural" authority in late nineteenth-century culture: "Gnomon implies interpretation and Greek geometry, but is placed curiously beside catechism" (*James Joyce* 28).

40 The famous problem of squaring the circle is not in the *Elements* but was raised early by Greek students of Euclid, along with two other unsolvable puzzles: "doubling the cube" and "trisecting the angle" (Kline, *Mathematics in Culture* 50).

41 See also Levin's first chapter, "Reality" (19–31). Edmund Wilson, in his influential early appreciation of Joyce's work in *Axel's Castle* (1931), similarly describes *Dubliners* as "French in its objectivity" (191) and considers both *Dubliners* and *A Portrait* as "straight work[s] of Naturalistic fiction" (192).

42 For an argument along these lines, see LaValley.

43 See, for example, Tindall, *Reader's Guide* 17–19, and Stone; see also apRoberts's attack on Stone and on symbolmania in Joyce criticism generally.

44 See Euclid 30–31, 119–23 (book 2, definition 2 and proposition 4; book 6, propositions 26–29). Neither Albert, Weir, nor Herring (3–5, 10–14), in three recent explorations of the Joycean gnomon, examines the structural significance of Euclid's figure for confirming Joyce's symbolic method in *Dubliners*; see also my earlier version of the present argument (Rice, "Geometry" 393–404) and note 34 to this chapter.

45 See Kenner's discussion of Joyce's use of this "Uncle Charles Principle"—the impersonal narrator's mimicking of the character's idiom—elsewhere in his fiction (*Joyce's Voices* 15–38 and passim).

46 See also Kline, *Mathematics in Culture* 144–58. Much has been written about Joyce's use of film techniques in his later work and his interest in the cinema generally (including his failed attempt to operate a film theater in Dublin in 1909 [JJII 300–311]), although no one has noticed this cinematic conclusion to "The Dead"; aside from comments on John Huston's film version (1987), Deane's essay "Motion Picture Techniques in James Joyce's 'The Dead' " is the sole discussion of the cinematic qualities of the story.

47 As Ellmann observes, by the autumn of 1906, after completing all but the final story of *Dubliners*, Joyce began to develop "a more indulgent view of Ireland" (JJII 230); Ellmann (231) quotes Joyce's 25 September letter to Stanislaus: "Sometimes thinking of Ireland it seems to me that I have been unnecessarily harsh. I have reproduced (in *Dubliners* at least) none of the attraction of the city for I have never felt at my ease in any city since I left it except in Paris. I have not reproduced its ingenuous insularity and its hospitality. The latter 'virtue' so far as I can see does not exist elsewhere in Europe" (*Letters II* 166).

CHAPTER 2: THE ALIMENTS OF JUMEANTRY IN *A PORTRAIT OF THE ARTIST AS A YOUNG MAN*

1 For Joyce's Roman period, see JJII 224–42; for more information on the origins of *Ulysses*, see Owen 1–15.

2 As Gabler makes clear in "The Seven Lost Years of *A Portrait*," Joyce continued work on his novel throughout the period from 1908 to 1915.

3 For the reception of Bonola's book, see Enriques and Carslaw.

4 See Kline's "The First Debacle: The Withering of Truth" (*Loss of Certainty* 69–99)

and Bachelard's "Dilemmas in the Philosophy of Geometry" (*New Scientific Spirit* 19–42).

5 Henderson's *Fourth Dimension* is an excellent historical survey of the impact of turn-of-the-century popular awareness of n-dimensional and non-Euclidean geometry on modern, predominantly visual, art.

6 For example, Cox and Dyson observe that the "revolution in physics . . . culminates in the publication of the special theory of relativity by Einstein in 1905" (x) and proceed to note the influence of this revolution on the fiction of James, Ford, and Conrad; S. Spencer, likewise, sees Einstein's influence as a fait accompli in 1905 (xvii and passim). For similar views, see Kenner (*Pound Era* 20, 153, and passim) and Glicksberg's chapter "The Tragic Vision and the Scientific Synthesis" (77–84). Kern proves to be a mild exception by devoting a few pages to the non-Euclidean revolution in *The Culture of Time and Space* (132–34), although most of his discussion of "the nature of space" in modern culture privileges the role of relativity theory (131–80).

7 For Riemann's influence on Einstein, see Farwell and Knee 104–5; Houzel 18–19; Pagels, *Cosmic Code* 28–31; and Torretti.

8 Larbaud was among the first to compare Joyce's new celebrity to Einstein's, in his lecture on *Ulysses* cited in the previous chapter (see also JJII 522); the "influence" of relativity theory on *Finnegans Wake* became a (misleading) commonplace early in its critical reception as well (e.g., Troy's "Notes on *Finnegans Wake*" [1939]). See also appendix A.

9 Bergonzi (25–34) suggests that Wells first became interested in the new geometries in 1887, when he may have heard a paper on the "fourth dimension" at the Royal College of Science and begun writing "The Chronic Argonauts" shortly after, a very early version of *The Time Machine*; "However," Bergonzi concludes, Wells's "geometrical speculations . . . are only incidental" to both works (34).

10 See also Henderson's selective bibliography, "The Popularization of the Non-Euclidean and n-Dimensional Geometries" (381–96).

11 By 1913 *Science and Hypothesis* had "been translated into six languages and . . . already had a circulation of over 20,000" (Poincaré x; Halsted published his English translation in 1905).

12 For an introductory discussion of Poincaré's "conventionalism," see Slosson 104–46, and for a brief survey of the life (1854–1912) and prolific work (over 500 titles) of Poincaré, the preeminent mathematician of his era and the greatest contemporary popularizer of mathematics as well, see Bell's chapter "The Last Universalist" (526–54). Joyce would have been aware of Poincaré's reputation and very likely knew something of his "conventionalist" philosophy; Stephen Dedalus's view of the doctrinal system of Roman Catholicism as "an absurdity which is logical and coherent" (P 244) distinctly echoes Poincaré's assertion in *Science and Hypothesis*, quoted here, that Euclidean geometry offers only a con-

vention for representing space. Joyce was well-positioned by his mathematical education to recognize, contemporaneous with his composition of *A Portrait*, that the entire concept of proof was under attack in axiomatic systems such as mathematics and philosophy. (This recognition informs his parody of "the idea of a taxonomic system itself" in the "Ithaca" chapter of *Ulysses* [Lawrence 195].) It is less certain, however, that Joyce knew the work of David Hilbert (1862–1943), Poincaré's rival for the title of preeminent mathematician of his era, the leader of the "axiomatic movement" in mathematics at the turn of the century, and the man whose attempts to formulate a metamathematical "proof theory" to demonstrate the consistency of mathematical systems, between 1900 and 1930, were finessed by Kurt Gödel's 1931 demonstration that "the consistency of any mathematical system . . . [can]not be established by . . . logical principles" (Kline, *Loss of Certainty* 261; see also Hofstadter, *Gödel, Escher, Bach*).

13 Books like Ball's *Mathematical Recreations* and Poincaré's *Science and Hypothesis*, presumably capitalizing on a large audience that, like Leopold Bloom of *Ulysses*, was interested in improving its knowledge of technical and scientific subjects, were extremely popular at the turn of the century (and remain popular today in the works, for example, of Martin Gardner and Ian Stewart). Among the best-known survivors, after Poincaré and Ball, are the four volumes of "mathematical recreations" published by Charles L. Dodgson ("Lewis Carroll"), *A Tangled Tale* (1885), *The Game of Logic* (1887), *Pillow Problems* (1893), and *Symbolic Logic* (1896), the last two of which appeared in four editions by 1895 and 1897, respectively, and all of which remain in print (*Mathematical Recreations of Lewis Carroll*).

14 See Henderson 25–31, 39, 245–99, and passim. See also Ouspensky, "The Fourth Dimension" 65–71 and passim; idem, *Tertium Organum* 1–2, 18–27 and passim; and note 41 to this chapter. Bergonzi traces Hinton's ultimate influence on the idea of the fourth dimension in both Wells's *Time Machine* and Wilde's "Canterville Ghost" (31–33).

15 See Bishop 146–47 and passim, and Solomon 119–29; for one of the most famous visual uses of the tesseract in modern art, see Salavador Dali's *Crucifixion* (1954) (Henderson, plate 114).

16 Henderson 31–33; Henderson (45) describes C. W. Leadbeater's assimilation of hyperspace into his conception of Theosophy in *The Other Side of Death* (1903).

17 Stephen Dedalus echoes Joyce's attitude toward Theosophy ("O, fie. Out on't! *Pfuiteufel*") in the "Scylla and Charybdis" episode of *Ulysses* (*U* 9.72; see also *U* 9.60–71); Joyce parodies accounts of "the other side of death" in "Cyclops" (*U* 12.338–373).

18 For additional discussions of Saccheri, see Bonola 22–44; Kline, *Mathematics in Culture* 412–14; idem, *Loss of Certainty* 80–81; and Torretti 45–53.

19 For a consideration of the impact of the subsequent development of non-Euclidean geometry on the reception of Kant's thought, see Hopkins's essay "Visual Geometry."

20 "From 1825 on [Lobatchevsky] presented his views on the foundations of geometry in many papers and two books. Johann Bolyai . . . published a twenty-six page paper, 'The Science of Absolute Space,' on non-Euclidean geometry, which he called absolute geometry . . . in 1832–33 and therefore after publications by Lobatchevsky[; however] Bolyai seems to have worked out his ideas on non-Euclidean geometry by 1825. . . . In a letter to his father dated November 23, 1823, Johann wrote, 'I have made such wonderful discoveries that I am myself lost in astonishment' " (Kline, *Loss of Certainty* 83).

21 For a recent account of the evolution of this "hyperbolic" geometry, from Plato and Euclid to Kant, Lobatchevsky, and Hilbert, see Trudeau's *Non-Euclidean Revolution*.

22 For fuller discussions of Riemann, see Bonola 129–80 and Torretti 85–109.

23 For recent overviews of the remarkable achievements of the German mathematical community in the mid-nineteenth century, under the profound influence of Gauss, see Jungnickel and McCormmach's *Torch of Mathematics* and Fauvel, Flood, and Wilson's *Möbius and His Band*.

24 For Helmholz's contributions, see Bonola 152–53 and passim, and Torretti 155–71 and passim; for a recent technical account of Riemannian geometry, see Willmore's *Riemannian Geometry*; and for the multiple historical and philosophical issues raised by the development of non-Euclidean geometry, see Boi, Flament, and Salanskis, *1830–1930: A Century of Geometry: Epistemology, History and Mathematics*.

25 For additional discussion of Clifford, see Bonola 200–215; Henderson 19–21; Richards, "Reception" 151–56; and Torretti. Barrow describes Clifford's anticipation of Einsteinian relativity in *Theories of Everything* 57–58.

26 Theodore Spencer, the editor of *Stephen Hero*, proves an exception among Joyce's critics, finding Stephen Daedalus in the earlier manuscript version of the novel to be "on the whole a more sympathetic person" than the Stephen of *A Portrait* (13).

27 For arguments along this line, see Scholes, "Stephen Dedalus," and Sharpless; for overviews of the problem of distance in *A Portrait*, see Anderson 446–54; Staley, "Strings in the Labyrinth"; and Sosnoski, which also includes a bibliographical checklist (1928–77) on the "controversy about esthetic distance" (59–63).

28 Stephen himself replicates this process of estrangement in his progressive loss of sympathy for others: from his father during the trip to Cork in the second chapter ("He listened without sympathy to his father's evocation of Cork" [P 87]), from his schoolmates at Belvedere in the third chapter ("The blundering answer stirred the embers of his contempt of his fellows" [P 104]), and from virtually everyone in the final two chapters.

29 John Paul Riquelme offers persuasive stylistic evidence for his assumption that the artist of *A Portrait* is a hypothetical future Stephen (48–85); to do so, however, he must ignore the narrator's ironies and rely on the readers remaining in sympathy, indeed identifying, with Stephen. Comens follows Riquelme in

viewing Stephen as the ultimate narrator of his text, although he remains "implicated in the narrative net he would escape" (309). The debate between sympathetic and ironic readings of *A Portrait* will probably be with us as long as we read the novel; Margot Norris, for example, counterbalances the responses of Riquelme and Comens by seeing Stephen as a "plebeian" aesthete and the novel as Joyce's "self-critique of [the] aestheticism" of modernism (*Joyce's Web* 58, 55).

30 For additional discussion of non-Euclidean geometry in "Ithaca," see McCarthy and Wilcox.

31 Henderson convincingly argues that "although the term *simultaneity* did gain acceptance among the Cubists" after the term was introduced at the exhibition of Italian futurist art in Paris in February 1912, and they employed this idea of simultaneity to describe "their juxtaposition of several views of an object, the term *space-time* does not occur in contemporary Cubist literature. Art historians interpreting Cubism in relation to Einstein's Theory of Relativity and [Hermann] Minkowski's four-dimensional space-time continuum [1909] simply adopted Minkowski's terminology and applied it to the element of time sensed by even the earliest observers of Cubism. . . . However, the Cubists were not influenced by Einstein's relativizing of simultaneity nor by Minkowski's ideas on 'space-time.' Instead, their 'fourth dimension' was an outgrowth of nineteenth-century n-dimensional geometry, a fact that provides a valuable insight into the time element in Cubist painting ('space-time') and the resultant juxtaposition of images ('simultaneity'). . . . The Cubists never interpreted the fourth dimension as time itself, . . . as it was later employed in discussions of four-dimensional space-time. Instead, Cubism's *durée* was simply the temporal means that enabled the artist to gather and synthesize information about the fourth dimension of space. As in n-dimensional geometry, time in Cubist painting plays only a supporting role, allowing the artist or geometer to accomplish the physical or mental movement necessary to form an idea of an object's total dimensionality" (89–90, 91); see also Henderson's extended discussion in "The Question of Cubism and Relativity" (353–65). Henderson's useful distinction between the cubist *durée* and the space-time continuum of relativity applies equally well to Joyce's spatial/temporal technique in the "Wandering Rocks" episode of *Ulysses*. As in the "cubist" *Portrait*, time proceeds linearly through the tenth episode of *Ulysses*, affording the artist the opportunity to arrange his narrative blocks, the wandering "rocks" of the nineteen mini-episodes, and to develop their "total dimensionality," which includes a "fourth" dimension (the intrusions from adjacent subsections of the episode).

32 See also Loss's excellent discussion of the correspondences between cubist techniques in the visual arts and the spatial form of *Ulysses* (41–65).

33 See Riquelme's description of Joyce's narrative strategies for representing Stephen's subjectivity (55–57); see also Brown 124–29.

34 Such is the primary definition of *empathy* in *Webster's New Collegiate Dictionary* (1976). Benjamin's term *Einfühlung* (150) conveys a sense of projection through the German *ein*-prefix that is missing in the more passive English words *sympathy* and *compassion*, Greek and Latin derivatives, respectively, communicating, like the German word Benjamin did *not* choose, *Mitgefühl*, the idea of shared feeling: sym/com/mit = "together" or "with"; pathy/passion/*Gefühl* = "feeling."

35 Joyce underlines Stephen's unreliability as an observer by pairing the motif of "watching" (e.g., P 8, 26, 68–69, 73, 87, 93, 100, 136, 154, 171, 185, 224, 232) with motifs of "vagueness," "gloom," and "shadows" (e.g., P 55, 64, 66, 68, 99, 101, 135–36, 140–41, 154–55, 158–61, 217, 233).

36 As in his *Dubliners* story "An Encounter," Joyce uses the motif of the encounter ironically in *A Portrait* to suggest the gap between an exotic fancy and an external (and perhaps perverse) reality; for example, see P 65, 99, 159, 252–53.

37 Kumar (103–38 and passim) has traced James's and Bergson's links to Joyce's fiction, but he overlooks the possibility that Joyce's analysis of subjectivism in *A Portrait* was a more direct response to the developments in mathematics and science that influenced all three men.

38 Ball (182–87) describes mazes, such as the Cretan labyrinth constructed by the architect and engineer Daedalus, in the general context of unicursal geometrical problems; see also Poundstone's discussions of rectilinear and circular mazes (160–76).

39 Stephen's aesthetic is an extrapolation from Euclid in much the same sense that Noon finds it to be "applied Aquinas" (28 [P 209]), particularly, as I will show, in Stephen's geometrical differentiation among the lyric, epic, and dramatic forms. As Noon remarks, "It may well be that a literary aesthetic along strict Thomistic lines drives one straight into a genre theory of literary forms and 'representations,' but before one commits St. Thomas to this view, it is well to keep in mind that he nowhere asserts such a position" (28); see also Staley, "Religious Elements" 162.

40 For a description of Fr. Arnall's "real-life counterpart," Fr. William Power, and "his distinctive teaching methods," see Bradley (41–44).

41 For more discussion of Stephen's Cartesian worldview, see Sicker. P. D. Ouspensky, reflecting the new consciousness of subjectivity resulting from the development of non-Euclidean geometries, sounds much like Stephen in the following observation: "It seems to us that if we should close our eyes, then the objective world would continue to exist, such as we just saw it; and if our inner life were to disappear, so would the subjective world disappear—yet the objective would exist as before, as it existed at the time when we were not. . . . But such a division of the subjective and objective world does not satisfy us. By means of reasoning we can establish the fact that in reality we know only our own sensations, perceptions and conceptions, and we cognize the objective world by

projecting outside of ourselves the causes of our sensations, presupposing them to contain those causes" (*Tertium Organum* 9); see also note 14 to this chapter.

42 See Tiles 58 and, for a similar dialectical resolution of the subject-object dualism, see Adorno, "Subject and Object."

CHAPTER 3: ULYSSES, CHAOS, AND COMPLEXITY

1 For the best general introductions to chaos theory, see Gleick's *Chaos*, Ruelle's *Chance and Chaos*, and Stewart's *Does God Play Dice?* Hall's essay collection *Exploring Chaos* provides a recent overview of the applications of chaos theory among the natural and social sciences. The only significant works of literary criticism that attempt to assimilate chaos theory, Hayles's *Chaos Bound* and her essay collection, *Chaos and Order*, both pursue a direction quite different from mine for reading chaos in fiction and seriously misrepresent the science and significance of chaos theory (see "Chaos as Nonsense II. N. Katherine Hayles," in Gross and Levitt's *Higher Superstition* [98–106]).

2 See Stewart's full discussion of Poincaré, "The Last Universalist" (*Does God Play Dice* 57–72), as well as Bell's chapter, also titled "The Last Universalist" (526–54); for Poincaré's influence on the popular awareness of non-Euclidean geometries in France, see Henderson 81–85, 93–99, and passim.

Throughout this chapter I use the term *nonlinear* both in "the intuitive sense" to describe irregular phenomena that "do not 'follow a straight line' " (Churchland 113) and in the strict mathematical sense. Heinz Pagels offers a useful clarification of the mathematical distinction between linearity and nonlinearity: "These terms simply refer to the properties of solutions to equations—whether or not you can add them up to get new solutions. If the equations describe some natural or social phenomena, then we can refer to those phenomena as linear or nonlinear as the case may be. . . . Most of the equations that describe phenomena in the natural world, human behavior, neurofunction, population dynamics, and many other areas, are nonlinear. In spite of the fact that these are extremely interesting phenomena that we would like to understand, the fact that nonlinear equations are usually mathematically intractable [made] them almost impossible to solve . . . previous to the deployment of the computer. . . . Nonlinear science is the study of phenomena that requires nonlinear equations for its mathematical language" (*Dreams of Reason* 72–73). One of the fundamental insights of Benoit Mandelbrot's fractal geometry—which I discuss later in this chapter—chaos science generally, and complexity science is that there is a direct relation between this mathematically defined nonlinearity and the rough irregularity of phenomena that appear nonlinear in the intuitive sense of the term.

3 For Poincaré's enormous impact on modern mathematics, see Browder's *Mathematical Heritage of Henri Poincaré*, which contains Aleksandrov's historical account of Poincaré's "grand scientific creation," topology.

4 Brian Wynne describes the ether controversy in late Victorian England as an ultimate test of the physicist's "*faith* in [an] all-unifying medium" (171); for the scientist, the loss of belief in "the ineffable, unseen ethereal basis of matter" meant the loss of "an ineffable spiritual and transcendent basis of social reality" (180). As Bell succinctly observes, "relativity put the complicated mathematics of the ether on the shelf" (528). See also the discussions of the field, relativity, and quantum theory in appendix B.

5 For a similar view of the perils of common sense in scientific thought, see Bachelard, *Philosophy of No* 90–114 and passim; see also Gramsci's distinctions between common sense and "good sense" (323–62).

6 Gross and Levitt note that chaos theory in fact "represents, in a major sense, the triumphant reemergence of Newtonian mechanics, *not . . . its overthrow*" (98), a basic point overlooked by those postmodern critics who have seen nonlinear mathematics as a subversion, a "negation" of the "intellectual life of the West since the Enlightenment" (72); "Newton's equations of planetary motion are, of course, nonlinear" (98).

7 Several recent critical studies, principally of contemporary American novelists, base their constructions of postmodernism on what Hofstadter calls the "pseudo-uncertainty principle" of quantum theory ("Heisenberg's Uncertainty Principle" 455); see, for example, Hayles's *Cosmic Web* and *Chaos Bound* and Strehle's *Fiction in the Quantum Universe*; despite Hayles's discussion of chaos in *Chaos Bound*, to date only Philip Kuberski (*Chaosmos*) and I (Rice "*Ulysses*" and "Complexity") have argued that chaos theory transcends the indeterminism of this postmodernist appropriation of the "quantum" view of reality and offers a new paradigm for critical theory.

8 Kuhn develops the concept of the "paradigm shift" in his *Structure of Scientific Revolutions*; see the introduction to the present book.

9 Without referring to chaos science, Riquelme describes a similarly "preposterous" strategy for the prospective and retrospective reading of *A Portrait* (60–61).

10 For an excellent summary of such interpretations, to the early 1970s, see Kain, "Significance."

11 The key to resolving this apparent conflict between entropy and evolution is the recognition that the world is *not* the ideal, closed system of thermodynamic theory; rather, it is an open, nonequilibrium, *dissipative* system (i.e., sustained by a constant source of energy). In *Order Out of Chaos*, for instance, Prigogine finds a model for an anti-entropic evolution in the study of chemical autocatalysis, a form of self-organization in dissipative dynamic systems far from equilibrium (see also Toffler xix–xx). Schaub argues, in his discriminating discussion of the idea of entropy in Thomas Pynchon's fiction (18–19 and passim), that Pynchon sees the energy of thought itself—the "control [of] entropy through feedback" of Norbert Wiener's cybernetic theory (Wiener 26)—as the force that keeps life in the world in its nonequilibrium state, forestalling entropy. In *Wonder-*

ful Life Gould suggests yet another resolution that redefines evolution as, in some senses, entropic. The paleontological study of the Burgess Shale demonstrates that the emergence of life did not in fact involve "increasing complexity and differentiation" of life forms at all (Gould 120; i.e., progressive evolution); rather, there was progressive extinction of variety (i.e., entropy) as life settled, by chance, into a relatively limited number of species: the history of life "has been a tale of decimation, not increasing variety of design" (120; Wells's hypothesis in *The Time Machine* turns out, like so many of his other speculations, to have been prescient). Gould also notes that Darwin himself viewed the now standard progressivist interpretation of evolution equivocally (257–58); see also Gould 277–91, 319–21, and passim, and Gell-Mann 215–60.

12 I should remind the reader here of my distinction between the idea of indeterminism in quantum theory as it has entered and influenced contemporary cultural studies and the much more complex and ultimately less indeterminate conception of uncertainty in the theory itself. Gross and Levitt not only assert that "the uncertainty principle is a very certain item indeed . . . *an objective truth about the world*" (52), but they point out that recent quantum research (by Dürr, Goldstein, and Zanghi) "bluntly contradict[s] the 'Copenhagen interpretation' of Bohr and Heisenberg," proving that "Einstein was right: God does not play dice with the cosmos" (261–62). This reestablishment of determinism, they note further, tends to confirm the metaphysical implications of chaos theory (262). For a fuller account of the origins of quantum theory and the Copenhagen interpretation of quantum theory, see appendix B.

13 For the novel philosophic consequences of quantum mechanics' status as a *nondeterministic* theory, see Passmore 330–42.

14 Berry describes the "emerging science" of "quantum chaology" that may map "the largely unexplored border country between quantum and classical [Newtonian] mechanics" (187, 195); for a recent formulation of quantum chaology, see Nakamura.

15 See, for example, Barrow, *World* 259–60, and Morris 3–5, 210–11; for an important critique of the methodological problems of this concept, see Popper, "Simplicity" (*Logic* 136–45).

16 See Gleick 321; Gleick provides an excellent overview of Lorenz's career (11–31 and passim).

17 For further comment on Poincaré's anticipation of the play of chance and determinism in the principle of sensitive dependence, see Peterson 143–69 and Ruelle 48–50.

18 As Joseph Kelly makes clear, Stanislaus Joyce, despite Ellmann's extensive reliance on his memory, is not an entirely reliable source of information, particularly for his recall of purported statements made by his brother. The kernel of Stanislaus's anecdote, however, concerning his brother's "idea of the signifi-

cance of trivial things" is, I think, indisputably true to Joyce's methods and consistent with his other remarks about the "trivial," whereas the concluding remark about "the two or three unfortunate wretches who may eventually read me" sounds suspiciously like the dyspeptic Stanislaus.

19 "In the first six episodes of *Ulysses*, as in Joyce's earlier fiction, the reader has learned to distinguish between presentations of action in a fictive external world and presentations of characters' thoughts. Such distinctions are not always easy to make in those early episodes, and they largely disappear during the middle ones. They are impossible to make in the final episode of Part II ['Circe']" (Riquelme 138).

20 Gleick provides a basic example of such "bifurcation" in his description of the biologist Robert May's graph of population fluctuations, his picture of the "boom and bust" behavior generated in a dynamic system by fluctuating rates of growth and the tendency for populations to "oscillate" in time among two or more alternating values (70): "The level of the parameter [representing increasing values for rate of growth] was plotted horizontally, increasing from left to right. The population was represented vertically. For each parameter, May plotted a point representing the final outcome, after the system reached equilibrium. At the left, where the parameter was low, this outcome would be just a point, so different parameters produced a line rising slightly from left to right. When the parameter passed the first critical point, May would have to plot two populations: the line would split in two, making a sideways Y or a pitchfork. This split corresponded to a population going from a one-year cycle to a two-year cycle. As the parameter rose further, the number of points doubled again, then again, then again. It was dumbfounding—such complex behavior, and yet so tantalizingly regular" (72).

21 As Hart makes clear (Introduction), Joyce—corresponding through Lucie and Paul Léon, the "amanuenses" responsible for the "idiosyncratic spelling" in this quotation (xiii n)—provided Budgen a number of ideas and suggestions for *James Joyce and the Making of "Ulysses,"* "turn[ing] some parts of it into a collaborative effort" (xiii). Budgen transports Joyce's suggestion directly into his concluding chapter: "In *Work in Progress* he creates his own [symbols], and these are intentionally trivial in the original, literal sense of the word. We are led by three ways to a place where the ways of departure are also three" (*James Joyce* 318). Although Budgen's definition somewhat complicates the picture, and may easily be misread as intersection of six branches at one point, the term *trivial* clearly refers to a fork in a road, a bifurcation, or as Oedipus, whose deterministic fate rested on a trivial, chance circumstance, would say, a "place where three roads join. . . . Chance rules our lives, and the future is all unknown" (Sophocles 48, 52).

22 Kauffman develops this view of the edge of chaos into a new interpretation of evolution in *The Origins of Order* (for a nontechnical introduction to this new in-

terpretation, see Kauffman's *At Home in the Universe*). Kauffman is a central figure in Lewin's and Waldrop's recent accounts of the developing sciences of complexity (q.v.); see also Brockman 333–43.

23 For various versions of the naming of the quark, see Morris 13, Boslough 655, and Gell-Mann 180–81; see also appendix B ("The Quark").

24 For additional views of the emergent "behavior" of *Ulysses*, see French, Goldman 74–117, and Riquelme 131–229.

25 See Pagels's discussion of cognition and consciousness (*Dreams of Reason* 180–240) and the survey of recent theories of consciousness in chapter 5 of the present work.

26 Waldrop discusses economist Brian Arthur's evolution of his heterodox theory of "increasing returns" and the VHS versus Beta competition (35–36 and passim); one of Arthur's most intriguing examples of the phenomenon of increasing returns is the emergence of the QWERTY keyboard, a deliberately awkward alignment of typewriter keys (meant to slow the typist and prevent jamming in early machines) that nevertheless came to dominate the industry, eliminating other and better formats and remaining the standard keyboard today (Waldrop 35). For similar applications of this idea to account for the railway industry's adoption of a standard rail gauge, the emergence of the "Silicon Valley" in Santa Clara, California, and the recent ascendancy of Japanese autos in the world economy, see Mainzer 262–65.

27 Both Pagels (*Dreams of Reason* 23) and Murdoch (26–31 and passim) argue that Wittgenstein does not, in fact, rule out metaphysics and theology in his *Tractatus*; he simply exposes the limits of logic. Proposition 6.41 actually implies that a higher design may exist (perhaps perceptible from the fourth dimension of non-Euclidean geometry?).

28 For a similar argument, see French 239; for the most extended reading of *Ulysses* in light of quantum theory, see Booker, and for a convincing argument for an aboriginal reality in the novel, beyond the influence or control of the observer, see Perlis; see also appendix A. There is no inconsistency between Stephen's assumption that the individual "ineluctably construct[s]" his own cognitive map "upon the incertitude of the void" (*U* 17.1014–15), his "quantum" view of reality, and my earlier recognitions of the metaphysical determinism embedded in Stephen's "Messenger" interpolation (*U* 7.762–65), his Maeterlinck quotation (*U* 9.1042–44), and his linear view of history ("was that only possible which came to pass?" [*U* 2.52]). For Stephen, metaphysical determinism is quite simply a conscious construct that he imposes on incertitude—much as he constructs Shakespeare's life and work in "Scylla and Charybdis"—rather than a mode of belief: "Do you believe your own theory?—No, Stephen said promptly" (*U* 9.1065–67).

29 This schema for the relations between literary theory and the paradigm shifts in

twentieth-century science is clearly more pertinent to the evolution of Anglo-American and French critical theory than to the development of central and eastern European critical theory. One could argue that Russian critics (e.g., Bakhtin) and the theorists of the Frankfurt school—as I observe at the conclusion of chapter 2 and note again in chapter 4—responded more immediately to the implications of new scientific conceptions. See also appendix B ("Relativity" and "The Copenhagen Interpretation").

30 Several of the essays and notes published in the 1993 "Joyce and Advertising" double issue of *James Joyce Quarterly*, edited by Garry Leonard—where Wicke's article appears—illustrate a similar consciousness of "complexity"; see, in particular, Connor; Leonard, "Joyce and Advertising"; idem, "Power"; and Tratner.

CHAPTER 4: FINNEGANS *WAKE*

1 See also Begnal, Begnal and Senn ix–xi, and Norris, *Decentered Universe* 1–9.

2 See also Suter 64; Joyce frequently used variants of this tunneling metaphor for his composition of the *Wake* in his letters to Harriet Shaw Weaver (see *Letters I* and *Letters III*).

3 See, respectively, Litz, *James Joyce* 99–100; Norris, *Decentered Universe* 10–22; Tindall, *Reader's Guide* 237; and Benstock, *Joyce-Again's Wake* 3.

4 For the principal introductions to the sciences of complexity, see Cohen and Stewart's *Collapse of Chaos* (1994), Lewin's *Complexity* (1992), Pagels's *Dreams of Reason* (1988), and Waldrop's *Complexity* (1992); for a rather more technical account of the current state of complexity science across many disciplines (physics, biology, neuroscience, computer technology, economics, and information systems), see Mainzer's *Thinking in Complexity* (1994). At the time of this writing, no work of literary criticism has explored the value of a complex-systems approach to the literary work; however, in *The Art of Excess* Tom LeClair comes close as he analyzes the masterworks of complexity in contemporary American fiction (e.g., Pynchon's *Gravity's Rainbow* and Gaddis's *J.R.*). LeClair approaches these novels armed with several concepts drawn from Ludwig von Bertalanffy's interdisciplinary general systems theory, a distant precursor of complexity theory (6–13). His contention that the "systems novels" he studies "are primarily reconstructive, showing how orders and forms in the world (and not just the artistic text) can arise out of seeming chaos" (21), resembles my view here of *Finnegans Wake* as a self-organized system.

5 For the best recent essay on the influence of modern technology on the *Wake*, concentrating on three fields that are also prominent in complexity studies—chemistry, mathematics, and mechanics—see Theall; see also appendix A.

6 See also appendix B ("Relativity" and "Quantum Theory"); Bachelard, *New Scientific Spirit* 61–72; and Canetti, *Crowds and Power* 29–30, 75 (Canetti took a degree in

chemistry from the University of Vienna). Two other obvious public "events" of the postwar era that intensified the communal sense of the unpredictable, uncontrollable, and apparently incomprehensible nature of social phenomena are the flu pandemic of the late 1910s and the worldwide Great Depression of the 1930s. I already mentioned (in chap. 3) how contemporary virologists have begun to apply the insights of complexity science to the study of epidemics; Klaus Mainzer describes how economic theory responded to the depression by formulating inadequate linear economic models for business cycles, models that recent economists have "easily reformulated in the framework of nonlinear systems" (257) to better understand global behaviors like the postwar crash or (an even more immediate stimulus) the oil crisis of the 1970s (254–65).

7 Kauffman applies the concepts of complexity science to study the integrated dynamical and regulatory behavior of genes—the middle-range between small-scale chemical synthesis of proteins and the large-scale phenomena of life—and to narrow further the gap between the study of genetics and the global theory of evolution (*Origins* 441–522 and passim).

8 "Recurrent networks" in the brain, Churchland writes, "display a feature . . . of being predictable only within statistical limits. The cycling sequences of [information flow] within a recurrent network are *nonlinear* in the intuitive sense that they do not 'follow a straight line.' A recurrent network's unfolding path [graphed in a multidimensional] activation space is a winding path—sometimes curving gently, sometimes zig-zagging sharply—a path that is at times stable against small perturbations, and at other times shows an exquisite sensitivity to infinitesimally small influences from any quarter. That is to say, a nonlinear system is one in which, at least occasionally, even the tiniest of differences in its current state will quickly be magnified into very large differences in its subsequent state. Since we can never have *infinitely* accurate information about the current state of any physical system, let alone for a system of the complexity of the living brain, we are doomed to be forever limited in what we can predict about such a system's unfolding behavior, even if there are, and even if we happen to know, the inviolable laws that govern the system's behavior. Such systems are strictly deterministic, in the sense of being law governed, but they are nevertheless unpredictable, beyond their statistical regularities, by any cognitive system within the same physical universe" (113).

9 Thus complexity theory in neuroscience effectively dismisses the long-standing Cartesian assumption of the *res cogitans*, the notion that there is a mind separate from and in control of the brain, a "deeper headquarters, any inner sanctum," or even a "*functional* center" that minds the mind (Dennett 106). See Dennett's entire discussion of the persistence of the concept of the "Cartesian theater," the image of a central locus in the brain where the mind "all comes together" (107), in the neurological and philosophical study of consciousness (101–38);

see also Damasio 94–96, 247–51, and Horkheimer's discussion of the *res cogitans* ("On the Problem of Truth" 408–9), quoted at the conclusion of chapter 2.

10 For a recent discussion of the shared problems of contemporary AI research and critical theory, see Herbert Simon's "Literary Criticism" and the thirty-three responses to his article, collected in Franchi and Güzeldere's "Bridging the Gap." For Searle's attack on the "basic assumption behind cognitive science . . . that the brain is a computer and mental processes are computational" (198), see his *Rediscovery of the Mind* (1992), 197–226 and passim. For sharp rejoinders to Searle, see Churchland 203–8, 244–46, and Dennett, who responds to earlier versions of his attack (435–40 and passim). In his best-seller *The Emperor's New Mind* (1989), physicist Roger Penrose speculates that the ultimate key to the origins of consciousness might be sought in "some more complete, but as yet undiscovered, theory" of quantum gravity (297) and a consequent "change in the very framework of quantum theory" (348). Picturing the mind as a " 'quantum computer,' " Penrose suggests that "there could conceivably be some relation between th[e] 'oneness' of consciousness and *quantum parallelism*" in the neuronic communication of the brain: "a large number of different activities, all occurring simultaneously" (399). Again, for rejoinders, see Churchland 246–50 and Brockman 248–57. Murray Gell-Mann succinctly states the case against Penrose's assumption that two things that we cannot understand, quantum gravity and consciousness, must be connected: "I can see absolutely no reason for imagining such a thing" (qtd. in Brockman 256).

11 Churchland describes the multidimensional complexity of the brain's processing of sensory phenomena—which we can represent graphically by "vector coding" in "activation space"—ranging from the relatively simple four-dimensional "taste-space," which may represent the four taste sensations (23), to the "at least twenty"-dimensional coding space that would be necessary to represent facial recognition (29). Any attempt to graphically represent "social space" (123–50) or intelligence in activation space would call for even higher dimensions: "we must keep in mind this fundamental point that intelligence is a high-dimensional vector rather than a one-dimensional magnitude" (255).

12 I should express here two caveats for my occasional use of the term "complexity theory": first, as an emergent interdisciplinary approach in the natural and social sciences, the sciences of complexity cannot yet be said to possess anything as formal as a unified theory and methodology; second, there already exists a branch of mathematical logic called "complexity theory," which, although a prominent influence on the study of complexity in systems (particularly for the concept of "algorithmic complexity," described later), should not be confused with the broader study of complexity.

13 See also Nicolis and Prigogine 196–97, 214, and Pagels, *Dreams of Reason* 45, 329.

14 Murdoch offers a penetrating analysis of the solipsistic implications of post-

structuralism (185–216); Riquelme makes subtle the postmodernist celebration of subjectivity by arguing that Joyce simultaneously undermines and reinforces the reader's sense of an origin in *Finnegans Wake* (34 and passim).

15 See, for example, the chapters on *Finnegans Wake* in Cheng's *Joyce, Race, and Empire*, Herr's *Joyce's Anatomy of Culture*, and Norris's *Joyce's Web*.

16 For additional discussion of the concept of the "edge of chaos," see Kauffman, *Origins* 208–27, 255–63, and *At Home* 86–92, 257–64; see also Lewin 44–62 and passim.

17 For a survey of the most ambitious applications of complexity theory to social phenomena such as the nonlinear "dynamics of an economy" and to the analysis of the social impact of technological innovations, urban growth, migration, and evolving "complex communication networks" (237–38), see Mainzer's chapter "Complex Systems and the Evolution of Human Society" (237–88); see also Kauffman, *At Home* 236–304.

18 Connor compares the half-ordered and half-chaotic text of *Finnegans Wake* to the "wondrous, often mysterious jumble of signal and noise, vastly fluid," of early radio broadcasts, which he suspects influenced Joyce's "audial" experiment (830). The concept of maximum information comes from Claude Shannon's *Mathematical Theory of Information* (1949), cited by Connor (825–26); for additional discussion of the information content of systems at the edge of chaos, see Lewin 52–55.

19 Although incompatible with the quantum theory that made it almost immediately obsolete, Rutherford's model of the atom has remained popular, primarily for ideological reasons: it offers a readily visualized picture (i.e., the Cartesian perceptual model), and it implies that a symmetry, a design, joins the microcosm to the macrocosm; see Pagels, *Cosmic Code* 51–53; for Joyce's interest in and allusions to Rutherford in *Finnegans Wake*, see Kuberski 58–62.

20 See Hardison's chapter "From Ajax to Eniac" (290–99) and Aspray's "Theory of Information Processing" (173–212). For an excellent historical survey of mechanical automata, from ancient China to the present, see Mazlish's "Man-Machine and Artificial Intelligence."

21 For the best introduction to this research field, see Levy's *Artificial Life*; for more discussion of Langton's project, see Levy 93–120 and Waldrop's chapter "Life at the Edge of Chaos" (198–240).

22 For a technical account of computer modeling strategies, see Vemuri's *Modeling of Complex Systems*.

23 For fuller discussion of the principal measures of complexity described here—algorithmic, physical, and logical complexity—see Pagels, *Dreams of Reason* 57–67.

24 See Hart, *Structure* 161–81 and passim; Hayman 36–55; and McHugh, *Sigla*.

25 See also Hart's discussion of the fundamental simplicity of Joyce's methods for his book (*Structure* 23–43).

26 Several recent books examine Joyce's reversal, unraveling, and recycling of his earlier techniques and themes in the *Wake*; see Devlin's *Wandering and Return in "Finnegans Wake,"* Hayman's *"Wake" in Transit*, and Norris's *Joyce's Web*.

27 For a fine discussion of the cultural significance of this question of the genre of the *Wake*, see Attridge, *Peculiar Language* 231–38; although Norris argued for "abandoning the novelistic approach to *Finnegans Wake*" in 1976 (*Decentered Universe* 22), her recent studies of Joyce's mediation of "social reality," in *Joyce's Web*, suggest that she now views the *Wake* as a "novel" in all but name.

28 For a good discussion of Joyce's "cagey" comments on "the relationship of *Finnegans Wake* to dreams and dreaming," see Bishop 6–9.

29 Besides cutting Weaver's remark, Ellmann provides no source for his earlier statement that, "as Joyce informed a friend later, he conceived of his book as [a] dream" (*JJII* 544), a claim on which he rests his unequivocal reading of the dream of *Finnegans Wake*. Although it is true that the usually reliable source of information about Joyce's intentions, Frank Budgen, assumes both that Joyce's book is a dream record and that he, himself, provided Joyce "the lightning flash of inspiration" ("Joyce's Chapters" 324), Budgen makes no claim that Joyce confided his conception of the *Wake* to him.

30 See Norris's Freudian reading of the "dream-work" of *Finnegans Wake* (*Decentered Universe* 5–9 and passim); see also Churchland's devastating critique, in terms of recent neuroscientific research, of the Freudian conception of the unconscious as overdetermined by the conscious (181–83): "Freud's theory" of the unconscious "was just commonsense psychology relocated one level down. It was also dubious in the extreme. The problem was not Freud's postulation of unconscious cognitive processes. Not at all. The vast majority of our cognitive activities take place at levels well below the conscious level. Rather, the problem was Freud's assumption that the *causal structure* of those unconscious cognitive activities is the same as the causal structure of our conscious cognitive activities, as represented in our commonsense prototypes for beliefs, desires, fears, and practical reasoning. . . . [Our] underlying cognitive activities are exceedingly unlikely to have such a sentence-like and inference-like structure" (182).

31 See "Hegemony, Relations of Force, Historical Bloc" in Gramsci 189–221; for Bachelard's immediate influence on Michel Foucault's conception of mutating epistemes in "the order of things," see Merquior 39–42. Despite the later dates of *Negative Dialectics* (1966) and *Crowds and Power* (1960), both Adorno and Canetti were developing their anti-Cartesian theses contemporaneous with Joyce's writing of "Work in Progress"; see Jameson's *Late Marxism* and Canetti's memoirs, *The Torch in My Ear* (1980) and *The Play of the Eyes* (1985).

WORKS CITED

Adams, Robert M. *James Joyce: Common Sense and Beyond.* New York: Random House, 1967.

———. *Surface and Symbol: The Consistency of James Joyce's "Ulysses."* New York: Oxford University Press, 1962.

Adorno, Theodor W. *Negative Dialectics (Negative Dialektik).* Trans. E. B. Ashton. New York: Continuum, 1973.

———. "Subject and Object." 1969. Trans. E. B. Ashton. *The Essential Frankfurt School Reader.* Ed. Andrew Arato and Eike Gebhardt. New York: Continuum, 1982. 497–511.

Albert, Leonard. "Gnomonology: Joyce's 'The Sisters.'" *James Joyce Quarterly* 27, no. 2 (1990): 353–64.

Aleksandrov, P. S. "Poincaré and Topology." *The Mathematical Heritage of Henri Poincaré.* Ed. Felix E. Browder. Providence: American Mathematical Society, 1983. 2:245–55.

Anderson, Chester G., ed. *"A Portrait of the Artist as a Young Man": Text, Criticism, and Notes.* New York: Viking, 1968.

apRoberts, Robert. "'Araby' and the Palimpsest of Criticism: Or, Through a Glass Eye Darkly." *Antioch Review* 26 (1966–67): 469–89.

Arnheim, Rudolf. *Art and Visual Perception: A Psychology of the Creative Eye.* Berkeley: University of California Press, 1969.

Aronowitz, Stanley. *Science as Power: Discourse and Ideology in Modern Society.* Minneapolis: University of Minnesota Press, 1988.

Aspray, William. *John von Neumann and the Origins of Modern Computing.* Cambridge, Mass.: MIT Press, 1990.

Atherton, James S. *The Books at the Wake: A Study of Literary Allusions in James Joyce's "Finnegans Wake."* New York: Viking, 1960.

———. "The Joyce of Dubliners." *James Joyce Today: Essays on the Major Works.* Ed. Thomas F. Staley. Bloomington: Indiana University Press, 1966. 28–53.

Attridge, Derek. "*Finnegans Wake*: The Dream of Interpretation." *James Joyce Quarterly* 27, no. 1 (1989): 11–29.

———. *Peculiar Language: Literature as Difference from the Renaissance to James Joyce*. Ithaca, N.Y.: Cornell University Press, 1988.

Attridge, Derek, and Daniel Ferrer, eds. *Post-Structuralist Joyce: Essays from the French*. Cambridge: Cambridge University Press, 1984.

Aubert, Jacques. "riverrun." *Post-Structuralist Joyce: Essays from the French*. Ed. Derek Attridge and Daniel Ferrer. Cambridge: Cambridge University Press, 1984. 69–77.

Bachelard, Gaston. *La Formation de l'espirit scientifique*. Paris: Vrin, 1938.

———. *The New Scientific Spirit (Le nouvel espirit scientifique)*. Trans. Arthur Goldhammer. Boston: Beacon, 1984.

———. *The Philosophy of No: A Philosophy of the New Scientific Mind*. Trans. G. C. Waterson. New York: Orion, 1968.

Baggott, Jim. *The Meaning of Quantum Theory*. Oxford: Oxford University Press, 1992.

Ball, W. W. Rouse. *Mathematical Recreations and Essays*. 10th ed. London: Macmillan, 1922.

Barrow, John D. *Pi in the Sky: Counting, Thinking, and Being*. Oxford: Clarendon, 1992.

———. *Theories of Everything: The Quest for Ultimate Explanation*. Oxford: Clarendon, 1991.

———. *The World within the World*. Oxford: Oxford University Press, 1988.

Bartley, W. W., III. Editor's Foreword. *The Open Universe: An Argument for Indeterminism*, by Karl Popper. Totowa, N.J.: Rowman and Littlefield, 1982. xi–xvi.

Beck, Warren. *Joyce's* Dubliners: *Substance, Vision, and Art*. Durham, N.C.: Duke University Press, 1969.

Beckett, Samuel, et al. *Our Exagmination round His Factification for Incamination of "Work in Progress."* Paris: Shakespeare and Co., 1929.

Begnal, Michael. Rev. of *The Sigla of "Finnegans Wake,"* by Roland McHugh. *James Joyce Quarterly* 15, no. 1 (1977): 96–97.

Begnal, Michael, and Fritz Senn. *A Conceptual Guide to "Finnegans Wake."* University Park: Pennsylvania State University Press, 1974.

Bell, E. T. *Men of Mathematics*. New York: Simon and Schuster, 1938.

Benjamin, Walter. "What Is Epic Theater?" *Illuminations: Essays and Reflections*. Trans. Harry Zohn. Ed. Hannah Arendt. New York: Schocken, 1968. 147–54.

Benstock, Bernard. *James Joyce*. New York: Ungar, 1985.

———. *Joyce-Again's Wake*. Seattle: University of Washington Press, 1965.

———, ed. *The Seventh of Joyce*. Bloomington: Indiana University Press, 1982.

Bergonzi, Bernard. *The Early H. G. Wells: A Study of the Scientific Romances*. Manchester: Manchester University Press, 1961.

Berry, Michael. "Quantum Physics at the Edge of Chaos." *Exploring Chaos: A Guide to the New Sciences of Disorder*. Ed. Nina Hall. New York: Norton, 1993. 184–95.

Best, Steven. "Chaos and Entropy: Metaphors in Postmodern Science and Social Theory." *Science as Culture* 2, no. 11 (1991): 188–226.

Bishop, John. *Joyce's Book of the Dark: "Finnegans Wake."* Madison: University of Wisconsin Press, 1986.

Blumenthal, Leonard M. *A Modern View of Geometry.* San Francisco: Freeman, 1961.
Boi, Luciano, Dominique Flament, and Jean-Michel Salanskis, eds. *1830–1930: A Century of Geometry: Epistemology, History and Mathematics.* Berlin: Springer, 1992.
Boldrini, Lucia. " 'The Sisters' and the *Inferno*: An Intertextual Network." *Style* 25, no. 3 (1991): 453–65.
Bonola, Roberto. *Non-Euclidean Geometry: A Critical and Historical Study of Its Development (La Geometria Non-Euclidea).* 2d rev. ed. Trans. H. S. Carslaw. LaSalle, Ill.: Open Court, 1938.
Booker, M. Keith. "Joyce, Planck, Einstein, and Heisenberg: A Relativistic Quantum Mechanical Discussion of *Ulysses*." *James Joyce Quarterly* 27, no. 3 (1990): 577–86.
Boslough, John. "Worlds within the Atom." *National Geographic* 167 (May 1985): 634–63.
Boyle, Robert, S.J. "Swiftian Allegory and Dantean Parody in Joyce's 'Grace.' " *James Joyce Quarterly* 7 (1969): 11–21.
Bradley, Bruce, S.J. *James Joyce's Schooldays.* New York: St. Martin's, 1982.
Brandabur, Edward. *A Scrupulous Meanness: A Study of Joyce's Early Work.* Urbana: University of Illinois Press, 1971.
Brecht, Bertolt. "Alienation Effects in Chinese Acting." *Brecht on Theatre: The Development of an Aesthetic.* Ed. and trans. John Willett. New York: Hill and Wang, 1964. 91–99.
Brockman, John. *The Third Culture: Beyond the Scientific Revolution.* New York: Simon and Schuster, 1995.
Browder, Felix E., ed. *The Mathematical Heritage of Henri Poincaré.* 2 vols. Providence, R.I.: American Mathematical Society, 1983.
Brown, Homer O. *James Joyce's Early Fiction: The Biography of a Form.* Cleveland: The Press of Case Western Reserve University, 1972.
Budgen, Frank. "Further Recollections of James Joyce." *James Joyce and the Making of "Ulysses" and Other Writings.* Ed. Clive Hart. London: Oxford University Press, 1972. 349–66.
———. "James Joyce." *James Joyce and the Making of "Ulysses" and Other Writings.* Ed. Clive Hart. London: Oxford University Press, 1972. 343–48.
———. *James Joyce and the Making of "Ulysses" and Other Writings.* Ed. Clive Hart. London: Oxford University Press, 1972.
———. "Joyce's Chapters of Going Forth by Day." *James Joyce and the Making of "Ulysses" and Other Writings.* Ed. Clive Hart. London: Oxford University Press, 1972. 323–42.
Burke, Kenneth. "Three Definitions." *Kenyon Review* 13 (1951): 173–92.
Butterfield, Herbert. *The Origins of Modern Science, 1300–1800.* Rev. ed. New York: Free Press, 1965.
Calder, Nigel. *Einstein's Universe.* New York: Greenwich House, 1979.
Canetti, Elias. *Crowds and Power (Masse und Macht).* Trans. Carol Stewart. London: Gollancz, 1962.
———. *The Play of the Eyes.* Trans. Ralph Manheim. New York: Farrar, Straus, Giroux, 1986.

———. *The Torch in My Ear.* Trans. Joachim Neugroschel. New York: Farrar, Straus, Giroux, 1982.

Capra, Fritjof. *The Tao of Physics: An Exploration of the Parallels between Modern Physics and Eastern Mysticism.* 3d ed. Boston: Shambhala, 1991.

Carroll, Lewis [pseud. of Charles L. Dodgson]. *Euclid and His Modern Rivals.* 2d ed., 1885. New York: Dover, 1973.

———. *Mathematical Recreations of Lewis Carroll.* 2 vols. New York: Dover, 1958.

Carslaw, H. S. Translator's Preface. *Non-Euclidean Geometry: A Critical and Historical Study of Its Development,* by Roberto Bonola. 2d rev. ed. Trans. Carslaw. LaSalle, Ill.: Open Court, 1938. v.

Casti, John L. *Complexification: Explaining a Paradoxical World through the Science of Surprise.* New York: HarperCollins, 1994.

Caton, Hiram. *The Origin of Subjectivity: An Essay on Descartes.* New Haven, Conn.: Yale University Press, 1973.

Cheng, Vincent J. *Joyce, Race, and Empire.* Cambridge: Cambridge University Press, 1995.

Church, Margaret. "*Dubliners* and Vico." *James Joyce Quarterly* 5 (1968): 150–56.

Churchland, Paul M. *The Engine of Reason, the Seat of the Soul: A Philosophical Journey into the Brain.* Cambridge, Mass.: MIT Press, 1995.

Cixous, Hélène. "Joyce: The (R)use of Writing." *Post-Structuralist Joyce: Essays from the French.* Ed. Derek Attridge and Daniel Ferrer. Cambridge: Cambridge University Press, 1984. 15–30.

Cohen, Jack, and Ian Stewart. *The Collapse of Chaos: Discovering Simplicity in a Complex World.* New York: Viking, 1994.

Comens, Bruce. "Narrative Nets and Lyric Flights in Joyce's *A Portrait.*" *James Joyce Quarterly* 29, no. 2 (1992): 297–314.

Connor, James A., S.J. "Radio Free Joyce: *Wake* Language and the Experience of Radio." *James Joyce Quarterly* 30, no. 4–31, no. 1 (1993): 825–43.

Conrad, Joseph. *Heart of Darkness. Joseph Conrad: "Heart of Darkness": A Case Study in Contemporary Criticism.* Ed. Ross C. Murfin. New York: St. Martin's, 1989. 17–94.

Conrad, Joseph, and Ford Madox Hueffer. *The Inheritors: An Extravagant Story.* London: Heinemann, 1901.

Copleston, Frederick, S.J. *Medieval Philosophy: Augustine to Bonaventure* and *Albert the Great to Duns Scotus.* 1950. Vol. 2, parts 1 and 2, of *A History of Philosophy.* 8 vols. Westminster, Md.: Newman, 1946–66.

———. *Modern Philosophy: Descartes to Leibniz.* 1960. Vol. 4 of *A History of Philosophy.* 8 vols. Westminster, Md.: Newman, 1946–66.

———. *Modern Philosophy: Kant.* 1960. Vol. 6, part 2, of *A History of Philosophy.* 8 vols. Westminster, Md.: Newman, 1946–66.

Corcoran, T., S.J. *The Clongowes Record, 1814 to 1932.* Dublin: Browne and Nolan, n.d.

Cox, C. B., and A. E. Dyson. 1900–1918. Vol. 1 of *The Twentieth-Century Mind.* 3 vols. London: Oxford University Press, 1972.

Damasio, Antonio R. *Descartes' Error: Emotion, Reason, and the Human Brain.* New York: Putnam's, 1994.

Dante. *The Divine Comedy of Dante Alighieri.* Ed. and trans. John D. Sinclair. 3 vols. New York: Oxford University Press, 1939.

Deane, Paul. "Motion Picture Techniques in James Joyce's 'The Dead.'" *James Joyce Quarterly* 6, no. 3 (1969): 231–36.

De Man, Paul. *Allegories of Reading: Figural Language in Rousseau, Nietzsche, Rilke, and Proust.* New Haven, Conn.: Yale University Press, 1979.

Deming, Robert H., ed. *James Joyce: The Critical Heritage.* 2 vols. London: Routledge, 1970.

Dennett, Daniel C. *Consciousness Explained.* Boston: Little, Brown, 1991.

Derrida, Jacques. *Of Grammatology (De la grammatologie).* Trans. Gayatri C. Spivak. Baltimore: Johns Hopkins University Press, 1976.

———. "Structure, Sign, and Play in the Discourse of the Human Sciences." Trans. Richard Macksey and Alan Bass. *Writing and Difference (L'Ecriture et la différence).* Ed. Bass. Chicago: University of Chicago Press, 1978. 278–93.

———. "Two Words for Joyce." *Post-Structuralist Joyce: Essays from the French.* Ed. Derek Attridge and Daniel Ferrer. Cambridge: Cambridge University Press, 1984. 145–59.

Descartes, René. *Discourse on the Method of Rightly Conducting the Reason and Seeking Truth in the Field of Science. Philosophical Essays.* Trans. Laurence J. Lafleur. Indianapolis: Bobbs-Merrill, 1964. 3–57.

Dettmar, Kevin J. H. "Selling *Ulysses.*" *James Joyce Quarterly* 30, no. 4–31, no. 1 (1993): 795–812.

Devlin, Kimberly J. *Wandering and Return in "Finnegans Wake": An Integrative Approach to Joyce's Fictions.* Princeton, N.J.: Princeton University Press, 1991.

Dewey, John. *Experience and Nature.* Chicago: Open Court, 1925.

———. *The Quest for Certainty.* New York: Minton, Balch, 1929.

DiBernard, Barbara. "Parallax as Parallel, Paradigm, and Paradox in *Ulysses.*" *Eire* 10, no. 1 (1975): 69–84.

Duffy, Charles F. "The Seating Arrangement in 'Grace.'" *James Joyce Quarterly* 9 (1972): 487–89.

Duffy, Enda. *The Subaltern "Ulysses."* Minneapolis: University of Minnesota Press, 1994.

Duszenko, Andrzej. *The Joyce of Science: New Physics in "Finnegans Wake."* Ann Arbor: UMI, 1989.

———. "The Relativity Theory in *Finnegans Wake.*" *James Joyce Quarterly* 32, no. 1 (1994): 61–70.

Eco, Umberto. *The Aesthetics of Chaosmos: The Middle Ages of James Joyce.* Trans. Ellen Esrock. No. 18 in the University of Tulsa Monograph Series. Tulsa, Okla.: University of Tulsa, 1982.

Eichenbaum, Boris. "The Theory of the 'Formal Method.'" *Russian Formalist Criticism: Four Essays.* Trans. and ed. Lee T. Lemon and Marion J. Reis. Lincoln: University of Nebraska Press, 1965. 99–139.

Ellmann, Richard. *The Consciousness of Joyce.* New York: Oxford University Press, 1977.

———. *James Joyce.* Rev. ed. New York: Oxford University Press, 1982.

———. *"Ulysses" on the Liffey.* New York: Oxford University Press, 1972.

Enriques, Federigo. Introduction. *Non-Euclidean Geometry: A Critical and Historical Study of Its Development,* by Roberto Bonola. 2d rev. ed. Trans. H. S. Carslaw. LaSalle, Ill.: Open Court, 1938. iii–iv.

Euclid. *The Thirteen Books of Euclid's Elements.* Trans. Thomas L. Heath. Chicago: Encyclopedia Britannica, 1951.

Farwell, Ruth, and Christopher Knee. "The Geometric Challenge of Riemann and Clifford." *1830–1930: A Century of Geometry: Epistemology, History and Mathematics.* Ed. Luciano Boi, Dominique Flament, and Jean-Michel Salanskis. Berlin: Springer, 1992. 98–106.

Fauvel, John, Raymond Flood, and Robin Wilson, eds. *Möbius and His Band.* Oxford: Oxford University Press, 1993.

Fleishman, Avrom. "Science in 'Ithaca': An Examination of the Physical Sciences in *Ulysses.*" *Fiction and the Ways of Knowing.* Austin: University of Texas Press, 1978. 136–48.

Fletcher, Angus. *Allegory: The Theory of a Symbolic Mode.* Ithaca, N.Y.: Cornell University Press, 1964.

Franchi, Stefano, and Güven Güzeldere, eds. "Bridging the Gap: Where Cognitive Science Meets Literary Criticism." *Stanford Humanities Review* 4, no. 1 (1995): n.p. (WWW: electronic journal).

———, eds. "Constructions of the Mind: Artificial Intelligence and the Humanities." *Stanford Humanities Review* 4, no. 2 (1995): n.p. (WWW: electronic journal).

———. "Mindless Mechanisms, Mindful Constructions." *Stanford Humanities Review* 4, no. 2 (1995): n.p. (WWW: electronic journal).

French, Marilyn. *The Book as World: James Joyce's "Ulysses."* Cambridge, Mass.: Harvard University Press, 1976.

Friedman, Alan J. "*Ulysses* and Modern Science." *The Seventh of Joyce.* Ed. Bernard Benstock. Bloomington: Indiana University Press, 1982. 198–206.

Gabler, Hans Walter. Preface. *James Joyce: "Dubliners": A Facsimile of Drafts & Manuscripts.* Arr. Gabler. New York: Garland, 1978. xxv–xxxi.

———. "The Seven Lost Years of *A Portrait of the Artist as a Young Man.*" *Approaches to Joyce's "Portrait": Ten Essays.* Ed. Thomas F. Staley and Bernard Benstock. Pittsburgh: University of Pittsburgh Press, 1976. 25–60.

Gell-Mann, Murray. *The Quark and the Jaguar: Adventures in the Simple and the Complex.* New York: Freeman, 1994.

Ghiselin, Brewster. "The Unity of Joyce's *Dubliners.*" *"Dubliners": Text, Criticism, and Notes.* Ed. Robert Scholes and A. Walton Litz. New York: Viking, 1969. 316–32.

Gifford, Don. *Joyce Annotated: Notes for "Dubliners" and "A Portrait of the Artist as a Young Man."* 2d rev. ed. Berkeley: University of California Press, 1982.

———. *"Ulysses" Annotated: Notes for James Joyce's* Ulysses. Rev. ed. Berkeley: University of California Press, 1988.

Gifford, Don, with Robert J. Seidman. *Notes for Joyce: An Annotation of James Joyce's "Ulysses."* New York: Dutton, 1974.

Gilbert, Stuart. *James Joyce's "Ulysses": A Study.* 2d ed. New York: Knopf, 1952.

Gillespie, Michael Patrick. "Kenner on Joyce." *Re-Viewing Classics of Joyce Criticism.* Ed. Janet Egleson Dunleavy. Urbana: University of Illinois Press, 1991. 142–54.

Gleick, James. *Chaos: Making a New Science.* New York: Viking, 1987.

Glicksberg, Charles I. *The Tragic Vision in Twentieth-Century Literature.* Carbondale: Southern Illinois University Press, 1963.

Goldman, Arnold. *The Joyce Paradox: Form and Freedom in his Fiction.* Evanston, Ill.: Northwestern University Press, 1966.

Gorman, Herbert S. *James Joyce.* Rev. ed. New York: Rinehart, 1948.

———. *James Joyce: His First Forty Years.* New York: Huebsch, 1924.

Gould, Stephen Jay. *Wonderful Life: The Burgess Shale and the Nature of History.* New York: Norton, 1989.

Gramsci, Antonio. *An Antonio Gramsci Reader: Selected Writings, 1916–1935.* Trans. William Boelhower, Quintin Hoare, and Geoffrey Nowell-Smith. Ed. David Forgacs. New York: Schocken, 1988.

Graves, Robert, and Alan Hodge. *The Long Week-End: A Social History of Great Britain, 1918–1939.* 2d ed. New York: Norton, 1963.

Groden, Michael. *"Ulysses" in Progress.* Princeton, N.J.: Princeton University Press, 1977.

Gross, Paul R., and Norman Levitt. *Higher Superstition: The Academic Left and Its Quarrels with Science.* Baltimore: Johns Hopkins University Press, 1994.

Hacking, Ian. "Experimentation and Scientific Realism." *Scientific Realism.* Ed. Jarrett Leplin. Berkeley: University of California Press, 1984. 154–72.

Hall, Nina, ed. *Exploring Chaos: A Guide to the New Sciences of Disorder.* New York: Norton, 1993.

Hardison, O. B., Jr. *Disappearing through the Skylight: Culture and Technology in the Twentieth Century.* New York: Viking, 1989.

Hardwick, Elizabeth. "A Lion at His Desk." *New Yorker* 8 May 1995: 85–89.

Hart, Clive. Introduction. *James Joyce and the Making of "Ulysses" and Other Writings.* Ed. Hart. London: Oxford University Press, 1972. vii–xix.

———. *Structure and Motif in "Finnegans Wake."* Evanston, Ill.: Northwestern University Press, 1962.

Hassan, Ihab. "Joyce and the Gnosis of Modern Science." *The Seventh of Joyce.* Ed. Bernard Benstock. Bloomington: Indiana University Press, 1982. 185–90.

Hawking, Stephen. *A Brief History of Time: From the Big Bang to Black Holes.* New York: Bantam, 1988.

Hayles, N. Katherine, ed. *Chaos and Order: Complex Dynamics in Literature and Science.* Chicago: University of Chicago Press, 1991.

———. *Chaos Bound: Orderly Disorder in Contemporary Literature and Science.* Ithaca, N.Y.: Cornell University Press, 1990.

———. *The Cosmic Web: Scientific Field Models and Literary Strategies in the Twentieth Century.* Ithaca, N.Y.: Cornell University Press, 1984.

Hayman, David. *The "Wake" in Transit.* Ithaca, N.Y.: Cornell University Press, 1990.

Healy, Richard. *The Philosophy of Quantum Mechanics: An Interactive Interpretation.* Cambridge: Cambridge University Press, 1989.

Heath, Stephen. "Ambiviolences: Notes for Reading Joyce." *Post-Structuralist Joyce: Essays from the French.* Ed. Derek Attridge and Daniel Ferrer. Cambridge: Cambridge University Press, 1984. 31–68.

Henderson, Linda Dalrymple. *The Fourth Dimension and Non-Euclidean Geometry in Modern Art.* Princeton, N.J.: Princeton University Press, 1983.

Henig, Robin Marantz. "Flu Pandemic." *New York Times Magazine* 29 November 1992.

Heppenheimer, T. A. "How von Neumann Showed the Way." *Invention & Technology* 6, no. 2 (Fall 1990): 8–16.

Herr, Cheryl. *Joyce's Anatomy of Culture.* Urbana: University of Illinois Press, 1986.

Herring, Phillip F. *Joyce's Uncertainty Principle.* Princeton, N.J.: Princeton University Press, 1987.

Heusel, Barbara Stevens. "Parallax as a Metaphor for the Structure of *Ulysses.*" *Novel* 15 (Summer 1983): 135–46.

Hinton, Charles Howard. *An Episode of Flatland: or, How a Plane Folk Discovered the Third Dimension; to Which Is Added an Outline of the History of Unaea.* London: Swan Sonnenschein, 1907.

———. *The Fourth Dimension.* London: Swan Sonnenschein, 1904.

———. *A New Era of Thought.* London: Swan Sonnenschein, 1888.

———. *Scientific Romances.* 1884–85, 1886, 1896. New York: Arno, 1976.

———. "What Is the Fourth Dimension?" *Dublin University Magazine* 96 (1880): 15–34.

Hofstadter, Douglas R. *Gödel, Escher, Bach: An Eternal Golden Braid.* New York: Basic, 1979.

———. "Heisenberg's Uncertainty Principle and the Many-Worlds Interpretation of Quantum Mechanics." *Metamagical Themas: Questing for the Essence of Mind and Pattern.* New York: Basic, 1985. 455–77.

Honner, John. *The Description of Nature: Niels Bohr and the Philosophy of Quantum Physics.* Oxford: Clarendon, 1987.

Hopkins, James. "Visual Geometry." *Kant on Pure Reason.* Ed. Ralph C. S. Walker. Oxford: Oxford University Press, 1982. 41–65.

Horkheimer, Max. "On the Problem of Truth." Trans. Maurice Goldbloom. *The Essential Frankfurt School Reader.* Ed. Andrew Arato and Eike Gebhardt. New York: Continuum, 1982. 407–43.

Horkheimer, Max, and Theodor W. Adorno. *Dialectic of Enlightenment (Dialektik der Aufklärung).* Trans. John Cumming. New York: Continuum, 1972.

Houzel, Christian. "The Birth of Non-Euclidean Geometry." *1830–1930: A Century of*

Geometry: Epistemology, History and Mathematics. Ed. Luciano Boi, Dominique Flament, and Jean-Michel Salanskis. Berlin: Springer, 1992. 3–21.

Hynes, Samuel. *The Edwardian Turn of Mind.* Princeton, N.J.: Princeton University Press, 1968.

Jameson, Fredric. *Late Marxism: Adorno, or, The Persistence of the Dialectic.* London: Verso, 1990.

Joyce, James. *The Critical Writings of James Joyce.* Ed. Ellsworth Mason and Richard Ellmann. New York: Viking, 1959.

———. *"Dubliners": Text, Criticism, and Notes.* Ed. Robert Scholes and A. Walton Litz. New York: Viking, 1969.

———. *Finnegans Wake.* New York: Viking, 1959.

———. *Joyce's "Ulysses" Notesheets in the British Museum.* Ed. Phillip F. Herring. Charlottesville: University Press of Virginia, 1972.

———. *The Letters of James Joyce.* Ed. Richard Ellmann. 2 vols. New York: Viking, 1966.

———. *The Letters of James Joyce.* Ed. Stuart Gilbert. New York: Viking, 1957.

———. *"A Portrait of the Artist as a Young Man": Text, Criticism, and Notes.* Ed. Chester G. Anderson. New York: Viking, 1968.

———. *Stephen Hero.* Ed. Theodore Spencer. New York: New Directions, 1959.

———. *Ulysses.* Ed. Hans Walter Gabler. New York: Random House, 1986.

Joyce, Stanislaus. *The Complete Dublin Diary of Stanislaus Joyce.* Ed. George H. Healey. Ithaca, N.Y.: Cornell University Press, 1971.

———. *My Brother's Keeper: James Joyce's Early Years.* Ed. Richard Ellmann. New York: Viking, 1958.

Jungnickel, Christa, and Russell McCormmach. *The Torch of Mathematics, 1800–1870.* Vol. 1 of *Intellectual Mastery of Nature: Theoretical Physics from Ohm to Einstein.* 2 vols. Chicago: University of Chicago Press, 1986.

Kain, Richard M. "'Grace.'" *James Joyce's "Dubliners": Critical Essays.* Ed. Clive Hart. London: Faber, 1969. 134–52.

———. "The Significance of Stephen's Meeting Bloom: A Survey of Interpretations." *James Joyce Quarterly* 10, no. 1 (1972): 147–60.

Kant, Immanuel. *Critique of Pure Reason.* 2d ed. Trans. J. M. D. Meiklejohn. London: Dent, 1934.

———. *Prolegomena to Any Future Metaphysics That Will Be Able to Present Itself as a Science.* Trans. Peter G. Lucas. Manchester: Manchester University Press, 1953.

Kauffman, Stuart. *At Home in the Universe: The Search for the Laws of Self-Organization and Complexity.* New York: Oxford University Press, 1995.

———. *The Origins of Order.* New York: Oxford University Press, 1993.

Kellert, Stephen H. *In the Wake of Chaos: Unpredictable Order in Dynamical Systems.* Chicago: University of Chicago Press, 1993.

Kelly, Joseph. "Stanislaus Joyce, Ellsworth Mason, and Richard Ellmann: The Making of James Joyce." *Joyce Studies Annual 1992.* Ed. Thomas F. Staley. Austin: University of Texas Press, 1992. 98–140.

Kemeny, John G. "Man Viewed as Machine." *Scientific American* April 1955: 58–67.

Kenner, Hugh. "The Cubist Portrait." *Approaches to Joyce's "Portrait": Ten Essays.* Ed. Thomas F. Staley and Bernard Benstock. Pittsburgh: University of Pittsburgh Press, 1976. 171–84.

———. *Dublin's Joyce.* Bloomington: Indiana University Press, 1956.

———. *Joyce's Voices.* Berkeley: University of California Press, 1978.

———. *The Pound Era.* Berkeley: University of California Press, 1971.

———. *"Ulysses."* London: Allen and Unwin, 1980.

Kern, Stephen. *The Culture of Time and Space, 1880–1918.* Cambridge: Harvard University Press, 1983.

Kershner, R. B. *Joyce, Bakhtin, and Popular Literature.* Chapel Hill: University of North Carolina Press, 1989.

Kline, Morris. *Mathematics in Western Culture.* London: Oxford University Press, 1953.

———. *Mathematics: The Loss of Certainty.* New York: Oxford University Press, 1980.

Krips, Henry. *The Metaphysics of Quantum Theory.* Oxford: Clarendon, 1987.

Krueger, Uwe, amd Heinz Wolf. *The Beauty of Chaos.* Digital file, World Wide Web site, http://i30www.ira.uka.de/˜ukrueger/fractals/.

———. *The Fractal Art of Uwe Krueger and Heinz Wolf.* Digital file, World Wide Web site, http://www.fractals.com/fractal_gallery/uwe_krueger/room3.html.

Kuberski, Philip. *Chaosmos: Literature, Science, and Theory.* Albany: State University of New York Press, 1994.

Kuhn, Thomas. *The Structure of Scientific Revolutions.* 2d ed. Chicago: University of Chicago Press, 1970.

Kuipers, A. "Model and Insight." *The Concept and the Role of the Model in Mathematics and Natural and Social Sciences.* Ed. B. H. Kazemier and D. Vuysje. Dordrecht, Netherlands: Reidel, 1961. 125–32.

Kumar, Shiv K. *Bergson and the Stream of Consciousness Novel.* New York: New York University Press, 1963.

Lachterman, David Rappaport. *The Ethics of Geometry: A Genealogy of Modernity.* New York: Routledge, 1989.

Lanczos, Cornelius. *Space through the Ages: The Evolution of Geometrical Ideas from Pythagoras to Hilbert and Einstein.* London: Academic, 1970.

Langdon, M. "Some Reflections of Physics in *Finnegans Wake.*" *James Joyce Quarterly* 17, no. 4 (1980): 359–77.

Larbaud, Valéry. "The *Ulysses* of James Joyce." *James Joyce: The Critical Heritage.* Ed. Robert H. Deming. London: Routledge, 1970. 252–62.

Latour, Bruno. *Science in Action: How to Follow Scientists and Engineers through Society.* Cambridge, Mass.: Harvard University Press, 1985.

LaValley, Albert J. "'Doublin Their Mumper': Some Thoughts on the Symbolist Drama of Joyce's *Dubliners.*" *Literary Studies: Essays in Memory of Francis A. Drumm.* Ed. John H. Dorenkamp. Worcester, Mass.: College of the Holy Cross, 1973. 172–90.

Lawrence, Karen. *The Odyssey of Style in "Ulysses."* Princeton, N.J.: Princeton University Press, 1981.

Leadbeater, C. W. *The Other Side of Death, Scientifically Examined and Carefully Described.* Chicago: Theosophical Book Concern, 1903.

LeClair, Tom. *The Art of Excess: Mastery in Contemporary American Fiction.* Urbana: University of Illinois Press, 1989.

Leonard, Garry. "Joyce and Advertising: Advertising and Commodity Culture in Joyce's Fiction." *James Joyce Quarterly* 30, no. 4–31, no. 1 (1993): 573–92.

———, ed. "Joyce and Advertising: Special Double Issue." *James Joyce Quarterly* 30, no. 4–31, no. 1 (1993): 573–843, 861–93.

———. "Power, Pornography, and the Problem of Pleasure: The Semerotics of Desire and Commodity Culture." *James Joyce Quarterly* 30, no. 4–31, no. 1 (1993): 615–65.

Leplin, Jarrett, ed. *Scientific Realism.* Berkeley: University of California Press, 1984.

Levin, Harry. *James Joyce: A Critical Introduction.* 2d rev. ed. New York: New Directions, 1960.

Levin, Richard, and Charles Shattuck. "First Flight to Ithaca: A New Reading of Joyce's *Dubliners.*" *James Joyce: Two Decades of Criticism.* Rev. ed. Ed. Seon Givens. New York: Vanguard, 1963. 47–94.

Levitt, Morton P. "Harry Levin's *James Joyce* and the Modernist Age: A Personal Reading." *Re-Viewing Classics of Joyce Criticism.* Ed. Janet Egleson Dunleavy. Urbana: University of Illinois Press, 1991. 90–105.

Levy, Steven. *Artificial Life: The Quest for a New Creation.* New York: Pantheon, 1992.

Lewin, Roger. *Complexity: Life at the Edge of Chaos.* New York: Macmillan, 1992.

Lewis, Wyndham. "Analysis of the Mind of James Joyce." *Time and Western Man.* London: Chatto and Windus, 1927. 91–130.

Littman, Mark E., and Charles A. Schweighauser. "Astronomical Allusions, Their Meaning and Purpose in *Ulysses.*" *James Joyce Quarterly* 2, no. 3 (1965): 238–46.

Litz, A. Walton. *The Art of James Joyce.* Rev. ed. London: Oxford University Press, 1964.

———. *James Joyce.* Rev. ed. New York: Twayne, 1972.

Lobner, Corinna del Greco. "Quincunxial Sherlockholmesing in 'Grace.'" *James Joyce Quarterly* 28 (1991): 445–50.

Lorenz, Edward. "Deterministic Nonperiodic Flow." *Journal of the Atmospheric Sciences* 20 (1963): 130–41.

Loss, Archie K. *Joyce's Visible Art: The Work of Joyce and the Visual Arts, 1904–1922.* Ann Arbor: UMI, 1984.

Lyons, J. B. *James Joyce & Medicine.* Dublin: Dolmen, 1973.

Macdonald, George. *Lilith: A Romance.* London: Chatto and Windus, 1895.

McCarthy, Patrick A. "Joyce's Unreliable Catechist: Mathematics and the Narration of 'Ithaca.'" *English Literary History* 51 (1984): 605–18.

McGee, Patrick. *Paperspace: Style as Ideology in Joyce's "Ulysses."* Lincoln: University of Nebraska Press, 1988.

McHugh, Roland. *Annotations to "Finnegans Wake."* Rev. ed. Baltimore: Johns Hopkins University Press, 1991.

———. *The Sigla of "Finnegans Wake."* Austin: University of Texas Press, 1976.

Madtes, Richard. *The "Ithaca" Chapter of Joyce's "Ulysses."* Ann Arbor: UMI, 1983.

Mainzer, Klaus. *Thinking in Complexity: The Complex Dynamics of Matter, Mind, and Mankind.* Berlin: Springer, 1994.

Mandelbrot, Benoit B. *The Fractal Geometry of Nature.* Rev. ed. New York: Freeman, 1983.

Marre, K. E. "Experimentation with a Symbol from Mythology: The Courses of the Comets in the 'Ithaca' Chapter of Ulysses." *Modern Fiction Studies* 20 (1974): 385–90.

Marshall, Brenda K. *Teaching the Postmodern: Fiction and Theory.* New York: Routledge, 1992.

Mazlish, Bruce. "The Man-Machine and Artificial Intelligence." *Stanford Humanities Review* 4, no. 2 (1995): n.p. (WWW: electronic journal).

Merquior, J. G. *Foucault.* Berkeley: University of California Press, 1985.

Mink, Louis O. "Reading *Finnegans Wake.*" *Southern Humanities Review* 9 (1975): 1–16.

Morris, Richard. *The Edges of Science: Crossing the Boundary from Physics to Metaphysics.* New York: Prentice Hall, 1990.

Morse, Stephen S., ed. *Emerging Viruses.* New York: Oxford University Press, 1993.

Murdoch, Iris. *Metaphysics as a Guide to Morals.* London: Chatto and Windus, 1992.

Nakamura, Katsuhiro. *Quantum Chaos: A New Paradigm of Nonlinear Dynamics.* Cambridge: Cambridge University Press, 1992.

Nicolis, Grégoire, and Ilya Prigogine. *Exploring Complexity: An Introduction.* New York: Freeman, 1989.

Niemeyer, Carl. " 'Grace' and Joyce's Method of Parody." *College English* 27 (1965): 196–201.

Noon, William T., S.J. *Joyce and Aquinas.* New Haven, Conn.: Yale University Press, 1957.

Norris, Margot. *The Decentered Universe of "Finnegans Wake."* Baltimore: Johns Hopkins University Press, 1976.

———. *Joyce's Web: The Social Unraveling of Modernism.* Austin: University of Texas Press, 1992.

———. Rev. of *A Conceptual Guide to "Finnegans Wake,"* by Michael Begnal and Fritz Senn. *James Joyce Quarterly* 13, no. 1 (1975): 116–19.

Nowak, Gregory. "Riemann's *Habilitationsvortrag* and the Synthetic *A Priori* Status of Geometry." *Ideas and Their Reception.* Vol. 1 of *The History of Modern Mathematics.* 2 vols. Ed. David E. Rowe and John McCleary. San Diego: Academic, 1989. 17–46.

Ouspensky, P. D. "The Fourth Dimension." *A New Model of the Universe: Principles of the Psychological Method in Its Applications to Problems of Science, Religion, and Art.* New York: Vintage, 1971. 61–100.

———. *Tertium Organum: The Third Canon of Thought: A Key to the Enigmas of the World.* Trans. Nicholas Bessaraboff and Claude Bragdon. 3d rev. ed. New York: Knopf, 1922.

Overstreet, David. "Oxymoronic Language and Logic in Quantum Mechanics and James Joyce." *SubStance* 28 (1980): 37–59.

Owen, Rodney W. *James Joyce and the Beginnings of "Ulysses."* Ann Arbor: UMI, 1983.

Pagels, Heinz R. *The Cosmic Code: Quantum Physics and the Language of Nature.* New York: Simon and Schuster, 1982.

———. *The Dreams of Reason: The Computer and the Rise of the Sciences of Complexity.* New York: Simon and Schuster, 1988.

———. *Perfect Symmetry: The Search for the Beginning of Time.* New York: Simon and Schuster, 1985.

Papin, Liliane. "This Is Not a Universe: Metaphor, Language, and Representation." *Publications of the Modern Language Association* 107, no. 5 (1992): 1253–65.

Passmore, John. *A Hundred Years of Philosophy.* 2d ed. Harmondsworth: Penguin, 1968.

Peake, C. H. *James Joyce: The Citizen and the Artist.* Stanford, Calif.: Stanford University Press, 1977.

Peat, F. David. *Einstein's Moon: Bell's Theorem and the Curious Quest for Quantum Reality.* Chicago: Contemporary, 1990.

———. *The Philosopher's Stone: Chaos, Synchronicity, and the Hidden Order of the World.* New York: Bantam, 1992.

Pendrick, Gerard. "Two Notes for *Ulysses.*" *James Joyce Quarterly* 32, no. 1 (1994): 105–7.

Penrose, Roger. *The Emperor's New Mind: Concerning Computers, Minds, and the Laws of Physics.* New York: Oxford University Press, 1989.

Perlis, Alan David. "The Newtonian Nightmare of *Ulysses.*" *The Seventh of Joyce.* Ed. Bernard Benstock. Bloomington: Indiana University Press, 1982. 191–97.

Perloff, Marjorie. "Modernist Studies." *Redrawing the Boundaries: The Transformation of English and American Literary Studies.* Ed. Stephen Greenblatt and Giles Gunn. New York: Modern Language Association, 1992. 154–78.

Peterson, Ivars. *Newton's Clock: Chaos in the Solar System.* New York: Freeman, 1993.

Plato. *Meno.* Trans. W. K. C. Guthrie. *Plato: The Collected Dialogues.* Ed. Edith Hamilton and Huntington Cairns. Princeton, N.J.: Princeton University Press, 1961. 353–84.

———. *Republic.* Trans. Paul Shorey. *Plato: The Collected Dialogues.* Ed. Edith Hamilton and Huntington Cairns. Princeton, N.J.: Princeton University Press, 1961. 575–844.

———. *Timaeus.* Trans. Benjamin Jowett. *Plato: The Collected Dialogues.* Ed. Edith Hamilton and Huntington Cairns. Princeton, N.J.: Princeton University Press, 1961. 1151–1211.

Poincaré, Jules Henri. *The Foundations of Science: Science and Hypothesis, The Value of Science, Science and Method.* Trans. George Bruce Halsted. New York: Science, 1913.

Popper, Karl. *The Logic of Scientific Discovery.* 1934. New York: Harper and Row, 1959.

———. *The Open Universe: An Argument for Indeterminism.* Ed. W. W. Bartley III. Totowa, N.J.: Rowman and Littlefield, 1982.

Pound, Ezra. "*Dubliners* and Mr James Joyce." *Literary Essays of Ezra Pound.* Ed. T. S. Eliot. New York: New Directions, 1968. 399–402.

Poundstone, William. *Labyrinths of Reason: Paradox, Puzzles, and the Frailty of Knowledge.* New York: Doubleday, 1988.

Prigogine, Ilya, and Isabelle Stengers. *Order out of Chaos: Man's New Dialogue with Nature.* New York: Bantam, 1984.

Purdy, S. B. "Let's Hear What Science Has to Say: *Finnegans Wake* and the Gnosis of Science." *The Seventh of Joyce.* Ed. Bernard Benstock. Bloomington: Indiana University Press, 1982. 207–18.

Rabaté, Jean-Michel. *James Joyce, Authorized Reader.* 1984. Baltimore: Johns Hopkins University Press, 1991.

———. "Lapsus ex machina." *Post-Structuralist Joyce: Essays from the French.* Ed. Derek Attridge and Daniel Ferrer. Cambridge: Cambridge University Press, 1984. 79–101.

Redhead, Michael. *From Physics to Metaphysics.* Cambridge: Cambridge University Press, 1995.

Reid, Constance. *A Long Way from Euclid.* New York: Crowell, 1963.

Reynolds, Mary T. *Joyce and Dante: The Shaping Imagination.* Princeton, N.J.: Princeton University Press, 1981.

Rice, Thomas J. "The Complexity of *Finnegans Wake.*" *Joyce Studies Annual 1995.* Ed. Thomas F. Staley. Austin: University of Texas Press, 1995. 79–98.

———. "Dante . . . Browning . Gabriel . . Joyce: Allusion and Structure in 'The Dead.'" *James Joyce Quarterly* 30 (1992): 29–40.

———. "The Geometry of Meaning in *Dubliners*: A Euclidean Approach." *Style* 25, no. 3 (1991): 393–404.

———. "Iris Murdoch and Chaos: *The Message to the Planet.*" *REAL: Yearbook of Research in English and American Literature.* Ed. Herbert Grabes, Winfried Fluck, and Jürgen Schlaeger. Vol. 9. Tübingen: Gunter Narr, 1993. 188–241.

———. "Paradigm Lost: 'Grace' and the Arrangement of *Dubliners.*" *Studies in Short Fiction* 32 (1995): 405–21 .

———. "The Reception of a Mathematical Theory: Non-Euclidean Geometry in England, 1868–1883." *Natural Order: Historical Studies of Scientific Culture.* Ed. Barry Barnes and Steven Shapin. Beverly Hills, Calif.: Sage, 1979. 143–66.

———. "*Ulysses*, Chaos, and Complexity." *James Joyce Quarterly* 31, no. 2 (1994): 41–54.

Richards, Joan L. *Mathematical Visions: The Pursuit of Geometry in Victorian England.* San Diego: Academic, 1988.

Riquelme, John Paul. *Teller and Tale in Joyce's Fiction: Oscillating Perspectives.* Baltimore: Johns Hopkins University Press, 1983.

Ross, Andrew. *Strange Weather: Culture, Science and Technology in the Age of Limits.* London: Verso, 1991.

Ross, W. D. *Aristotle: A Complete Exposition of His Works and Thought.* Cleveland: World, 1959.

Ruelle, David. *Chance and Chaos.* Princeton, N.J.: Princeton University Press, 1991.

Russell, Bertrand. *An Essay on the Foundations of Geometry.* Cambridge: Cambridge University Press, 1897.

Salvadori, Mario, and Myron Schwartzman. "Musemathematics: The Literary Use of Science and Mathematics in Joyce's *Ulysses.*" *James Joyce Quarterly* 29, no. 2 (1992): 339–55.

Schaub, Thomas H. *Pynchon: The Voice of Ambiguity.* Urbana: University of Illinois Press, 1981.

Scholes, Robert. "Further Observations on the Text of *Dubliners.*" *Studies in Bibliography* 17 (1964): 107–22.

———. "Grant Richards to James Joyce." *Studies in Bibliography* 16 (1963): 139–60.

———. "Some Observations on the Text of *Dubliners*: 'The Dead.' " *Studies in Bibliography* 15 (1962): 191–205.

———. "Stephen Dedalus: *Eiron* and *Alazon.*" *Texas Studies in Literature and Language* 3 (1961): 8–15.

Scholes, Robert, and A. Walton Litz, eds. *"Dubliners": Text, Criticism, and Notes.* New York: Viking, 1969.

Searle, John R. *Rediscovery of the Mind.* Cambridge, Mass.: MIT Press, 1992.

Seyffert, Oskar. "Euclides." *A Dictionary of Classical Antiquities.* 3d rev. ed. Ed. Henry Nettleship and J. E. Sandys. London: Glaisher, 1894.

Shannon, Claude. *Mathematical Theory of Information.* Urbana: University of Illinois Press, 1949.

Sharpless, F. Parvin. "Irony in Joyce's *Portrait*: The Stasis of Pity." *James Joyce Quarterly* 4, no. 4 (1967): 320–30.

Shklovsky, Victor. "Art as Technique." *Russian Formalist Criticism: Four Essays.* Trans. and ed. Lee T. Lemon and Marion J. Reis. Lincoln: University of Nebraska Press, 1965. 3–24.

Sicker, Philip. "Shades of Descartes: An Approach to Stephen's Dream in *Ulysses.*" *James Joyce Quarterly* 22, no. 1 (1984): 7–24.

Simon, Herbert. "Literary Criticism: A Cognitive Approach." *Stanford Humanities Review* 4, no. 1 (1995): n.p. (WWW: electronic journal).

[Simson, Robert.] *Euclid in Paragraphs. The Elements of Euclid: Containing the First Six Books and the First Twenty-One Propositions of the Eleventh Book.* Cambridge: Stevenson, 1845.

Slosson, Edwin E. *Major Prophets of Today.* Freeport, N.Y.: Books for Libraries, 1968.

Smith, Paul Jordan. *A Key to the "Ulysses" of James Joyce.* Chicago: Covici, 1927.

Smith, Thomas. *Euclid: His Life and System.* Edinburgh: T. & T. Clark, 1902.

Smith, Vincent Edward. *St. Thomas on the Object of Geometry.* Milwaukee.: Marquette University Press, 1954.

Snow, C. P. *The Two Cultures: And a Second Look.* Cambridge: Cambridge University Press, 1963.

Solomon, Margaret C. *Eternal Geomater: The Sexual Universe of "Finnegans Wake."* Carbondale: Southern Illinois University Press, 1969.

Sommerville, Duncan M.Y., ed. *Bibliography of Non-Euclidean Geometry, Including the Theory of Parallels, the Foundations of Geometry, and Space of n-Dimensions.* London: Harrison, 1911.

Sophocles. *The Theban Plays.* Trans. E. F. Watling. Harmondsworth, Britain: Penguin, 1947.

Sosnoski, James J. "Reading Acts and Reading Warrants: Some Implications for

Readers Responding to Joyce's Portrait of Stephen." *James Joyce Quarterly* 16, nos. 1–2 (1978–79): 43–63.

Spencer, Sharon. *Space, Time and Structure in the Modern Novel*. Chicago: Swallow, 1971.

Spencer, Theodore. Introduction. *Stephen Hero*, by James Joyce. Ed. Spencer. New York: New Directions, 1959. 7–18.

Spoo, Robert. "Joyce's Attitudes toward History: Rome, 1906–07." *Journal of Modern Literature* 14, no. 4 (1988): 481–97.

Staley, Thomas F. "Religious Elements and Thomistic Encounters." *Re-Viewing Classics of Joyce Criticism*. Ed. Janet Egleson Dunleavy. Urbana: University of Illinois Press, 1991. 155–68.

———. "Strings in the Labyrinth: Sixty Years with Joyce's *Portrait*." *Approaches to Joyce's "Portrait": Ten Essays*. Ed. Staley and Bernard Benstock. Pittsburgh: University of Pittsburgh Press, 1976. 3–24.

Stewart, Ian. *Does God Play Dice?: The Mathematics of Chaos*. Oxford: Blackwell, 1989.

———. "Portraits of Chaos." *Exploring Chaos: A Guide to the New Sciences of Disorder*. Ed. Nina Hall. New York: Norton, 1993. 44–58.

Stone, Harry. " 'Araby' and the Writings of James Joyce." *Antioch Review* 25 (1965): 375–410.

Strehle, Susan. *Fiction in the Quantum Universe*. Chapel Hill: University of North Carolina Press, 1992.

Sullivan, Kevin. *Joyce among the Jesuits*. New York: Columbia University Press, 1958.

Suter, August. "Some Reminiscences of James Joyce." Trans. Fritz Senn. *Portraits of the Artist in Exile: Recollections of James Joyce by Europeans*. Ed. Willard Potts. Seattle: University of Washington Press, 1979. 61–66.

Theall, Donald F. "The Hieroglyphs of Engined Egypsians: Machines, Media, and Modes of Communication in *Finnegans Wake*." *Joyce Studies Annual 1991*. Ed. Thomas F. Staley. Austin: University of Texas Press, 1991. 129–52.

Thomas, Brook. "Preserving and Keeping Order by Killing Time in *Heart of Darkness*." *Joseph Conrad: "Heart of Darkness": A Case Study in Contemporary Criticism*. Ed. Ross C. Murfin. New York: St. Martin's, 1989. 237–55.

Thomas, David Wayne. "Gödel's Theorem and Postmodern Theory." *Publications of the Modern Language Association* 110, no. 2 (1995): 248–61.

Thornton, Weldon. *Allusions in "Ulysses."* Chapel Hill: University of North Carolina Press, 1961.

Tiles, Mary. *Bachelard: Science and Objectivity*. Cambridge: Cambridge University Press, 1984.

Tindall, William York. *James Joyce: His Way of Interpreting the Modern World*. New York: Scribner's, 1950.

———. *A Reader's Guide to James Joyce*. New York: Noonday, 1959.

Todorov, Tzvetan. *Symbolism and Interpretation*. Trans. Catherine Porter. Ithaca, N.Y.: Cornell University Press, 1982.

Toffler, Alvin. Foreword: Science and Change. *Order out of Chaos: Man's New Dialogue with Nature*, by Ilya Prigogine and Isabelle Stengers. New York: Bantam, 1984. xi–xxvi.

Torretti, Roberto. *Philosophy of Geometry from Riemann to Poincaré*. Dordrecht, Netherlands: Reidel, 1978.

Tratner, Michael. "Sex and Credit: Consumer Capitalism in *Ulysses*." *James Joyce Quarterly* 30, no. 4–31, no. 1 (1993): 695–716.

Troy, William. "Notes on *Finnegans Wake*." *Partisan Review* 6 (Summer 1939): 97–110.

Trudeau, Richard J. *The Non-Euclidean Revolution*. Boston: Birkhauser, 1987.

Tymoczko, Maria. *The Irish "Ulysses."* Berkeley: University of California Press, 1994.

Ubbink, J. B. "Model, Description and Knowledge." *The Concept and the Role of the Model in Mathematics and Natural and Social Sciences*. Ed. B. H. Kazemier and D. Vuysje. Dordrecht, Netherlands: Reidel, 1961. 178–94.

Valente, Joseph. "Examining Uncertainty." *Style* 25, no. 3 (1991): 506–13.

Vemuri, V. *Modeling of Complex Systems: An Introduction*. New York: Academic, 1978.

von Neumann, John. *The Computer and the Brain*. New Haven, Conn.: Yale University Press, 1958.

———. *Theory of Self-Reproducing Automata*. Ed. Arthur W. Burks. Urbana: University of Illinois Press, 1966.

Waddington, C. H. *Tools for Thought: How to Understand and Apply the Latest Scientific Techniques of Problem Solving*. New York: Basic, 1977.

Waldrop, M. Mitchell. *Complexity: The Emerging Science at the Edge of Order and Chaos*. New York: Simon and Schuster, 1992.

Walzl, Florence L. "Gabriel and Michael: The Conclusion of 'The Dead.'" *James Joyce Quarterly* 4, no. 1 (1966): 17–31.

Watson, Edward A. "Stoom-Bloom: Scientific Objectivity versus Romantic Subjectivity in the 'Ithaca' Episode of Joyce's *Ulysses*." *University of Windsor Review* 2, no. 1 (1966): 11–25.

Weinstein, Norman. "The 'Ithaca' Chapter of *Ulysses*: Notes on Science, Number and Poetic Structure." *Southern Review* 12 (1979): 3–22.

Weir, David. "Gnomon Is an Island: Euclid and Bruno in Joyce's Narrative Practice." *James Joyce Quarterly* 28, no. 2 (1991): 343–60.

Wells, H. G. *The Definitive "Time Machine."* Ed. Harry M. Geduld. Bloomington: Indiana University Press, 1987.

———. *The Invisible Man: A Grotesque Romance*. London: Pearson, 1897.

———. "The Rediscovery of the Unique." *"The Time Machine," "The War of the Worlds": A Critical Edition*. Ed. Frank D. McConnell. New York: Oxford University Press, 1977. 335–44.

———. *Selected Short Stories*. Harmondsworth: Penguin, 1979.

Wells, Norman J. "Descartes and the Scholastics Briefly Revisited." *New Scholasticism* 2 (1961): 172–90.

Wells, Webster, and Walter W. Hart. *Progressive Plane Geometry*. Boston: Heath, 1943.

Wentworth, George A. *Elements of Analytic Geometry.* Boston: Ginn, 1886.

White, David A. *The Grand Continuum: Reflections on Joyce and Metaphysics.* Pittsburgh: University of Pittsburgh Press, 1983.

Whitehead, Alfred North. *Science and the Modern World: Lowell Lectures, 1925.* New York: Macmillan, 1947.

Wicke, Jennifer. "Modernity Must Advertise: Aura, Desire, and Decolonization in Joyce." *James Joyce Quarterly* 30, no. 4–31, no. 1 (1993): 593–613.

Wiener, Norbert. *The Human Use of Human Beings: Cybernetics and Society.* New York: Houghton Mifflin, 1950.

Wigginton, B. Eliot. "*Dubliners* in Order." *James Joyce Quarterly* 7 (1970): 297–314.

Wilcox, Joan Parisi. "Joyce, Euclid, and 'Ithaca.'" *James Joyce Quarterly* 28, no. 3 (1991): 643–49.

Wilde, Oscar. "The Canterville Ghost." *The Works of Oscar Wilde.* 15 vols. New York: Lamb, 1909. 4:89–152.

Willmore, T. J. *Riemannian Geometry.* London: Oxford University Press, 1993.

Wilson, Edmund. "James Joyce." *Axel's Castle: A Study in the Imaginative Literature of 1870–1930.* New York: Scribner's, 1931. 191–236.

Wittgenstein, Ludwig. *Tractatus Logico-Philosophicus.* Trans. D. F. Pears and B. F. McGuinness. London: Routledge & Kegan Paul, 1961.

Wynne, Brian. "Physics and Psychics: Science, Symbolic Action, and Social Control in Late Victorian England." *Natural Order: Historical Studies of Scientific Culture.* Ed. Barry Barnes and Steven Shapin. Beverly Hills, Calif.: Sage, 1979. 167–89.

Young, Richard O. "'Where Even the Trees Come and Go': D. H. Lawrence and the Fourth Dimension." *D. H. Lawrence Review* 13, no. 1 (1980): 30–44.

Zola, Emile. "The Experimental Novel." Trans. George J. Becker. *Documents of Modern Literary Realism.* Ed. Becker. Princeton, N.J.: Princeton University Press, 1963. 162–96.

INDEX

THOMAS JACKSON RICE, professor of English and director of graduate studies at the University of South Carolina, was educated at the University of Delaware and Princeton University, where he received his Ph.D. degree in English literature. He is the author of eight books and more than seventy articles and papers on nineteenth- and twentieth-century British and American fiction, including *James Joyce: A Guide to Research* (1982) and *James Joyce: Life, Work, and Criticism* (1985). He is currently working on a book-length study of the fiction and philosophy of Iris Murdoch.